Barmaids

Studies in Australian History

Series editors: Alan Gilbert, Patricia Grimshaw and Peter Spearritt *for Zoë*

The Bar, painting by John Brack, 1954. (Courtesy of the artist, painting in private collection.)

Barmaids

A History of Women's Work in Pubs

Diane Kirkby

PUBLISHED BY THE PRESS SYNDICATE OF THE UNIVERSITY OF CAMBRIDGE
The Pitt Building, Trumpington Street, Cambridge CB2 1RP, United Kingdom

CAMBRIDGE UNIVERSITY PRESS
The Edinburgh Building, Cambridge CB2 2RU, United Kingdom
40 West 20th Street, New York, NY 10011–4211, USA
10 Stamford Road, Oakleigh, Melbourne 3166, Australia

First published 1997

Printed in Australia by Brown Prior Anderson

Typeset in ITC Garamond 10/12 pt

National Library of Australia Cataloguing in Publication data

Kirkby, Diane.
Barmaids: a history of women's work in pubs.
Bibliography.
Includes index.
ISBN 0 521 56038 1.
ISBN 0 521 56868 4 (pbk.).
1. Bartenders. 2. Women – Employment – Australia.
3. Bartending – Social aspects – Australia. 4. Sex role in the
work environment. 5. Bars (Drinking establishments) –
Social aspects – Australia. I. Title.
331.4816479594

Library of Congress Cataloguing in Publication data

Kirkby, Diane Elizabeth.
Barmaids: a history of women's work in pubs/Diane Kirkby.
    p.   cm.
Includes bibliographical references and index.
ISBN 0 521 56038 1 (alk. paper). – ISBN 0 521 56868 4 (pbk.
alk. paper).
1. Cocktail servers – Australia – History. 2. Bartenders –
Australia – History. 3. Feminism – Australia – History. 4. Bars
(Drinking establishments) – Australia – History. I. Title.
TX950.59.A8K57   1997   97–17304
305.43′642–dc21

A catalogue record for this book is available from the British Library

ISBN 0 521 56038 1 hardback
ISBN 0 521 56868 4 paperback

Contents

Figures

Acknowledgements

My interest in this subject, I now realise, was first stirred by the experiences I had growing up in a fairly isolated part of rural Australia. There, on our occasional visits to town on hot summer afternoons, as the temperature regularly soared above the century, my sisters and I would stand in the dirt road that constituted the main street, red dust blowing across our cleaned shoes and socks, to watch the comings and goings at the pub. There weren't many buildings in the town: a general store, one end of which was the post office; a police station; butcher's shop; bush nurses' quarters; a Memorial Hall made of corrugated iron; and dominating them all, on the corner of the main road into town, was the pub in all its unlovely splendour. There the men drank in the public bar from which we quickly learnt that children and women were excluded; the few women (sisters and wives of the men drinking) sat alone in the hot, sparsely furnished and extraordinarily named 'Ladies Lounge'. The only woman who was exempt from this segregation was the licensee, a woman we called 'Mrs Gascoyne', who served behind the bar and whose control over the pub's male clientele we children never doubted. She certainly had us in awe. When I now reflect on that small town and its population I realise that all those small businesses were run by women – Mrs W. in the general store, continually pregnant; Mrs M. in the post office whose name I could never pronounce; Mrs D. in the butcher's shop, mother of five gigantic sons; the bush nurse – all women whose work was vital to the existence of the town. From those beginnings has developed a scholarly interest in the meaning and significance of women's work, of the power relations that relegate women to the 'Ladies Lounge', of the dominance of pub culture and men's drinking habits in shaping the lives and experience of women and children.

It is not really possible to give full acknowledgement to all the people who have assisted and encouraged me along the way with this book. Over the course of more than ten years I have incurred many debts. First, the research could not have been undertaken without the benefit of research grants from the Australian Research Council and La Trobe

University's Faculties of Humanities and Social Sciences, which enabled me to travel and collect photographs and documents from all over Australia. I am grateful to the library staffs of the John Oxley Library, Brisbane; the Battye Library, Perth (in particular Joanna Sassoon); the State Library, and Museum, particularly Vicki Farmery, of Tasmania; the Mortlock Library of South Australia; the Mitchell Library, Sydney; the State Library, and the Museum, of Victoria. Maureen Purtell of the Noel Butlin Archives of Business and Labour at the Australian National University, Maryanne McCubbin and Susanne Fairbanks of Melbourne University Archives guided me expertly through their collections.

In addition I received valuable assistance from the New South Wales and Queensland branches of the Australian Hotels Association; and from Eugene Fry of the Western Australian branch of the Australian Federated Liquor Hospitality and Miscellaneous Workers Union. Shirley Mellor of the Queensland branch of this union was particularly generous in giving her time and her unique insights drawn from personal experience working behind the bar. For that I am much indebted. Alleyn Best who wrote the union's history shared his notes and gave me valuable leads. It was he who first drew my attention to the photo collection of the social history unit of the Museum of Victoria.

I benefited from an Australian–American Education Foundation (Fulbright) Postdoctoral Award in the early stage of the research, which enabled me to visit the University of Wisconsin, Madison for part of a semester. There I endured weather conditions that severely tested my interest in Wisconsin brewery workers but my discomfort was mitigated by the hospitality I received from the History Department, especially John Cooper, Linda Gordon and Stanley Katz. Time spent at the Humanities Institute at SUNY Stony Brook, in the autumn of 1993, was more climatically hospitable and there my project benefited from comments and conversations with Temma Kaplan, Susan Squier, Judith Walkowitz and Barbara Weinstein. I am very grateful to Anne Kaplan for facilitating the Fellowship that enabled me to take advantage of such rich resources.

Finding the material on which I could construct this history has been a daunting task. In that I have been very ably and energetically assisted: Hilary Kent got me started with some crucial evidence that gave me leads for subsequent further research; Adele Murdolo put in many hours following up much unpromising-looking material; Tanja Luckins provided sources that brought the subject to life in new ways; and Cathy Coleborne was unfailingly thorough, resourceful and always cheerfully prepared to handle requests for material and proofread at short notice.

I have also been overwhelmed by the generosity of my peers. Postgraduate students – Louise Walker, Suzanne Lloyd-Jones, Wendy Bastalich, Helen Hamley – shared their research with me; Liz Conor,

Susanne Davies, Rae Frances and Marilyn Lake passed on references, or snippets found in the course of their own research. Others – Patricia Grimshaw, Hilary Golder, Judith Smart – read long passages of typescript and made incisive and pertinent suggestions that saved me making gross errors. Rosemary Hunter was always willing to confer; Fiona Paisley to offer ideas and suggestions. I am also grateful to Kitty Sklar for her encouragement, and especially to Eileen Boris, Sue Cobble and Alice Kessler-Harris who read the manuscript in its entirety. Christopher Tomlins has always been willing to offer strategic support.

I am especially indebted to those who helped with the visual sources. Helen Young brought John Brack's painting to my attention; Jeni Thornley graciously lent me her own copy of the photo of Newcastle barmaids after I had spent months tracking it down, a very generous gesture for which I am most grateful; Jill White was similarly helpful in making available photographs taken by Max Dupain. Meeting with such generosity of spirit has been one of the joys of doing this book. Rhys Isaac gave me a wonderful poster of John Collett's eighteenth-century painting, *The Pretty Bar Maid*, which unfortunately could not be included but which graces my wall in constant reminder of Rhys' support and encouragement over many years.

Phillipa McGuinness of Cambridge University Press guided the project through its final stages with a firm hand. Without her clear vision of the project it might well have wilted under its own weight. Jane Farago was very professional; Katherine Steward's painstaking and thoughtful copy-editing gave me an opportunity to clarify my intentions.

My mother, Marjorie Kirkby, and my sisters, Helen and Robyn, gave me love and encouragement and always took an interest. My children, Michael and Zoë, showed fortitude and restraint in the face of immense provocation. They sacrificed pleasures and tolerated disruptions so that I could complete my task according to schedule. Alec has lived with this project since its inception, and borne with me when my expectations exceeded what was reasonable. I am grateful for the unwavering strength of his support. Alison, Sandy and Julie can always be counted on to enrich and sustain; my friend Sam has been a stalwart in my life for over thirty years. With such riches the meaning of my work is constantly enhanced.

Introduction

In the winter of 1995 patrons at the Croxton Park hotel in suburban Melbourne mourned the loss of their barmaid. Jean Dent, 67 years old, had worked behind the bar for twenty years. Although she had started her working life as a cake decorator, and she had owned and run a succession of milk bars, it was work behind the hotel bar that she loved. She had, she claimed, 'never aspired to do anything else'. Her employer described her as efficient, friendly, punctual and adaptable, her customers thought she was 'irreplaceable', 'the life and soul of the ... public bar'. Both bar patrons and staff were 'devastated' when she died unexpectedly. The new licensee considered dedicating a room to her memory and customers and the previous management placed 'in memoriam' notices in the metropolitan press. The local paper reported the day 'had an eerie symbolism about it. It was Melbourne's coldest and most miserable day for 94 years.'[1]

Jean Dent was typical of many barmaids in the pleasure she took in her work and in the high esteem in which she was held. The sense of loss her customers and employers expressed at her passing could just as well have been an expression of the larger public's feeling about the demise of a unique occupation. In 1995 'Sydney's most popular barmaid', Brenda Fletcher, retired from the city pub she worked in after forty-six years in the industry. She was treated as a celebrity, 'she's a real lady', her departure noted and regretted by a wide group of people.[2]

Barmaids have long held a special place in the imaginations of Australians. They have been the mainstay of the hotel trade, and the subject of paintings, plays and films in a way that no other group of workers has. In 1945 they were thought to be inseparable from the industry in which they were employed: 'The barmaid is an English and Australian institution ... as old as the trade and a popular unit of it', an industry paper claimed. Drawing a contrast with the American trade, the *Hotel Review of Western Australia* was surprised to find that the barmaid was not similarly important there. The Australian pub and the American saloon certainly had much in common in the nineteenth century but by 1945 their

histories had significantly diverged. The growth of a temperance movement opposed to the sale and consumption of alcohol altered the
character of public drinking houses in both countries. Over the course
of the twentieth century the place of the barmaid took on a cultural
and political significance in Australian pub life that went beyond the
economic importance of their work.

Now, in the 1990s, barmaids are 'a dying breed'.[3] Major changes in the
industry and a restructured workforce mean 'the barmaid' as she was
understood to be in 1945, is disappearing. 'Once they were legends. They
could make a pub, or break it. They could stop a fight, mend a broken
heart, then pull another beer. Now their world is fast disappearing.
They're not even called barmaids anymore, they're food and beverage
attendants.'[4] There has been a crescendo of protest in the press about this
loss to popular culture, an attention to barmaids that mirrors past times
when 'the barmaid' occupied central stage in public debates.

This book is a study of barmaids and of the meaning of 'the barmaid'
in Australian culture. It is an exploration of an occupational category, of
the means by which it came into being, and of how it changed over the
course of two centuries. It starts from Judith Walkowitz's observation that
'what is socially peripheral is so frequently symbolically central'.[5] It is the
story of how women's work behind the bar has figured in wider public
discussions, and of the way women workers have had to negotiate the
cultural meanings attached to being a barmaid. It is a study of the
dynamics of work and leisure, of sexual difference and sexuality in the
workplace, of pubs and drinking cultures, and the creation of a gendered
and racialised national cultural identity.

It seems extraordinary that there has been no previous study of
these issues. Pubs have played a crucial part in the Anglo-European
domination of Australia. They were central institutions in colonising the
continent in the early nineteenth century and, through a series of laws
and exclusions, they were significant in the twentieth century in the
creation of an 'Australian' culture that was both racially exclusive and
androcentric.[6] Both Aboriginal people and women were forbidden to
drink in them. By the middle of the twentieth century pubs were being
celebrated as icons of the national culture, repositories of the myth-
ologies of national identity, and symbolic of 'the Australian way of life'.
Drinking copiously, noisily, in the company of other sporty, gambling,
culturally homogeneous and like-minded men became synonymous in
the mid-twentieth century with being archetypically Australian. Drinking
beer was represented as the national pastime and the way of defining
masculinity.[7] Masculinity and national identity were thus interwoven with
pub culture, and the ethnic and sexual exclusivity of that culture was
celebrated.

Writing in 1952 author Paul McGuire set the tone when he pointed to the centrality of hotelkeeping in colonising the continent. 'Melbourne was conceived in an innkeeper's brain and bar', he said. It was hotelkeepers 'who built the roads and bridges ... put coaches on our roads ... built our first ships, opened our trade, founded newspapers and libraries, endowed churches, schools, and university colleges', he claimed, as they 'fed and bedded the advancing waves of population as they spread out to occupy the land'. McGuire's study had begun as a study of the peopling of Australia, but he found that whether he was looking at religion, transport, roads, education, art, trade, industry or politics, he was constantly turning up accounts of inns, hotels and taverns: 'from Sydney to the deepest bush' the economy and the social life of the young country revolved around them in a most extraordinary way. According to McGuire, 'even the English inn ... has [not] played such a part in the national life as the inn and innkeeper played in Australia'. Graphically he declared, 'if you take the inn out of our history, you leave it filleted'.[8]

McGuire's history was an unproblematic celebration of the spread of Anglo-European people and English institutions in the making of 'Australia'. Not surprisingly, he found public houses and inns at the core of that history because, by the mid-twentieth century, pubs were playing a vital part in the way the history of Australia was being imagined. The uniqueness of the Australian pub as an institution became the stuff of folklore. 'Every local pub ... has its own romance and legend. Every old country pub has a bushranger story, every inner city pub built before 1850 has a convict or smuggler story', J. M. Freeland enthused as he sought to capture the character and culture of this colonial institution. 'The pub is one of the most socially significant, historically valuable, architecturally interesting, and colourful features of Australian society.' Pubkeeping was an 'enterprise ... with characteristics and practices uniquely Australian', he claimed, one that meant pubs have been 'involved in practically every phase of Australia's historical development'. Describing the pub as 'a national phenomenon ... a broad and complex subject with a wide range of detailed interplay', Freeland lamented that the pub itself 'has never been looked upon ... as a cultural achievement'.[9]

This project restores the pub's place as a creation of Australian culture. But it does so through a focus on the pub as cultural icon and workplace, as gendered space, where knowledge of sexual difference was created and performed through workplace interactions and as men and women pursued their pleasure. It is, first and foremost, a history of work.

Working behind the bar, either as licensees or as barmaids, has been a very important source of income-earning for women in Australia. Yet women have been invisible in the mythologising of pubs except as creations of men's fantasies, as objects of desire to a masculine gaze.

Women's presence in the pub was not part of the celebration of national identity except in their capacity as 'The Barmaid', a sexualised identity created out of pub culture. 'The barmaid, like the prostitute, ... occupies a special, trite place in male mythology', theatre critic Angela Bennie pointed out recently, 'friend, confidante, surrogate wife-mother, good sport with a heart of gold/slut, servant, object, there to serve man's appetites ...'[10] She was intrinsic to men's pleasure, at the core of the pub's masculine culture.

This book is intended to restore to visibility the women who worked in Australia's pubs as barmaids. But it is also intended to illuminate the culture that created the identity of 'The Barmaid' by revealing the mythologising of pubs and barmaids that has occurred in the national culture, and by exploring the different means by which knowledge of women's work as barmaids was created and disseminated.

Through an exhaustive study of the texts – the photographs, legislative debates, governmental inquiries, autobiographies, newspaper reports, census statistics, the publications of union and temperance organisations, the hoteliers associations, the parliamentarians and the press – which created the occupation and category of 'the barmaid', this book addresses key questions in the history of women's work. By examining the activities of key players in defining, protesting and advocating bar work, it reveals the particular nature of the work and the meanings it has had for women and womanhood throughout more than a century of Anglo-European culture in Australia. It is, implicitly, by inference also an exploration, in a small way, of Australia's drinking culture, a topic as yet unexplored in Australian history.[11]

The 1950s was a key decade for the imagining of a unique Australian culture and pubs and their barmaids figured prominently. Two years after McGuire's book on innkeepers was published, Melbourne artist John Brack exhibited his painting of a barmaid in a suburban pub during the 6 o'clock rush (see frontispiece). Brack's study was a direct reference to French artist Edouard Manet's 1881 painting, *A Bar at the Folies Bergère*, 'one of the most famous icons of the modern movement in art'. Hailed by reviewers at the time for its satirisation of 'a world familiar to us all', Brack's painting has been praised subsequently for both its ironic social comment and its execution. It was a major work in a prominent young artist's career. Brack believed Manet would never have chosen an Australian bar as his subject. Yet in doing so Brack was recognising the social and cultural significance of pub life in mid-century Australia. By substituting 'the dry, hard-faced' barmaid for the 'beautiful but melancholy Parisian' barmaid of Manet's imagination, Brack also captured something of the distance that representations of barmaids had travelled in eighty years. Nevertheless he chose for his model not an actual worker in a pub but a milk-bar attendant, as she 'seemed to fit my conception better than the real thing'.[12]

Something of the importance of 'the barmaid' to Australia's self-definition is also conveyed by the enormous popular success of Ray Lawler's play *Summer of the Seventeenth Doll*, first performed in 1955, and part of a trilogy that was completed twenty years later. The status of this play, according to theatre critic John McCallum, 'is so immense that it must be unreal: it is not simply the Great Australian Play, it is a cultural phenomenon which has accrued qualities which are not of itself but part of the self-perpetuating nature of Fame'. It is the most studied Australian play in schools and tertiary institutions and has had an enormous impact on the theatrical repertoire.[13] In 1959 it was made into a film starring Ernest Borgnine and John Mills, and in 1996 it was turned into an opera for performance at the Melbourne Festival.

'The interest in the characters and setting of the *Doll* seems to have stemmed partly from their being so quintessentially "us"', according to McCallum, who with earlier critics saw in the play a confrontation between the Australianness of the Bush legend and the realities of modern, urbanised industrialised Australia. The play revolves around the relationships between two Queensland canecutters and their female companions in Melbourne during the seasonal lay-off. Lawler 'has presented us with some of the most lively and perceptive female characters in our drama ... often strong, energetic and capable of great insight into their condition', they are now thought to be more significant than the male characters.[14] The play has spawned almost an industry of literary criticism, most interestingly around the meaning of the central female character, Olive. In an intriguing feminist reading of the *Doll*, Kerryn Goldsworthy challenges previous readings which saw the kewpie doll of the title as the symbol of Olive's childlessness, and therefore her immaturity, as 'a male misreading of female culture' in which dolls are not baby substitutes but objects of play capable of teaching many things to little girls who play with them. Kewpie dolls – an American invention – represent Cupid, that is, Eros, and are indeed the representation of sexual desire, both male and female. Goldsworthy suggests there is a complexity to the sexual suggestiveness of the kewpie doll that can best be read as the central couple's mutual desire for 'sexuality unconstrained by habit, unsanctioned by marriage, and unconfirmed by the presence of offspring: desire carrying those suggestions of the illicit, the anarchic and the magical which are associated with carnival ...' And, I would add, with the escapism and fantasy the pub offers.

It has gone unremarked that in depicting two women who would embark on such a relationship Lawler chose his female characters to be barmaids. Yet this is no coincidence. Pearl, 'a widowed barmaid with an innocent eighteen-year-old daughter, a good black dress, and no enduring objections to falling into bed with Barney' is, according to Goldsworthy, 'a triumph of dramatic construction ... she lives ... on a number of borders; between working class and middle class; between respectability and licentiousness; between the play's audience and the rest of the characters ... her sexual status, like her social status ... an unstable proposition with a deceptive surface'. Goldsworthy also points out that Olive manifests a marked maturity in taking responsibility for her own survival: 'without the social, financial and emotional security of marriage ... she is and has always been financially independent' and even in the last emotional moment of the play, goes off to work.[15]

The *Doll*, 'the most canonical play we have by a long way',[16] therefore captures much of the cultural meaning of 'the barmaid' in Australia: financially, sexually and socially independent, simultaneously respectable as a woman battling to make her own way in the world yet suspiciously having too close a knowledge of too many men. When Katherine Thompson's play *Barmaids* was performed (first in Perth in 1991, then in Sydney in 1992 and again in 1995) it provided another chance for cultural critics to locate 'the barmaid'. Significantly men and women reviewers reacted differently. 'Barmaids play an ambiguous role in Australian society', one male reviewer ambiguously observed; another wrote 'pubs were ... male preserves ruled with a rod of iron by those archetypal mother/whore figures'. A female reviewer, however, pointed out that Thompson's play was not about barmaids at all: 'It's about men, as they are seen through female eyes', she wrote, and 'What better female-type to use for the female perspective ... than the barmaid ... who sees the male in all his dull *flagrante undelicioso*.' Another female reviewer concentrated on the fact that barmaids were workers: 'Think for a moment about the working life of a barmaid: social worker, confessor, mother figure, psychological punching bag ... you'd really have to like it to stick at it', she said. She then pointed out that, indeed, 'most barmaids loved their job'.[17]

There is then a complex story to be told about barmaids and their place in Australian culture and history. No other occupation has carried the larger cultural significance that women's work behind the bar has done over the course of Australia's history. And no other occupation has attracted the attention from reformers that 'the barmaid' and her workplace consequently did at the turn of the century. 'Where, more than anywhere else in the world are women out of place?' Sarah Perkins of the New Zealand Woman's Christian Temperance Union asked rhetorically in 1902. 'Unhappily', she said there was 'more than one career ... in which women tend to lose their womanly qualities and to degenerate; but the one place above all others in which they are most apt to injure their own best selves and often do a fatal amount of harm to others, is a public-house bar.' While protesting vehemently about the nature of the work, Perkins also drew attention to its place in the context of British imperial culture. 'If we of the British Empire were not blunted to it by custom and habit, the sight of a woman in such a place as this would revolt us, and public opinion would rise and sweep at least this evil away at once', she continued.[18] The ensuing debate about the desirability of such work for women had important repercussions.

Bar work for women was an occupation that originated in the pubs of London and very quickly spread throughout England's imperial possessions. But in Australia it became 'quintessentially us', in John McCallum's phrase. The Australian pub became a domain historically identified and protected by law and custom as men's recreational space, where women's place was to provide (always cheerful) service. It was, therefore, a workplace for women that was a site dominated by the presence of men pursuing their leisure. That gives the nature and characteristics of bar work particular meaning compared with most other occupations women have followed. It has also been an occupation pursued by men, a factor which has similarly placed women's bar work in a unique category. The sexual division of labour has ensured women's employment has generally been concentrated in female-dominated workplaces. Yet pubs have challenged this division and created spaces where women could define themselves as workers alongside men while simultaneously perpetuating the myth of male exclusiveness.

Australian pubs and their workers have not been studied by historians, and no study has been undertaken of their drinking practices. There have been only a few celebratory books produced for non-academic readers, and Freeland's very comprehensive architectural history, now thirty years old. That, as the only academic study ever undertaken of Australian pubs, has been enormously useful but is limited by its preoccupation with architecture. Neither has there been a specific study of the temperance movement published, or a history written of the Woman's Christian Temperance Union in Australia. Several theses have explored temperance, others the development of brewing industries in various states. There are some histories of brewing in the United Kingdom, and British historians have written on alehouses and taverns, as they have on drinking customs and the temperance movement.[19] Similarly several United States historians have explored the saloon and its significance in American history, and bartending as an occupation has rated a passing mention in other studies.[20] In none of the historical literature in Australia or overseas have pubs been looked upon as workplaces, and only one other historian has written on the occupation of barmaid, and that briefly.[21]

Yet pubs were significant workplaces in the past, partly because, particularly in the late nineteenth century, they were so numerous, and partly because, as small family-owned businesses, they provided more self-employment in the Australian colonies than any other kind of business. As the nineteenth century ended they were also becoming important as employers of wage labour, especially for women with no other trade training, a practice which continued in the twentieth century. Today they remain a very labour-intensive workplace, one where new technologies have barely reached. There is therefore a significant gap in the historical literature both in Australia and overseas, given the importance and prevalence of pubs and the significance of drinking to working-class recreation. This study is intended to address that gap but to do so in broader terms than labour history has traditionally employed.

American and Australian historians have been calling for new approaches to the study of work and the working class.[22] In particular they have sought to bring fresh insights to labour history from new theoretical perspectives. My approach was inspired by the argument of Patrick Joyce that work is a cultural activity rather than just an economic one.[23] To Joyce work is intensely subjective and ideological, imbued with meaning it is the historian's task to unravel. Joyce was particularly concerned with the meanings of work held by the working people themselves and the significance and meaning they brought to the labour experience. While I share his concern, I have an additional interest in the meaning some kinds of work and occupations have beyond the workplace. Women's work – paid and unpaid – has this kind of meaning. It has been problematic for labour history for no single narrative has been able to account for both men's and women's separate experiences of work, and at work. As a result, one historian has pointed out, women's labour narratives have 'revolved around the related but separate themes of the sexual division of labour and the separation of spheres' that enabled the development of parallel but separate men's and women's labour histories.[24]

This project began in the 1980s as a study of a manufacturing workplace, the brewing industry. At that time feminist scholars were seeking to explain the sexual division of labour which saw women concentrated in particular jobs, at the lowest levels of the hierarchy, and always subjected to an inequitable distribution of rewards. Drawing on a Marxist/ socialist/materialist explanation, feminists looked to the division of labour between the public world of paid work and the private world of home and family that occurred with industrialisation as the foundational experience in women's oppression. Numerous empirical studies of manufacturing industries were then undertaken, demonstrating or challenging the timing of the change from household production to factory work, to locate the moment when women's work was effectively separated from men's, and the cause of women's oppression could be pinpointed.

In this spirit I set out to explore an industry that was predominantly male in the hope that by examining an industry in which women did not work, I might uncover some understanding of the processes by which women were systematically excluded from paid labour. Having read a report by the Womens Trade Union League on brewery employees in Milwaukee (USA) in 1912, the brewing industry seemed a logical choice for my study. In the United States (and the United Kingdom) women were employed in brewing, but only in the bottle shop alongside adolescent boys, and only after the introduction of mechanical bottling. There they were left unorganised by the Brewery Workers Union, a militant industrial union with strong German-Socialist credentials, despite the discussion of the 'woman question' within socialist circles and the commitment to structural change contained within socialist political belief.

I very quickly discovered that brewing was a very scientifically based industry, relying on chemical processes for the completion of its product, and heavy manual unskilled labour for the transportation and carriage of the product to wholesale and retail distributors.[25] Not too many secrets there about the exclusion of women. Challenged by a lunchtime conversation I had with Gerda Lerner during a semester I spent at the University of Wisconsin, Madison, about the viability of looking only at an absence, I began to rethink my project. As I looked deeper into the history of the brewing industry in the United States, I also began to think about brewing in Australia.

I became aware that in Australia, where the consumption of beer has been such an intrinsic part of national culture, women were never employed in the manufacture or bottling of beer, but they were always employed in service occupations in the distribution side of the industry. Hotels were often tied, through ownership or lease arrangements, to breweries. It was then that my focus began to shift. Having always been sceptical about the Marxist meta-narrative about the separation of work from households as the overriding explanation for the ongoing nature of women's participation in the paid workforce, I now found I was exploring a workplace where the public–private divide was not clear-cut, that home and work and leisure fused in ways that old theories did not address. It was a service rather than a manufacturing industry that other studies had not explored. By now Joan Scott had pioneered a new kind of labour history, one that rendered visible the way knowledge of sexual difference was manifested. Alice Kessler-Harris explored the payment of wages as a system of meaning.[26] The influence of their work on mine will be apparent in the course of this book. My research was in good company as other feminist scholars were also turning away from manufacturing industries and the masculine model of 'work' on which so much theorising had been based. To find women's employment, as Rosemary Pringle and Jill Matthews have pointed out, it is necessary to look in other places.[27] Focusing on an occupation rather than an industry, one that was a service rather than a manufacturing trade, was one of those other places.

More recent scholarship has focused on women working 'in other places'. The literature on women's working experience has burgeoned in the last decade as scholars have moved away from the definition of 'work' as only paid labour and redefined the workplace and the home in ways that overcame the dichotomous public–private division of earlier theorising.[28] Problematising the domestic character of paid workplaces, and rendering visible the paid and unpaid work women have performed in and from the home, feminist scholars have opened up the field of labour history in new and exciting ways. Particularly influential for my study was Rosemary Pringle's book, *Secretaries Talk: Sexuality, Power and Work*, which appeared in 1988. So much of what Pringle wrote about the significance of secretaries as a group, of secretarial work as an occupation, and of the importance and difficulties secretaries present for feminists, could as easily be said of barmaids.

Like secretaries barmaids, too, are defined more by what they are than what they do. As in the office, so too in the pub, 'far from being marginal to the workplace, sexuality is everywhere . . . alluded to in dress and self-presentation, in jokes and gossip, looks and flirtations, secret affairs and dalliances, in fantasy, and in . . . sexual harassment . . . Sex at work is very much on display.' As Pringle points out, 'gender and sexuality are central not only in the boss–secretary relation but in all workplace power relations'.[29] This book, then, is intended as a contribution to this new feminist literature. Although it draws heavily on empirical material from Australia, the issues raised here about work, workers, sexuality, power and sexual difference have implications and reverberations beyond the limitations of national boundaries.

As Lisa Adkins argued recently, there has been a growing recognition since the 1980s of the connections between sexuality and the gendering of the labour market that is particularly pertinent to service occupations in tourism and hospitality. The emphasis placed on customer interaction with the worker means that service work is to be distinguished from other forms of wage labour. Service work involves a degree of mediation, the worker's task is to ensure that specific requirements of customers or clients are met, and the worker therefore has a certain degree of autonomy to ensure customer satisfaction. There is more than an economic meaning to this work. For in meeting the customer's expectations, the service worker is also bringing about a state of affairs that conforms to certain general values and codes, that are acceptable to the customer and that (re)produce the social structure.[30] Particularly (but not only) where women perform services mainly to a male clientele, sexuality and gendered power relations are deeply implicated.

This is, however, an historical study. Historical examination of women's service work in pubs casts new light on contemporary issues of sexuality in the workplace and yet has a significance beyond the narrowly defined field of labour history. The very fact of women earning money has, by definition, significant implications for sexual difference that British feminist Eleanor Rathbone recognised in 1930: she pointed out that it wasn't women's working *per se* that caused men consternation, it was only when they were being paid for it.[31]

This study also draws heavily on non-traditional sources as it attempts to explore the cultural symbolism of women's work behind the bar. Historians seeking workers' experiences have often encountered a problem in finding sufficient and adequate sources for their task. Working people have not as a rule left voluminous quantities of letters, diaries, and autobiographies. Historians usually rely on more indirect sources: government inquiries where workers have given evidence, participant observation studies by investigative journalists, trade union campaigns for improved conditions, cases argued before industrial tribunals. This study of barmaids uses all these. In addition it relies heavily on photographs and other visual representations of bar work. New theoretical developments over the past fifteen years have highlighted the significance of visual representation in constructing knowledge. For historians of work, photographs are sometimes the only sources available. As Boyd Tonkin pointed out, photographs have particular significance for people who rely on oral traditions for their collective memories.[32] But photographs are also an important source for understanding the meanings of work and the ways work has been represented.

Photography was a particularly nineteenth-century cultural form. The technology was invented in the early decades of the century and although it drew on the existing cultural conventions of image-making in portrait painting, its technological innovation gave photography a whole new meaning. Photographs produced in the nineteenth century embody the beliefs of their makers in the value of science and objectivity associated with mechanical reproduction. Photography enabled the democratisation of 'art' as first portraiture and then cameras themselves became increasingly accessible to the population at large. Photography provides a unique and particularly valuable means of reading the nineteenth century.

The important place photography held in the Australian colonial consciousness in the second half of the nineteenth century is revealed in this plea from a mother in rural Queensland, who, in the 1890s, wondered why more photographers were not travelling in the bush. She wrote, 'I have been saving my pin-money for the last two years to get my little family taken for the ' "old folks at home" ... I am one of the many mothers out west, whose means are too limited to take their children to town, but who would part with their last shilling at home to make glad the hearts of grandmamma or grandpapa in the old country.'[33] This mother was dependent on commercial photographers but amateur photography had become a very popular pastime in the later nineteenth century, and many amateur clubs were formed. Hand-held cameras were introduced in Australia in 1895, which widened the market and expanded the possibilities of photography. It meant more and more amateur enthusiasts could enjoy the activity and build up their family photo albums, some of which have become sources for historical narratives.

Photographs, however, must be approached with the same critical awareness as other historical texts, with knowledge of who is creating the document, why and when. And they must be approached with some awareness of the conventions and aesthetics of the form. Historians are usually interested in the subject or content of the photographic image rather than the form in which the image is created, but a critical awareness of the form is essential to analysis of the subject. For example, on one level paintings and photographs are not interchangeable sources of evidence, yet on another level they are, as the techniques and conventions of one influenced the other. Family photograph albums serve a particular purpose in constructing a family's identity and self-representation and they tend to be used in an uncritical evidentiary way by the families they belong to, as a depiction of a past 'reality'. Historians, however, need to exercise caution in collecting and reading such photographs, they need to be alert to the cultural forms of representations and their meanings.

Like paintings, photographs are not just objective unmediated reality. They actually cause the viewer to see in a new way and thereby 'to present a reality in a way that the mind does not ordinarily perceive it'.[34] But they are 'evidence' of something historical. Their connection to reality gives photographs an authority of authenticity denied to other texts, which is perpetuated today in the popular use of photography and in the discipline of history when photographs are not read critically, as texts. Historians traditionally have not used photographs as anything more than illustrations, of the period, or the person. Yet in using them as illustrations we are using them as evidence of an unmediated reality as though 'looking at a photograph is looking at life itself'.[35] The uncritical use historians make of photographs perpetuates the ideology of scientific objectivity that prevailed in the nineteenth-century construction of the image. There is political danger in this untheorised, uncritical usage that I and others are setting out to disrupt. However the ideology of scientific objectivity contained within the image is also the subject of scrutiny.

Because photography enjoys a privileged relationship to the idea of reality historians (and others) tend to believe 'strongly in its reporting, identifying and documenting function', one feminist photographer has written: 'a photograph promises reality and truth and scientific precision'.[36] But photographs are always an expression of the photographer's vision; the object of that vision is never just out there waiting to be framed but is something 'dynamically produced in the act of representation and reception ... highly mediated and densely coded', a construction not a reflection of 'reality'.[37] The meaning of the photograph is as much contained in its reception by its audience as it is in the actions of the photographer.

Similarly important for this study of barmaids have been legal texts. Law has shaped the meaning and experience of work for women in ways that have not been true for men. Through industrial legislation supposed to be protective in its intent, women's working experience has been shaped and circumscribed since the first Factory Acts were passed in the United Kingdom in 1842. There is now an abundant literature on the impact of this labour legislation on women workers, and on women's campaigns to have the legislation passed or subsequently repealed.[38] Most of this legislation referred to manufacturing industries, or specifically to hours and wages of (usually women) workers. Within Australian labour history, legalism has also operated within the industrial relations system of compulsory arbitration as well as in the legislature and the courts. Thus there is a key focus in this book on legal materials as historical sources, on law's definition of 'the barmaid', on the campaigns for legislative interventions in women's work behind the bar, and on the impact of that for subsequent experience. The nature of the occupation generated prolonged debates and a specific legal response. This study extends the scope of previous studies in the field of protective labour legislation through its inclusion of a legalistic industrial relations system, and its examination as a workplace of what was also a leisure site. Legislation shaping work in pubs also shaped leisure and cultural practices, something previous studies of labour law have not addressed.

Like photography, law also has the power to define and create images of reality. Like other texts, legislation generates a knowledge of sexual difference through its power to set boundaries and proscribe transgressions. In reading legal instrumentalities as texts I have been much influenced by the work of historian Natalie Zemon Davis in 'allowing the "fictional" aspects of these documents [to] be the center of the analysis'.[39]

By that Davis means the way narratives are crafted in the documents under investigation. Her concern is with court records – letters of remission – in sixteenth-century France, but it is an approach that can also be applied to reading legislative debates in twentieth-century Australia. By 'attending closely to the means and settings for producing the stories and to the interests held by both narrator and audience in the storytelling event', parliamentary debates can be read for the cultural meaning they embody as stories of 'the barmaid' told within a particular forum.

Statutes, once enacted, do not contain the same story-telling properties as court depositions but they do create a fictive reality that has all the properties of fidelity to 'truth' that many novels have. Laws that forbade women to be present and drink alcohol except in certain prescribed venues had a material effect on women's drinking practices, in the same way that laws proscribing women's employment behind the bar materially affected women's wage-earning capacity. But at the same time they also created a knowledge of 'appropriate' womanhood that became inscribed in the minds and daily practices of people inside and outside pub culture. How faithful that was to the experience and sense of identity of those women who found employment behind the bar is part of the story of this book. To borrow from Natalie Zemon Davis, I 'ask what relation [law's] truth-telling had to the outcome of the stories' for the women workers in the workplace, 'and what truth status' law's stories had for sexual difference in society outside the workplace.[40]

In Australia, citizenship and public drinking rights have historically been closely correlated.[41] At the turn of the century, feminists within the Woman's Christian Temperance Union were concerned at the effect that alcohol had on homes and families. As they campaigned to enfranchise women they simultaneously campaigned to reduce men's access to alcohol in licensed premises.[42] They succeeded on both counts, but the effect was to strengthen sexual difference: to re-inscribe the pub as a masculine space from which women as customers were systematically excluded. Not surprisingly perhaps, drinking practices and pubs were one of the first targets of a revitalised feminist movement in the 1970s. And in the 1990s they have become the subjects of feminist academic enquiry.

This, then, is a study of a unique occupation in a particular kind of workplace. As work itself undergoes revolutionary changes in the closing decades of the twentieth century historical studies of workplaces, of 'woman' as 'worker' in the nineteenth and twentieth centuries, will have more than a scholarly value. This is a social history of work blended with the cultural history of an occupation, and a study of the meanings embedded in both, for the past as well as for the future.

The sheer quantity of material across the temporal and geographical scope of this subject inevitably means there are gaps and biases and much yet to explore. A thorough exhaustive study of licensing laws across all states over the time period would have been of considerable assistance. I can do no more here than allude to matters of historical significance as I see them, and trust that other scholars will share my enthusiasm for the topic and pursue it further.

PART I
The Nineteenth Century

CHAPTER ONE

'No Place for a Woman'?
Pubkeeping in Colonial Times

'It's a man's country ... it's no place for a woman', Mayse Young's father was told when he wanted to move north in search of work in 1929.[1] No explanation was offered. It was enough that the Northern Territory was the last part of the continent to be colonised, and colonising was a male experience. Roads and railways had to be built, industries established, the Aboriginal people quietened, the machinery of government set in place. There was no room for femininity in imagining the masculine adventure of colonisation. 'There weren't many white women in the Northern Territory in those days', Mayse recalled in a brief reference to the consequences of this gendering, 'and many white men took up with Aboriginal girls'. But Anglo-European women were there, even if only in small numbers. Mayse Young's mother packed her four children, the dogs, chickens and a few household possessions in the back of the car and drove them – with her husband in the truck in front – across the rough roads and unknown country to their new life, keeping a pub. Pubkeeping both was, and was not, a place for a woman.

Pubkeeping had a central place in the process of colonisation. As pubs provided accommodation, refreshment and social contacts to travellers and outlying settlers, they became the nucleus of towns and the centres of European identity. It was often women who ran them. Something of the racial and gendered meanings of colonialism that pubs therefore contained was captured in the reminiscences of Rosa Praed. In *My Australian Girlhood*, published in England in 1902, she wrote evocatively of 'the unloveliness of the Boonah hotel' in far north Queensland. The town was a railway terminus, consisting of a few huts, a store, a primary school and a school of arts. 'The hotel dominates all', she said: 'a two tiered pine-box with ill joined partitions and a zinc cover. It faces west, and the afternoon sun glares into the sitting-room' where strips of carpet 'bulge up with every gust of hot wind'. There were no outside blinds, she recalled, 'and one fancies something almost of indecency in the bareness, the publicity of it beneath the unshrinking stare of the sun'.

Rosa Praed was recounting an episode in the 1870s when it was market day and the customers were ribald and rowdy, causing the landlady to apologetically distance herself from them. 'I've done my best to raise the tone', she said. 'I daresay I manage them better than one in their own position, for they recognise that I'm superior ... if any one gets rowdy, it's enough for me to say a word, the others will back me up ... Still, of course, ... it's not the life I should have chosen.' She claimed she had been raised in a wealthy family in Victoria, but now, being a widow and 'with no man to help me', she had 'come down' to keeping a public house in the bush, where she was glad of market days for the custom they brought but embarrassed by her association with uncouth behaviour. That occasion, and a meeting with another woman in straitened circumstances, led Rosa Praed to reflect on the lot of women in the harsh reality of Australian bush life: 'It is difficult to find anything poetic in the mean hardships which fall upon gracious women, who in their springtime had reasonably expected something better out of life.'[2]

To Rosa Praed pubkeeping was not for 'gracious' women. Yet it obviously could be a means of economic survival. And in isolated communities it was a place for social contact. Over fifty years later, when Mayse Young's family arrived in Pine Creek in the Northern Territory to take over the hotel there, she found the pub 'had an atmosphere of hospitality and bush comfort, a haven of shade and cool refreshments ... where good humour and relaxed company could be found to relieve the isolation and heat of the outback'. Made of timber and galvanised iron, with a cement floor, unlined interior, and wide verandahs all the way around, it was 'a comfortable-looking old place', but hardly luxurious. To sixteen-year-old Mayse, who had lived in a tent most of her life, it seemed like a palace, with real beds to sleep in and a stove to cook on. It was her first real home and she learnt what it was like to live in a community and make permanent friends.

Adjusting to pubkeeping was a little more difficult. They had been taught always to 'look the other way' when they passed a hotel, and yet now she found herself not only living in one but also working for her parents making beds, waiting on tables and serving behind the bar. She came to love the work, and under the guidance of a 'very competent woman', who had had experience in a big hotel in the city and had worked for the previous owner, she developed a real skill at the business. By the end of her working life she owned three hotels in different parts of the Northern Territory. Economically pubkeeping was undoubtedly a wise choice. She was good at the business and could earn a decent living from it. The ambiguity of her social status remained. She often, though not invariably, found that other women would socially 'look the other way', that a hotel was not regarded as a suitable place for a woman, and she could be made to feel like a second-class citizen. She believed the tone of the hotel was set 'by the lady behind the bar' and she set out to create an atmosphere where women felt as welcome as men.

These stories of personal experiences highlight the complex and ambiguous relationship between women and pubs in colonial Australia, and the ironies of that work for 'the lady behind the bar'. While ideas of respectability and appropriate femininity decreed certain spaces to be off-limits, economic demands and the imperatives of colonialism decreed otherwise. Respectability and unrespectability worked together to create the pub. To the youthful Mayse Young the pub provided her family with the first settled home they'd had and subsequent economic security. They in turn provided homely comforts – accommodation, refreshment and social contact – for isolated settlers. While these were thought to be womanly skills, and were welcomed, the women who provided them were somehow tainted by the fact they did so.

Rosa Praed, forced to spend time in the little bush township of Boonah, reflected ironically on 'the march of civilisation' that brought the Salvation Army, temperance and godliness to one Aboriginal man, but that also brought women and pubs together in an unlikely place at the forefront of colonialism. The meanings of these relationships, and the pub culture that arose from them, provides the context for understanding women's work behind the bar. That culture had its origins in English and Irish drinking practices, but it was shaped by the circumstances of imperial expansion, the colonial enterprise. And in turn it shaped the

Figure 1.1 Colonial pubkeeping is represented as isolated and remote in this portrayal of a woman and child on the veranda of the hotel at Borroloola, Northern Territory, 1901–04. (National Library of Australia)

colonial culture of 'Australia'. The story of women's work in pubs is as old as beer selling itself.

Origins of the public house

Public drinking houses first appeared in England in the late Middle Ages as ale selling grew. Beer was part of the daily diet, even for small children, so brewing was a domestic task and probably all adult women were skilled at it. A minority of women brewed beer for commercial sale. Large households brewed for their own consumption, and some produced extra for their neighbours in small households. Unlike most other trades where wives generally helped their husbands and continued the trade when their husbands died, brewing beer was originally and 'chiefly, if not entirely' a craft carried on by women. Ale-selling, an intermittent, seasonal activity carried on after the harvest, was also largely carried on by women.[3]

In the sixteenth century laws were passed to separate the production of beer from its sale, and women were gradually forced out of brewing except for domestic purposes – their own households and, sometimes, other families. However they managed to remain in the retail trade where running a licensed house was regarded as 'suitable provision for invalids and widows who might otherwise require assistance from the rates'. Alice Clark points out that very rarely were doubts raised about the propriety of the trade for women, for although complaints were made at times about the conduct of some alewives (e.g. those receiving stolen goods) others wrote admiringly of them. Nevertheless magistrates began to ban victualling by women aged between 14 and 40 years of age, and by the middle of the seventeenth century very few alehouse keepers were women.[4] This was not so in the colony of New South Wales. There the circumstances of colonisation created a place for women as pubkeepers.

'The blessings of civilisation', J. M. Freeland ironically called them, 'a flag, gunfire and alcohol' came to Australia as 'symbols of the European Age of Enlightenment [and] marked . . . the beginning of the building of a nation in New South Wales'. Very quickly alcohol was 'at the centre of things, the very keystone to the structure of the society', but it was spirits, not ale or beer, and it was largely sold and distributed illegally.[5] The story of how beer came to be valued as a defence against drunkenness and to be historically, indelibly associated with developing the colonial identity begins with that illegal trade in spirits.

It was a British naval and military tradition to supply the troops with rum and this continued in the new settlement. For the troops rum was provided as part of their ration, for the convicts, as a reward for good behaviour. This meant that initially brewing was not a major interest in the colony. But when the officers of the New South Wales Corps took control of the distribution of rum away from the governors' authority, an alternative means of controlling the supply of spirits was sought. The authorities regarded beer as less harmful than spirits. It was thought not to be the cause of drunkenness but rather a healthy and nutritious supplement to working people's diet. Were beer to be readily available in the colony, the monopoly of the 'Rum Corps' (as the New South Wales Corps had become known) over the supply of alcohol could be broken and the degree of drunkenness reduced.

Successive governors thus sought to overcome this illegal trading and to encourage a trade in beer rather than rum. Governors Hunter and Bligh imposed strict port regulations, heavy duties and expensive spirit retail licences to break the power of the Rum Corps, but to no avail. The next governor, King, turned to brewing beer. In 1804 he built a government brewery at Parramatta, which lasted two years before being turned over to private enterprise. Subsequent governors continued to support private breweries through a reduced licence fee (25 pounds to brew it, and 5 pounds to sell it compared with 30 pounds to sell spirits). Breweries established by government patronage in the first forty years of settlement were owned by respected merchants who often had extensive interests in other businesses. There was a period of rapid expansion that culminated in 1835 with the opening of Newnham and Tooth's Kent Brewery in Sydney.[6] Tooths was to rise to a position of dominance in the trade in New South Wales and to last another 130 years. At the same time other breweries were being established in other colonies. Brewing and beer were now firmly identified with the colony's prosperity. It was only in the retail trade that women became part of the story.

'The first inns in Australia appeared with the first free men', Paul McGuire claimed in his history *Inns in Australia*, but it was women who ran them: soldiers' wives and the female friends and agents of officers of the New South Wales Corps. Perhaps this was a convenient means by which officers evaded the regulations prohibiting them from retailing spirits.[7] Nevertheless it gave these women an important means of income. From the time wine and spirit licences were first subjected to government regulation women were a small but significant minority of all licensees, especially in urban areas. Given the subsequent importance of hotels to Australian colonialism, this meant that, from the beginning, women played a significant part in the conquest of the Australian continent.

In the colony

The first licence approved for the sale of liquor in the colony of New South Wales was issued in 1792, four years after the arrival of the First

Fleet, to two men, Essex Henry Bond and Thomas Reiby. While Reiby successfully ran a trading business, his wife, Mary, ran the retail store and pub, and during a very long widowhood built up a substantial fortune. As Mayse Young was to in a later period, Mary Reiby found the liquor trade the key to economic success. The first licence issued directly to a woman to run a public house was granted to Sarah Bird in 1797, and two years after that two more licences were issued to women.[8] In 1815 there were ninety-six licences issued for the Sydney area, twelve of them to women.

The first colonies in Australia, New South Wales and Tasmania, were settled as convict colonies. The demand for women convicts' labour was largely as domestic servants to the officers and free settlers, though many also worked in other trades, laundering and sewing clothes for their fellow convicts, for example. Convict women could not hold a licence until they were pardoned or had served out their time. Marrying a free man automatically gained them their freedom. Spouses of convicts, male or female, could, however, hold a licence, and so some convict women ran public houses for which their husbands held the licence. Other licences were held by single women running the house in conjunction with their lovers. Mary Ford, for example, was the former mistress of prominent colonist Samuel Terry and became the licensee of his pub.[9] In 1820 some of these women were refused licences by Governor Macquarie for running houses of ill-repute too near the convict barracks. Mary Plowright was first on his list: there were frequent complaints about the disorderly nature of her establishment.[10]

While the number of free settlers in the colony remained small, so did the demand for lodgings and accommodation. But as the number of free settlers arriving increased, the opportunities for women to set up boarding houses or inns expanded. Sarah Thornton was a needlewoman sentenced to transportation for life for stealing some lace. She arrived in the colony in 1814, and a few months later her husband arrived to join her. Four years later they had a liquor licence: 'With the greatest frugality ... we collected together a small sum sufficient to buy a little house. I then applied to the Gentlemen of the Colony, for a Licence.' In 1820 she wrote home that she had arrived 'at a state of comfort' and that year was granted a conditional pardon.[11] About half the women involved in running licensed houses were freed ex-convicts which, Monica Perrot points out, may have been a very small proportion of the overall ex-convict population, yet was significant for the opportunity it gave those women.[12] Sarah Thornton thought 'not one in twenty who is sent here, obtains even the necessaries of life, by their own industry'.

During the early convict period the number of licences issued to women increased each year. Although originally run by convict or ex-convict women, by the end of the 1820s there were also growing numbers of free women running hotels and inns. In 1799 fourteen licences were issued, 2 of them to women; in 1809 fifty-three were issued, 5 of them to women, a year later 8 women were granted licences. In 1813 fifty-six licences were issued, 14 of them to women and in 1821 fifty-two were issued, 10 of them to women. In 1819 there were fifty-four public houses in Sydney Town, 11 of them were in the hands of women.[13]

As the number of free settlers in New South Wales increased, so the proportion of women gaining licences fell compared with men. By the 1828 census in New South Wales there were only nine independent women innkeepers and publicans, mainly widows of former publicans. This was a ratio of about one in twenty-four. Although in 1854 when the issuing of licences also covered Moreton Bay (later called Queensland) the ratio was about one in eighteen, the proportion of women gaining licences compared with men was declining.[14] In Tasmania, the proportion of female licensees remained constant though the overall number was increasing: while in 1845 the number of women licensees was ten, five years later it had more than doubled, to twenty-two, and those who were taking up new licences were tending to keep them longer. The average term of a licence was three years; from about 1865 onwards it was nine years and, in at least two instances, women ran the same licence for over twenty years, without a husband to assist them.[15]

Acquiring a licence and running a public house required little training but needed 'a good business head, a pleasant manner, and sufficient capital'.[16] In the early colonial days, hotels tended to be ephemeral, the number of female licensees was small and their average term short. Women often took over a licence when they were widowed. Elizabeth Graham was such a widow of a former convict; left in 1810 with eight children to support, she successfully petitioned the New South Wales governor for renewal of the licence so she could continue to run the business.[17] Similarly, the first woman in Tasmania to take up a licence was an ex-convict whose husband died in the year (1813) she opened her hotel. Three years later she remarried and her new husband took over the licence. A few licensees were women who came free to the colony.[18] As Katrina Alford has pointed out, running a public house was one occupation that was compatible with the task of caring for children, a particular concern for women who were widows. The second woman licensee in Tasmania ran a hotel for only a short time (1818); the third briefly took over a licensed premises on her husband's death; and the fourth opened a new hotel and ran it for seven years on her own.

Women were nevertheless a definite minority among the number of liquor licence holders in the early years of the colony. Alison Alexander has calculated that by 1865 the number of hotels in Tasmania had risen to 387 and remained at approximately 400 until 1914, and that the number of female licensees averaged forty-four per year or approximately 11 per cent of the total number of licences issued.[19]

Despite their small numbers, running licensed premises remained a very real economic option for women. Convict women were significantly outnumbered by convict men and they found it harder to return to Britain when they had served their time. Once they had served their sentence they could expect to spend the remainder of their life in the colony. This may have been only a few years as many women died young. Sarah Thornton, who had done so well in getting her licence, lived only two years after she was fully pardoned. Although most female convicts were sentenced to shorter terms than the men, for many of them transportation for seven years meant, effectively, transportation for life. It was, however, possible for women to obtain their freedom by marrying a free man.[20]

All women, convict or free, were thus at a severe disadvantage economically in the new settlement. There was a demand for men's labour for building colonial enterprises, but virtually none for women's, except as domestic servants or housekeepers. With a very small population, there was not enough demand for this even to occupy all the women convicts. Keeping a licensed house, providing accommodation and meals to travellers, was one way women could both use their skills in domestic service and make an independent living. In a climate where demands for accommodation for travellers and new arrivals was constant and expanding, and thirsts were great, obtaining a liquor licence and keeping a hotel made good economic sense. It was one way women could gain entry into a business where the rewards were potentially quite substantial, as exemplified in the story of Mary Reiby. Most women ran boarding houses and lodgings that were unlicensed.[21] Some combined their liquor licence with running a brothel. The line between holding a liquor licence for legitimate accommodation purposes and using it as a cover to run a brothel was not always clearly defined, and law's role was crucial in defining the boundaries. Public perceptions of women publicans often did not acknowledge the difference.

Creating the Australian pub

Eighteenth-century English drinking establishments fell into three categories: inns, which were usually large, fashionable premises offering lodging, wine, ale, beer and elaborate food to prosperous travellers; taverns, which sold wine to wealthy patrons, but didn't offer extensive accommodation; and alehouses, which were normally smaller premises serving ale or beer (and later spirits) that provided rather basic food and accommodation and were patronised by 'the lower orders'. These different categories were enshrined in laws dating from the sixteenth century, which stipulated the ways in which premises were licensed and the legal obligations of their landlords.[22]

In the new colony, the tavern, the alehouse and the inn fused to become a distinctively new institution. Essentially a drinking establishment, the public house in the colony catered to both locals and travellers, and it provided accommodation and food when it was profitable.[23] The Australian pub, therefore, had a unique character, which made it difficult to be precise about terminology. It wasn't quite the equivalent of the English inn, tavern, alehouse or hotel, it was indeed all of them. It was, perhaps, closer to the alehouse, 'the most popular drinking place in pre-industrial England and the direct forerunner of the Victorian [era] pub';[24] but it was colonial legislation that created it.

From the earliest days of settlement governors had tried to control the traffic in liquor through statutory or regulatory provisions. Governors also distributed licences for the retail sale of alcohol, and it was this licensing system that created 'the Australian pub' as a distinctive entity. In 1816 Governor Macquarie passed regulations in New South Wales requiring people receiving spirit licences to also take a beer licence, while simultaneously preventing brewers from retailing beer. These regulations created a public house where customers could obtain any kind of drink they wanted. Their choice of pub was no longer determined by the type of drink they wanted but by considerations of service, atmosphere and location. Having thereby 'killed the alehouse', in 1830 a new Act 'killed the tavern', leaving the Australian equivalent of the English inn as the sole supplier of liquor in the colony. The Beer Act of 1830 in England had a similarly profound impact on the development of English pubs.[25] The New South Wales Act of 1830 required that every licensed premises should provide accommodation – apart from that provided for the family of the publican – 'of at least two sitting rooms and two sleeping rooms' for use by the public. Later legislation specified the size had to be moderate. Amendments were needed to the Act throughout the 1830s to overcome loopholes that noncompliant publicans were able to find.

More notably, in addition to requiring the provision of accommodation, the 1833 Act also separated out general retailing – of farm equipment, tools, food, et cetera – from the selling of liquor for consumption on the premises. From then on the hotel was a shop that could sell liquor only. The Australian pub as it has since existed was basically determined. It offered both accommodation and refreshments in a private parlour to resident guests, and served a variety of drinks to the casual passing customer in a public bar opening on to the street. There was to be no legislative change to this basic pattern for another eighty years. The importance of beer as the primary beverage served did, however, grow. By the 1830s the brewing industry had taken hold. It needed only customer tastes to develop the demand.

In country districts licensing laws operated a little differently from the city. In 1818 Governor Macquarie had recognised the essential part that wayside inns would play in developing the country and how impossible it would be to police the licensing laws outside the towns. He therefore exempted them from the requirement to hold a liquor licence. Consequently, 'trading hours in the inns were determined only by the presence of the customers and the ability of the proprietor to stay awake. Many of them', Freeland claimed, 'were little better than grog shops.' Given a fillip by the beginning of the coach trade in the 1820s, these inns thrived 'in what was to become the best Australian country pub tradition'.[26]

The pattern of Australia's colonisation was thus crucial in giving the Australian pub both its unique form and its significant place in subsequent history. Pubs spearheaded the conquest of new areas. They were often built before any churches or other public buildings and they became the first theatres and meeting places for religious worship as pastoralists, miners and farmers spread over the continent. The pub was sometimes the only building that indicated the site of a town, and was always one of the best: 'invariably the most substantial, the most solid, ambitious, and resplendent building in the neighbourhood'. Pubs occupied the best sites and could be found on practically every corner (until displaced by the banks.) 'Raw and unrefined, socially outcast but ubiquitous' the colonial pub was subsequently celebrated for the essential part it played in the development and growth of 'Australia' as it came to be.[27] Only now are women being seen as key actors in that story.

Many of the rural pubs were run by women. There were four ways women were involved in the hotel trade: as owner of a freehold title, as lessee, as licensee, or as employee.[28] They sometimes had them built specially. The *Town and Country Journal* in December 1875 reported that a hotel had been built for a Mrs Glassock in Rockhampton, North Queensland, ten years earlier. Married women by law could not hold property or keep their earnings until the passage of the Married Women's Property Acts, beginning in the 1870s. Even then they were only allowed to do so if they were not financially dependent on their husband, if they were legally separated or he was insane. So only widows and single women could own or lease a hotel property. Holding a licence was a different matter. Married women and widows could take over their husband's licence or take up a new licence. Unmarried women – and men – were not legally permitted to hold a liquor licence, a restriction still in force in Queensland in the 1960s.

There were ways around these restrictions, however. In the colonies the letter of the law was sometimes interpreted loosely in the larger economic and social interests of the new society. As already shown, women frequently ran hotels in 'silent partnerships' with their husbands, lovers, relatives or friends. Single women would manage a hotel for which another member of their family (e.g. a brother-in-law) would have nominated for the licence. Women were also known to act as nominees for a single man, an unmarried brother, for example. As late as the 1930s women sometimes held licences on behalf of their husbands.[29]

Figure 1.2, *On Church Hill*, a watercolour by George William Roberts of Ann Bushby and the Dove and Olive Branch pub in 1845, represents 'the woman publican' in early colonial Australia. 'Ann Bushby' is clearly the licensee, her name is prominently displayed over the door in large letters and it appears again on the sign bearing the hotel's name. The figure of the woman is central to the picture: she stands framed by a doorway, in the centre of the painting, directly under the licensee's name. She is surrounded by signs promoting the spirits and liquors she has for sale. Her hospitality is portrayed by her positioning in the doorway, on the front step, arms outstretched.

This is a portrait of hotelkeeping as hospitality, and hospitality as domesticated femininity. Ann Bushby is a business proprietor, and seemingly successful given the substantial establishment she is proprietor of, but her business is domesticated service. And we can see the clientele for

Figure 1.2 *On Church Hill*, watercolour by George William Roberts of Ann Bushby and the Dove and Olive Branch pub, 1845. (Dixson Library, State Library of New South Wales)

whom she provides this service. Leaning against the barrier of the fence, which marks out public boundaries from private, is the rather ambiguous figure of a man. He is outside the fence, but his leaning on it suggests a desire to be inside it. The woman is turned towards him, her outstretched arms possibly inviting him in. His stance is harder to read. He is turned from her, shoulders hunched, arms and legs crossed. He could be sulking, he could be drunk, he is certainly reluctant to approach her but not walking away. The literal and metaphorical space between them is conveyed by the lamp post, which effectively divides the image into two (almost equal) parts, his and hers: she being inside the building, he being outside the domestic sphere visually represented by the fence. She is, however, the stronger image, more comfortable with her surroundings; he looks surly, sullen, perhaps hungry. He has the want, she has the means to provide for his need. Perhaps he was a convict. Convicts were frequent visitors to public houses, although they could be charged with consuming alcohol and the licensee could be charged with allowing it.[30]

One woman who tried to enter the hotel trade on her own was Isabella Kelly, the only single woman landholder among the early settlers on the Manning River in northern New South Wales. In 1841, in anticipation of a township being built at a site near a river crossing, she built a magnificent inn and advertised for custom. But the town was never built. Other river crossings were opened up and she had to give up her plans for running an inn. Hotels were built along transport routes, in the very early days along horse and coach routes. Later, when the railway came, they were built at the terminus or near the station. One inn might be the only accommodation available between two major urban centres, and also provide the venue for court hearings, coronial inquiries, business transactions, and various local administrative (e.g. Land Board) meetings and social functions. Sometimes hotelkeepers set up adjoining premises of a store and post office, or combined it with trading in building materials or butchery. One hotelkeeper who ran a busy establishment on a major traveller's route wrote home to her sister in England of the demands when a coach arrived: horses had to be changed, the travellers fed, and the long-awaited post distributed among the eager, waiting locals. This particular woman bore most of the responsibility for running the hotel when her husband became incapacitated, but as her children grew up she was able, with their help, to keep the business going for another twenty years, by which time she was 80 years old.[31]

The 1840s saw Sydney's 'entry into manhood' according to Freeland, when 'Sydney left its Colonial youth behind'. The 'small intimate colonial inn', as depicted in the painting of Ann Bushby, had been 'in tune with Sydney's character' for the first fifty years of settlement. Now it was 'no longer adequate in size, efficiency or standards'.[32] The discovery of gold brought other opportunities to women pubkeepers.

On the goldfields

When gold was first discovered in 1850, men rushed to the diggings. When one field ran out, they moved on to another, and it was often some time before they drifted back to the towns and their families. Wives had to fend for themselves and raise their children as best they could. But there were also women who found their way to the goldfields; some to try mining (mainly fossicking) for themselves, some to work as prostitutes, some to launder and labour for the men they were attached to, and others to set up shop selling liquor. Within a decade the proportion of women to men on the goldfields was nearly the same as in the population generally (about 39 per cent). At first, in an attempt to control drunkenness on the diggings, the colonial government outlawed the presence of hotels on the goldfields, a ban that lasted for several years. Not surprisingly, almost immediately 'grog shops sprang up magically among the heaps of spoil. Housed in tents, shanties or weatherboard sheds hastily knocked together, they provided a rough-and-ready kind of entertainment'.[33] Selling liquor either legally or illegally was one means by which women were able to support themselves and their children (this was how bushranger Ned Kelly's mother, Ellen, supported her family after she was widowed).[34]

There were consequently many women licensees of pubs in and around the goldfields. Indeed, there were more women working in hotels or as hotelkeepers in the mining districts of Victoria in the 1850s and 1860s than there were in other parts of the state.[35] Their presence there was documented in photographs. The camera arrived in Australia in 1840, within a year of the first daguerreotype, and therefore virtually simultaneously with the colonisation of much of the continent. In the next decade the population rush that the discovery of gold brought provided subject matter, a rationale and an expanded market for this new technology.

The photo in Figure 1.3 was taken in 1867 in the Victorian gold-rush town of Ballarat. Now located in a museum, it probably came from a personal collection or family photo album. It belongs to the genre of Australian 'frontier' photography, those 'highly specific, highly localised and personalised images' that were produced 'purely for immediate and local consumption'.[36] The men and women who stood outside their houses and shops and were the subjects of the photographs were also the clients who purchased them. These images were not for public exhibition. They were an extension of the portrait, icons of pride in new status and new possessions. Having your portrait done was a way of making your economic success and rising social status visible to yourself and to others.[37] They were, nevertheless, commodities, for which there was a socially defined demand. These images were valued in the nineteenth century for their 'realism'; for their directness, their detail and the exhaustiveness of their documentation.[38]

Historians can read a photograph such as this as evidence that women were on the goldfields (which reading you would not get from traditional Australian history narratives); and we can infer from the careful position-ing of the woman, to the left of a building on the street outside but in front of an open door, that she was not simply a passerby, but that she had some connection to it. The photograph has been composed to include the entire building including the name, indicating that this was a hotel, she, most likely, the licensee. Photographic conventions of the period, which included photographing proprietors outside their establish-ments, and the fact that a licence for the Pennyweight was issued in the same year that the photo was taken, support the reading that this is the licensee herself.

Reading this photograph in the realist aesthetic of the time in which it was taken, and in the uncritical evidentiary way of history, it challenges the masculinist national narrative of Australian history in which women's

Figure 1.3 The Pennyweight Hotel, Levy Street, Ballarat, 1867. An example of Australian frontier photography. (#00044, Collection 012, Courtesy of the Museum of Victoria Council)

work as innkeepers on the goldfields was rendered invisible. But we can also read it as a representation whose meaning for us today comes from the image of the woman that is depicted. This woman is looking directly into the camera although we can't really see her face. The adoption of a pose looking directly into the camera can also tell us something about her as subject and agent of her own history. At the very least, as Pierre Bourdieu has said, 'striking a pose means respecting oneself and demanding respect'.[39] Having one's image made in the nineteenth century carried an importance that came through in the picture. The subject of this photograph, however mediated, was not only a creation of the photographer's fantasy. The nineteenth-century technology was such that the subject had to stand still for long periods and poses were often very formal. The conventions of photographic forms were as much a result of this technology as they were of aesthetic sensibilities. The technology alone required the cooperation of the subject with the photographer: the intractability of the tripod-mounted camera, the relative slowness of exposure, and the fixed position that had to be maintained.

This woman is the only person in the photograph. She has a small dog beside her. The hotel is not a grand one, it is barely more than a house, a wooden construction with a front room reminiscent of a family parlour at a time when 'city pubs were reaching to four floors, balconies were provided' and 'curved corrugated iron' had become fashionable.[40] There were fashionable grand pubs in Ballarat by 1867. This woman is the proprietor of a small establishment that was neither fashionable nor very prosperous. It seems not to have been located on a corner or a hill or in any other prime location as the better pubs were. She was probably struggling to make a viable living. Her dress and demeanour speak of a life of hard work and little spare cash. There are no luxuries in sight either in the hotel fixtures or in her dress. Her stance, however, is proud and determined. She is standing firmly, both feet solidly on the ground, hands by her side, looking front on to the camera in the way Pierre Bourdieu describes as commanding respect. Photographic historian Anne-Marie Willis has spoken of how the photograph allows the viewer to dwell on the 'specifics of the moment and the minutiae of the local ... the rough dirt roads, the coarse grain of timber houses, the crude but practical construction of the buildings'. It also, from the perspective of historical distance, 'senses the poignancy of disjunctions ... in the sometimes confident, sometimes awkward poses, the stances of swaggering pride in relation to what is materially so slight' that is found in these early frontier photographs.[41]

What is also visible, then, in this image of a woman licensee, is the meaning of economic independence in a colony where 'work' was a male prerogative. As we have seen, 'business women did not abound in the colonial economy', and by and large their enterprises were small and did not require large amounts of capital.[42] Hotelkeeping was the principal industry in which they were involved but even there women were a minority. This image of a real woman looking back into the camera's gaze is a challenge to dominant narratives eliding or constructing 'woman' as either passive or invisible in the colonial economy.[43] This is also an image of self-assertion and pride in independence in a culture of frontier colonialism, where men outnumbered women four to one, and paid work for women was available only in a narrow range of employments. Running a commercial enterprise carried importance grounded in, but beyond, simple economic survival. For women without men it would also have meant considerable personal freedom. 'Freedom' and 'respectability' were often incompatible concepts in the nineteenth century and careful negotiation was needed to straddle both.

Gold discoveries continued to simultaneously disrupt and bring wealth and population to other parts of the continent. In 1870 gold was discovered in Gympie, Queensland, and photographers were there to record the work of women hotelkeepers. Photographs of public houses and their licensees were, as I have said, usually produced for the owners of the business but they have come to us as historical sources on which knowledge is and was built. Photography was playing an increasingly significant part in the culture of colonial Australia as the century progressed, and in the crucial period of nation-building.

Anne-Marie Willis has discussed how photographers, self-consciously portraying an 'Australian' vision for public consumption, positioned the women and children 'as those who wait, patiently and faithfully, for the return of husband and father'.[44] Figure 1.4 shows an example of this practice, another in the frontier genre of photography. That this woman is the proprietor of this establishment is indicated by her positioning in and of the premises whose name so prominently displayed makes it the subject of the image rather than her. Yet she is at an angle to the camera; she is positioned in relation to her children and in a doorway, sheltered by the building, suggesting a reluctance to leave the domesticated space of the interior for the exposed street (the public world) outside. The business is therefore dominant in the frame, she is not. She is subservient to it, suggesting her significance to the enterprise is not central but as helpmeet. She could well be pregnant. This and the presence of the children prompts questions about a father. Signs of economic hardship and her subordination to the business name in the frame indicate a more important figure is absent, a worker, a breadwinner. We are therefore made conscious of a man's absence, made to expect that a man's presence is being waited for. The street in front of the building is masculine space, but it is empty and she has not stepped forward into it as the woman in front of the Pennyweight Hotel did. Indeed her expression (as much as we can tell) is watchful, anxious, her stance uncertain, and, in the absence of a man, hesitancy, anxiety and uncertainty is the dominant mood of this photograph, compared with the determination and boldness of the image in Figure 1.3.

This image is representing 'woman as licensee' as mother/widow/past, present and future wife. Widowhood and wife desertion were very prevalent in the Australian colonies, and family sizes were much larger than in Europe or the United Kingdom. Women therefore often struggled to raise very large families in a harsh environment without assistance from extended kin.[45] Struggle rather than independence is the dominant sense being conveyed in this image.

Keeping a pub

Some women licensees were quite young; most did not employ staff but ran their hotels either alone or with the help of relatives.[46] The work was very physically demanding. Far from being an easy way to make a living, it was quite arduous and the tasks were many. Responsibilities involved running the residential and dining facilities (providing meals for maybe twenty or thirty people at a time) managing the laundry of all the bed and

Figure 1.4 Morse's Bendigo Hotel, Gympie, Queensland, *c.* 1872. Another example of Australian frontier photography. (Collection: John Oxley Library, Brisbane)

table linen, as well as tending the bar. Colonial laws often permitted liquor to be served from 4 a.m. until midnight six days a week. There was more limited trading on Sundays, but travellers could still purchase liquor twenty-four hours a day, seven days a week. Later laws reduced the hours of trading (from 6 a.m. to 11 p.m.) and banned Sunday trading for all but bona fide travellers, but extensive flouting of this law meant even Sundays were not free. As one licensee said of his clientele, 'If you didn't serve them a drink on Sundays, they would tear the place down.'[47]

Having difficulty with a rough clientele was one of the hazards of the trade. Mary Doyle, who ran various pubs over the course of thirty years, had her nose broken when she intervened in a brawl between her customers, and Mayse Young coolly declared, 'of course there were punch-ups every now and then'. On one occasion, she said, 'the drains around the hotel ran red with blood and our bush nurse was called in to attend the wounded'.[48]

From the 1860s onwards hotels increasingly became family businesses, with different members of the one family holding the licence, and passing it on to the next generation. This was a period of greater stability after the transience of the early colonial period and the disruption of the gold decades.

The photograph in Figure 1.5 shows an example of a pub in rural New South Wales. The premises again are a simple single-storey wooden building. This would seem to be an establishment providing an income for a widow and her extended family. The licensee is most probably the woman dressed very conspicuously and placed in the centre of the rather large group. It is reasonable to suppose the two young women seated on either side of her are her daughters or daughters-in-law, and the girl seated on the far right is her daughter. The man leaning in a familiar, intimate way on the shoulder of the young woman on the left was perhaps her husband or, given his youthful appearance and demeanour, was more probably her brother. The four small children are grouped as one, suggesting they belong to one or both of the young women, and perhaps the more neatly dressed and sober-looking man (second from right) standing immediately behind the girl is a husband. The other men holding up their bottles and glasses are undoubtedly customers and show considerably more jollity than the rest of the group. The young women are very demurely dressed, only the older woman proprietor is distinguished in her appearance. There is another figure, standing on the roof, separating himself from the group in the way perhaps a younger son would, but he is chopped off at the top of the picture.

There is, however, one employee featured in this photograph, which is rare for its inclusion of an Aboriginal man. His positioning – in the front row with the family owning the pub, but off a little distance to the left of

Figure 1.5 Gold Diggers Arms, Moonan Brook, New South Wales, 1880. (Bicentennial Copying Project, State Library of New South Wales)

them – suggests he was neither customer nor family but was probably employed. The number of Aboriginal people who worked in or around pubs in the nineteenth century is unknown. There is evidence in the twentieth century of Aboriginal women laundering and cleaning in hotels, or helping with the proprietors' children.[49] However, as early as 1838 laws had been passed prohibiting or restricting Aboriginal people's consumption of alcohol and these provisions were extended over the course of the century to cover their very presence in and around licensed premises.

This is a very unexplored aspect of Australian history. As Ann McGrath has pointed out, Aboriginal men's inability to enter a pub freely alongside other (white) men was a constant reminder of inequality, for only via the patronage of white men could they obtain access to liquor.[50] The history of alcohol and Aboriginal people in Australia is one of 'much sorry business' in Marcia Langton's phrase. It is also a direct consequence of colonialism. From the days of the rum trade through to the end of the nineteenth century a national cultural identity had developed around alcohol consumption and participation in drinking rituals. By the time of Federation in 1901, drinking 'demarcated full citizenship, [and] full membership in the nation'. This was 'intrinsically a male domain' but the systematic exclusion of Aboriginal men as well as women made it a racially exclusive domain too. Ann McGrath has pointed out that the liberalisation of the laws in various states between 1957 and 1972, which gave Aboriginal people the right to drink, was perhaps more significant for some than the less tangible arrival of political citizenship. 'But then maybe grog *was* citizenship' for it gave Aboriginal men the right to be admitted into 'that bastion of white male supremacy, the pub ... the locus of power in the townships'. Thus access to alcohol carried different meanings for Aboriginal men and for women: for Aboriginal men it promised access to power and status alongside white men. For women, whose relationship to white men was different, 'the combination of grog and western-style marriage was a violent sometimes lethal one'. Drink and protection from it also provided justification for missionaries and governments to exert control over Aboriginal women. Today public drunkenness is one of the prime reasons for arrest and incarceration of Aboriginal men, a very direct consequence of colonialism. Aboriginal women have developed a critique of men's drinking and are waging campaigns to free their communities of alcohol.[51]

Pubkeeping cannot therefore be separated from the colonialist project. Pubs providing accommodation and refreshments facilitated the spread of settlement into Aboriginal country, and brought alcohol and drinking culture to the people who were displaced. White women, although in a minority, were active participants in this process. Yet pubs and drinking were increasingly identified with masculinity and the same dynamics of exclusion worked against Anglo-European women as against Aboriginal people.

Pubkeeping has thus had a vital part to play in the sexual and racial dynamics of Australian culture. Women are important to the history of pubkeeping and pubkeeping is important to the history of women in Australia. It was a source of self-employment and business proprietorship where others often didn't exist and by the 1890s provided more opportunities for self-employment than any other industry. In 1891 13 per cent of the New South Wales female labour force (nearly 5000 women) were self-employed (compared with 1200 men or 7 per cent of the male labour force). Of these, three-fifths of the women and well over half the males were hotel and innkeepers, or board and lodging house keepers. Women also ran some quite substantial and important hotels in the cities, of necessity employing staff. Mrs. Leah Johnson's Commercial Hotel in Queensland was very grand.[52] Women employers were the smallest category in the New South Wales census of 1891. Virtually all of the slightly more than five hundred women employers were providing some form of accommodation and hospitality to paying customers.

In isolated rural areas with a fluctuating and itinerant population, hotels were important social centres as well as places providing accommodation for travellers and transient workers. In the far north-west of

Western Australia, a 'respectable' woman could become a postmistress, teacher, nurse or the 'manageress or proprietress of boarding houses and hostels'. A small group also ran hotels, 'a fairly respectable profession' for mainly middle-class women, and their numbers were growing by the end of the century. From an isolated one woman hotel licensee listed in the 1881 census, the number had increased to thirteen by 1891. But 'it was a constant battle' to keep hotels distinguished in reputation from the bawdy gambling houses and brothels also run by women.[53] Some boarding houses listed in the census statistics were no doubt disguising prostitution and brothel-keeping. 'Respectability' and 'unrespectability' were key concepts for establishing boundaries and appropriate conduct. As the adventures and new freedoms of colonialism were explored, hotels were one site where they were played out.

There were also many hotels where women were involved as part of the family business. In Tasmania in 1891, approximately half (112) of the 217 women working in hotels were employers or working on their own account, the other half were 'relatives assisting' other family members. In 1891 the colonial census-takers had reclassified wives and adult children working on family farms and in family enterprises as 'not workers', as 'relatives assisting' a single (male) breadwinner.[54] Most of the females and nearly all the males (i.e. 588 of 723) described in the New South Wales census as 'relatives assisting' were working in hotels and inns. Ten years later, when either the 1890s depression had taken its toll, or the census statisticians had classified them differently, two-thirds of the women working for themselves in Tasmania had disappeared and the number of 'relatives assisting' had increased by more than the same amount.[55]

Hotelkeeping was undoubtedly a source of economic survival, even prosperity, for colonial women and their families. It was also one colonialist enterprise in which women could participate. It facilitated their adventure into unknown regions and carried with it elements of risk and danger that some found exciting. In the nineteenth century pubs were important as places of entertainment. Hotels provided some recreation and leisure for women as well as men, although at present very little is known about this in Australia. This development was unmistakably connected to changing leisure customs as towns and cities grew.

By the mid-nineteenth century, urban pubs were the centre of life and recreation. They offered entertainment, games like skittle and billiards, nightly sing-songs and sociability, 'friendship and cordial relationships ... [they were] a place for public contests and rivalries'.[56] Gradually the term 'bar' came into usage in the colony. By the end of the 1840s, Freeland claims, although they were to change their character somewhat over the next hundred years, the four terms and types of bar that were to become the standard of the Australian pub had been established: the saloon bar;

Figure 1.6 Cherry's Carlton Club Hotel, Hobart, *c.* 1888, showing the centrality of pubs to urban social life. (W. L. Crowther Library, State Library of Tasmania)

the private bar; the parlour bar, which had privacy and comfortable seats and tables; and the public bar, which from then on 'was fixed and immutable'.[57] The public bar was the one directly accessible from the street where liquor was served to any passing customer who popped in: men, women and sometimes children fetching for their parents, some to stay and drink, others to fill a jug and take it home. The number, type and quality of these bars depended on the particular house. Grand city hotels, corner suburban locals and country inns catered for their own clientele and provided facilities accordingly. The class of patrons was clearly significant. In urban working-class localities the corner pub catered for a regular drop-in trade in the public bar. The seasonal nature of work in rural areas, which meant work was casual and intermittent for many city workers also, was more likely to lead to bouts of binge drinking.[58] City pubs catered for the professional and commercial classes after work or an evening in the theatre. They provided several interior, sometimes upstairs bars in order to cater to their middle-class clientele as distinct from their public-bar patrons. Middle-class patronage of public houses was on the increase by the last quarter of the nineteenth century, and the spatial arrangements of pubs began to reflect both class and gender differences.[59] These developments provided the context for the emergence of barmaids. As pubs underwent change they became a more significant source of employment for wage labour. And it is in the employment of wage labour that we see the development of the occupational category of barmaid.

The new prosperity and population growth in the second half of the nineteenth century created more – and more varied – work opportunities for women than had been available previously. The heavily agricultural, mining and pastoral economy, with its very high ratio of men to women, that had been characteristic in the early nineteenth century, gave way over the following decades to more urban development. The impetus of the gold boom enabled the colonial economy to diversify. With diversification and economic prosperity came further population increase and a growth in trades and industries that opened up the labour market. Most spectacular was the rise in population of the major cities.

With the influx of families and the growth of towns, work opportunities for women now expanded. There was a demand for services such as laundering and schooling that women provided, and there was a growth in the development of manufacturing for local consumption in the clothing, footwear and food industries. As a consequence, although domestic service remained the major source of paid employment for women until the end of the century, there was a big increase in women's participation in other forms of paid labour. Many women leaving domestic service were moving into manufacturing industries. In 1871, well over half of women working were domestic servants. Forty years later that proportion were employed in manufacturing trades.[60]

Particularly significant for women's changing employment opportunities in the second half of the nineteenth century was the growth of towns, with their schools and commercial enterprises, their shops, boarding houses, laundries and licensed public houses. The biggest rise, then, was in professional and commercial occupations. Overall, Australian women workers were more likely than their British counterparts to be employed in service industries than manufacturing trades. The nature of colonial settlement and the later mechanisation of manufacturing trades in the colonies meant the number of women engaged in commerce was much greater and the proportion who were active in occupations involving food, drink and running lodgings was larger in Australia than it was in the United Kingdom in the same period.[61]

As the colonial population grew and expanded, and hotels became increasingly numerous, they became a significant source of wage employment for women. Eighty-one per cent of the female labour force (31 000 women) identified in the New South Wales census in 1891 were wage-earners, of whom 4537 were employees 'of various kinds' working in hotels and inns. Many of these would have been undertaking cleaning and cooking tasks, perhaps occasionally serving behind the bar. But from the 1850s onwards women were also being employed specifically to serve in the bar. For along with the expansion of towns, wage labour and an increasing labour market, grew occupations associated with new, urban, commercialised, recreational pursuits. One of these was the occupation of barmaid. It is to this change that I now turn.

CHAPTER TWO

'The Photographer and the Barmaid': Narrating Women's Work

Bartending for women in Australia first appears as a distinct occupation in the convict indents. A very small number of convict women transported to the Australian colonies in the early nineteenth century gave 'bar attendant' as their occupation on boarding ship.[1] It was not until much later that the distinctiveness of the occupation became apparent.

In 1885 a poem called 'The Photographer and the Barmaid' was published in a Queensland newspaper.[2] It assumed knowledge of the occupations of 'the barmaid' and 'the photographer' in a way that was not possible fifty years earlier. Both occupations were a creation of nineteenth-century social and labour market changes. They had first appeared in the middle of the century and were well known by its end. Most of the readers of this particular newspaper had probably had their 'image taken' by 1890. Being a barmaid was an occupational choice increasingly available to young women. Seeing the barmaid as sexualised object of the photographer's intentions would also reverberate with popular knowledge. This poem was similar to a lot of poetry published in the popular press at this time; barmaids were, by then, a favourite subject.

What is interesting about the poem is the humour with which it spoke in the usual, if metaphorical, way of the dangers of paid work for young women. This particular poem told the story of a pretty barmaid seduced into having her image taken by a wily young photographer who then abandoned her. Here 'the barmaid' was represented as the sorry victim of commercial trade, experiencing loss and humiliation as, it was often suggested, would the numerous other such girls entering the paid labour force in this period. It was an allegory of sexual danger, a familiar nineteenth-century narrative about women working outside their own or somebody else's home. Casting 'the barmaid' as another working girl innocent of, but vulnerable to, the dangers of public commerce resonated with a prevailing discourse about young women seeking paid employment. 'The attraction of girlish inexperience, a pretty face and a pretty figure ... make a bar seductive', one report said. But the seducer was the male photographer, not the barmaid: 'the general youthfulness of barmaids' means that 'they are almost always innocent ... their part ... is at least at first that of the seduced, not the seducer'.[3]

Canadian historian Peter Bailey has claimed that 'the modern barmaid was a product of the transformation of the urban public house' in England when, beginning in the 1830s, the tavern was replaced by a new drinking establishment, the gin palace. This new-style drinking establishment, 'with its dramatic innovations of scale, plan, management and style', according to Bailey, 'needed the barmaid both as staff ... and as a further item of allurement among its mirrors and mahogany, its brassware and coloured tile'. Increasing competition in the licensed trade and a clientele that was 'more numerous, transitory and anonymous' in urban centres than in old long-settled neighbourhoods meant an attractive woman became necessary to attract trade.[4] The Australian colonies didn't experience these changes as disruptions. There were no old long-settled neighbourhoods or gin palaces. Certainly urban centres were growing apace and pubs proliferated. But the idea of woman as an 'item of allurement' – the barmaid as the seducer – seems to have become significant only in hindsight.

The presence of women as barmaids did cause concerns about the mixing of the sexes in public, as it did in all workplaces. I suspect the emergence of 'the barmaid' as an occupational category was more directly tied to changes in occupational specialisation that occurred in all kinds of workplaces, than it was to her sex and sexuality. The economic factors shaping women's participation in paid labour (as workers) are conveniently denied as they are subsumed into women's identity as their sex (as women) as necessarily different. This way knowledge of the harsh realities of economic differences between men and women is established and maintained. Women's employment in hotels continued to be in areas where they were expected to carry out a variety of tasks, while men's became more specialised into occupations that were paid more. Work behind the bar was available to both and only gradually did it become a specific occupation with sexual identity. Occupational specialisation was a way of marking out and maintaining sexual difference as women moved into paid labour in public workplaces. It created the sexual division of labour as sexual difference was renegotiated in the workplace. Marking the work of women behind the bar, as barmaids, as sexual work marked out the boundaries of sexual difference. Historians have tended to accept uncritically subsequent characterisations of barmaids without tracing their origins.

From Servant to Barmaid

Serving alcohol was part of the work of servants in English taverns and alehouses, and only one of their tasks. In the mid-nineteenth century increased customer demand and the changing skills needed for serving meant the work became more limited to the specific task of serving behind the bar. The first significant change came in the nature of the public drinking house and its physical layout. Until the early nineteenth century standard English taverns were barely distinguishable from the houses around them and consisted of five rooms: the public parlour, tap room and bar, which were accessible to the public, and a kitchen and private parlour which were not. Working men were served in the tap room which was furnished with fixed wooden benches around the walls. More genteel customers were served in the public parlour which had superior furnishings and chairs. No one was served in the bar area. Food and drink were brought to the tap room or the public parlour by female servants and 'tapboys'.

Under this design the public house was more of a *house*, where the owner made some of his rooms available to guests. He was the host, and they were looked after by his servants according to their status, as they would be in a private house.[5] Then public houses began to include spirit stores or dram shops in their premises. These had been established in the eighteenth century as separate shops, dispensing mainly cheap gin, but with no parlours, no tap room, no seats and no food. In the early nineteenth century taverns began to install counters behind which they kept glasses, tankards and the drink that was not in the cellar, which they then sold to the public.

The introduction of this bar counter was the most significant inno-vation of pub design in the nineteenth century. Similar to the counter in retail department stores, which emerged much later, the bar symbolically converted the patrons from 'guests' into 'customers', a more impersonal and formalised selling relationship than had previously existed. As a large impenetrable barrier, the bar across the entire room very effectively divided customers from workers. And it created the category of special-ised bar attendant: the woman servant turned into a barmaid. These changes were mirrored in the Australian colonies.

Like so much else, 'the barmaid' was supposedly brought to Melbourne with the gold rushes. In 1856 the English company Spiers and Pond set up a refreshment bar at their city theatre in Melbourne and employed women as barmaids to serve drinks at intermission.[6] The Theatre Royal 'was the place to find everybody who was anybody in those days, and to be found by them', an article in *Table Talk* claimed in

1893. The women employed by Spiers and Pond were, in language suggestive of fruit and other edibles, 'the pick of the basket': young, pretty, and, unlike the women who hung about theatres for the purposes of prostitution, 'respectable'. 'It was a sight good for the eyes to see eight lady-like girls down the stairs and one in the cafe above, all habited alike in neat black dresses with white collars to neck and ditto cuffs to the wrists. They were as good as they looked in their behaviour, which was alike to everybody.' To a population of largely single young men, the presence of the barmaids made a visit to the theatre an 'every-evening resort' for they 'found attractions in these pretty barmaids not to be found in their boarding houses'. Regrettably, 'such a selection of nice girls as were made in the fifties could not be found now', *Table Talk* lamented.[7]

While this reminiscence is interesting for its nostalgia about the barmaids of a past era, it is also a rare source for reconstructing something of the history of 'the barmaid' in Australia. It is significant that it was written so many years after the event, and at a time when public interest in barmaids was at its height. Most importantly, according to this account, the young women working for Spiers and Pond were deliberately employed *because* of their personal attributes. Their employment was predicated on their provision of a service that hinted at, but was not, prostitution. That it took place in a theatre also was suggestive for the meanings attached to the work and the workers. By the 1890s barmaids were undoubtedly associated with sexual titillation, especially in the temperance literature, discussed in subsequent chapters.

This deliberate manipulation of commercialised sex and the linkages to prostitution was part and parcel of the definition of the occupation of barmaid by the time this piece was written. Juxtaposing the barmaids' explicit sexuality with their respectability was defining women's employment in a public space in a new, highly charged way. It created a sense of heightened excitement: 'There was more than drink to be had' and the population of Melbourne in the 1850s, youthful and largely single, 'enjoyed a freedom and unrestraint to which they had been elsewhere unaccustomed'.[8] It is not clear that barmaids' sexuality was as important in the 1850s as this account indicates. Nevertheless the occupation soon spread beyond the theatre bars to hotels.

The Australian pub differed from its English progenitor, and it provided a ready environment for 'the barmaid' to flourish. While town inns existed primarily as private houses offering hospitality to paying guests, the colonial equivalent of taverns were a different proposition. They had developed bar counters as early as 1825 and, by 1835, had them as a standard feature. The tap room was for storage only and by the 1850s the term 'tap room' had died out and been replaced by 'bar'. The counter bar enabled speedy service and a watchful eye to be kept over customers, no doubt a necessity in a primarily convict population.[9] As hotels proliferated and other colonial work opportunities expanded in the later nineteenth century, so did the number of bars and the chances for work behind them for young women.

For some time barmaids and servants were counted together in the census records. 'Servant' as used in the census earlier in the nineteenth century usually meant an unskilled employee who may have undertaken domestic or other duties attached to the enterprise. Skilled workers were identified by their trade (e.g. stonemason) but the only categories for unskilled workers were as 'labourer' or 'servant', often to an employer identified by an occupation. For example, in the 1828 census in New South Wales, one James Bannister was described as servant to William Ikin, innkeeper, and Henry Barlow as servant to William Jones, publican. Some women were 'servants' to grocers' shops. Clearly the employer's trade was included because it affected the sort of servant the respondent was, and tasks could include selling as well as cleaning, fetching and carrying.[10] The term 'barmaid' was not in current use in England before the late 1830s and although it had begun to be used in the colonies following the Spiers and Pond experiment in the 1850s it still took some time for the category to turn up in census classifications. For quite a long time, as was the case in England, there was no clear-cut distinction made between the domestic duties servants were expected to perform in an employer's household and work in their business or trade. Servants did not have specialised duties, a feature that would be particularly true in innkeeping and would continue in small family-owned establishments.[11] In 1856 it was reported in the Hobart *Mercury* that a 14-year-old servant had been left in charge of her employer's hotel and had served a customer beer. Advertisements for servants could specify a range of expected duties, including looking after children and serving behind the bar.[12]

'Barmaids' were not, therefore, listed separately in the censuses taken in Victoria in 1871 and 1881, although we can see a decline (of 469) in the number of men working as 'inn, clubhouse and eating house servants' and a corresponding rise (of 411) in the number of women working in these capacities in that decade. By 1881 there were 1500 men and over 3000 women hotel servants in Victoria. Barmaids and barmen were indexed separately in the 1871 Queensland census but in the text were grouped in with other occupations; in 1881 there were 724 males and only 52 females 'dealing in drinks and stimulants' in Queensland. In South Australia there was no separate category either; in 1871 there were 482 innkeepers and their servants, in 1881, 626 male servants and 334 female servants in hotels, probably many of whom also worked at least part of the day in the bar. Hotel servants also included those employed to wait on tables in the dining room.

Bar staff were not a separate category until 1891 in Western Australia. The census-takers had recorded only 7 women hotelkeepers in 1881 and 106 men 'hotelkeepers, barmen etc.' In 1891 numbers were very small, there were 42 barmen to 12 barmaids. But single working-class women 'were in demand all over the north' to work as barmaids and waitresses as hotels and public houses sprang up in coastal towns and the inland gold-rush regions of Western Australia. The number of hotels in Western Australia more than trebled between 1895 and 1910: from 217 to 721.[13] Barmaids were first mentioned separately in Tasmania in the census of 1881 when 31 barmaids were listed; twenty years later this number had more than doubled, to 68.[14] In small establishments and in rural areas people continued working as servants and only sometimes serving behind the bar, but from this time on working specifically and only behind the bar increasingly became a distinct category of occupation that took women employees out of the category of 'servant'. A wages book from a Melbourne hotel in 1870 clearly differentiates the wages (3 pounds) paid to 'Miss Higgins, Miss Kelly, barmaid' from those of the housemaids and pantry maid who were paid less than half that. In England there were more barmen than barmaids although the numbers were almost equal, but by the 1890s in New South Wales, barmaids (402) outnumbered barmen (275), in the cities (281:160) more so than in the country (120:113).[15]

The census figures thus show increasing numbers of women being employed to work behind the bar, not in their own family businesses, or as 'relatives assisting', but as wage-earners, independent of their families.

English barmaids were largely recruited from among the daughters of shopkeepers, tradesmen and mechanics. Many had previously worked as domestic servants.[16] As could be expected, barmaids in Australia were essentially recruited from the same group of workers as most other domestic servants. In the 1901 New South Wales census a high proportion of barmaids were Catholics, suggesting they were probably Irish.[17] Though not actually middle class, young women working as barmaids were a higher order of servant than most: they had personal qualities of appearance and manner that could command higher wages, and they could, therefore, leave domestic service for the better conditions of work behind the bar.

One young woman who began work as a barmaid in the 1870s published her autobiography in 1891.[18] Her account gives some idea of the reasons other women were turning to bar work. 'I was born in the month of December, 1860', she began, and with a little schooling and having reached the age of twelve years, 'my mother said it was time I did something for my living'. She began working as a 'nursegirl' in a doctor's house and benefited from 'presents of cast-off finery' from the mistress of the house, who frequently complimented her on her personal appearance. 'This circumstance somewhat put high notions into my head, and made me think I was destined to distinguish myself in a grade somewhat higher [than] that of a menial.' The other servants, too, fuelled her aspirations, the cook 'pleasantly telling me that I was "the makings of a regular lady". At this time I was rather tall for my age and (so people told me) good-looking.' Here we see the emphasis on physical attributes ('tall', 'good-looking') as well as personal appearance and demeanour ('a regular lady').

Her father was a fireman on a coastal steamer and her mother took in washing. Both of them spent 'a very considerable portion of' any money earned at the corner pub. Physical attributes, some intelligence, and the ability to model herself on and learn from her social superiors, were virtually all she could take with her into the colonial workforce of 1872. Domestic service was still the main employment prospect but one experience found her 'half-starved, overworked, and ... always [having] considerable difficulty in getting what little I earned'. At the age of fifteen 'tall, and ... prepossessing in appearance' her family decided she 'should seek a position as an assistant in a shop or hotel and eschew menial labour altogether'. Her mother was clearly most instrumental in the decision: 'You were never made for rough work, my dear, ... besides the pay will be much better' she told her daughter.

Thus this particular young woman found her way into the occupation of barmaid when she responded to the advertisement, 'Wanted a respectable young person as Barmaid ...' What motivated her was ambition for better working conditions and higher pay; what helped her succeed was some schooling (she was 'tolerably proficient in the three R's'), an obvious intelligence, and a confidence that she was capable of, and destined for, better things due to her superior physical and personal qualities – unlike another candidate who was 'more of a floor-scrubber than a barmaid'. She already had some familiarity with a public house for she used to fetch for her parents as a child. She described one of the other candidates applying for her first job as 'a fragile young creature, who evidently felt uncomfortable, it being most likely the first time she was ever in a public-house'.[19]

The work

Hotels drew women as a labour force because the nature and conditions of the work were superior to domestic service. Hotels provided opportunities for a form of domestic labour that was consistent with women's domestic skills and experience. Many of the tasks the bar staff were required to carry out were cleaning or household-management tasks. In the period before customers arrived, for example, the bar, sideboard and the engine for drawing beer had to be cleaned and made to shine, glasses had to be washed and polished, and everything made neat and tidy. After the bar was closed in the evening, bottles and decanters had to be refilled, measures taken of the level of consumption, an inventory made of the entire stock – 'The cigars and biscuits are counted, the cheese weighed, the rolls, the butter pats, sausages, and pies reckoned up' – and the accounts made up.[20] This was a big responsibility. The barmaid had to account for missing or depleted stock and was held responsible for any breakages.

The work could be also be gruelling, according to an English account: as well as serving at the counter, barmaids had to clean the glasses, scour the floors, rub up the pewters and polish any marble-tops. Although this particular description of the barmaids' work played up the horrors of life behind the bar in order to downplay the glamour associated with them, it did emphasise the work involved in contrast with the portrait of barmaids as simply attractions to trade. 'The life is the life of a slave', barmaids were 'hard-working exemplary girls', held responsible for maintaining custom, expected to dress in accordance with the position of their employer, and not allowed to complain because their position could easily be taken by someone else. There was no average wage and no regulation as to hours of work. Employed for only a few shillings a week and engaged mainly when very young, they were vulnerable to their 'desperate battle for bread' the journalist declared.[21]

Yet women wanted the work. However domesticated the tasks were, the work was done outside the individualised domestic service of private families. One young woman liked the 'life and freedom' behind the bar compared with the 'tainted atmosphere of the sweating room or the repugnant drudgery of kitchen slavery' where it was 'goodbye to my healthy cheek and chances of a husband'.[22] Another said it was not a heavenly job but was a way to earn a living. They received better treatment than domestic servants and were addressed as 'Miss', a mark of respect.[23] Another supporter of barmaids pointed out they had regular time off every week, they had rooms to themselves, could sit at tables and be waited on, and, in the course of their work, met 'the most respectable men in the city', some of them subsequently making very happy marriages with people they could not possibly have met in their own homes. Men who would not marry domestic servants married barmaids.[24]

One American wholesaler even liked to fancy that barmaids – 'Upstanding, handsome girls, keen as needles, generally of splendid figure, well groomed, well paid' – were the most powerful members of the hotel establishment. The proprietor was indifferent about whose whisky he bought or sold, the customers simply asked for 'Scotch' or 'beer', regardless of brand, so it was the barmaid who selected which brands were used. 'I realised the power of the barmaid element and without any undue extravagance, secured their assistance', and within a month his product was selling in hundreds of bars in Melbourne.[25] However exaggerated this story was, knowing the quality of the liquor she sold and what her customers would want was one of the most important skills a barmaid had.

The skills the employer – 'the ordinary, moderate, sensible retailer' – was looking for in a barmaid were 'a woman endowed with common sense; virtuous, without being a prude or a shrew; polite to customers; self-respecting; of easy, confident manners; without any fussy conscious-ness; making everybody feel at home, and creating respect from everybody'.[26] Being called 'Miss' represented this respect. There were three classifications into which a barmaid could fit: the first group were 'highly-skilled women, strictly respectable, such as are employed in the best residential hotels in town and country'; the second group were 'young women whose characters ranged from frivolous to doubtful, and whose chief value [was] their power of attracting customers'; and the third group were 'women identified with low-class public houses and wine bodegas whose characters [were] not discussable'. This subdivision within the occupation meant that investigative journalist Beatrix Tracy, who set out to experience the work of the barmaid first-hand, could not easily step into the work; she hadn't the references to fit into the first group and the other two groups meant 'traversing territory too dangerous'. She had to settle for relieving in a bar for a few hours during the busy period. 'The labors of bar-employment I found most trying', Tracy reported. Kept on her feet constantly, but with no real exercise, coping with nauseating and injurious tobacco and alcohol fumes, and sharing accommodation with other barmaids that was unhealthy and uncomfortable, she found the hours were too long, and the high wages were insufficient compensation.[27]

Those who stressed the difficulties of the job were usually opposed to the idea of women doing it. Bar work was nevertheless attractive to young women because it paid better than most other work available to them. In Melbourne in 1895 housemaids were earning between 30 and 35 pounds a year while waitresses earned 15 to 20 shillings a week (approximately 50 pounds a year if employed for the whole year) and barmaids earned from 15 to 25 shillings per week (or up to 63 pounds a year if employed for the whole year). Barmen and waiters earned 20 to 30 shillings a week, that is, up to 75 pounds a year for the whole year.[28] Comparative wages for men and women differed considerably. In 1912 in most industries women earned from 37 to 47 per cent of the male wage except in the textile weaver's trade where the pay was equal, in the shop assistants' trade where women earned 57 per cent of the male wage, and in the hotel trade where women earned from 65 to 75 per cent of what men earned.[29]

Work behind the bar also had more regulated hours than domestic service, and it gave workers more autonomy than other kinds of work. In the Australian colonies barmaids' conditions were regulated and standardised, unlike those of household servants. After the turn of the century, under the Victorian Factories Act, a barmaid was technically considered to be a waitress and her hours were set at sixty per week with one half-holiday per week from 2 p.m. one weekday.[30] Employers could be fined for overworking them, even if the barmaids themselves agreed to work the extra hours.[31] Therefore 'young, bright girls have an aversion to work as general servants', the Women's Employment Agency (WEA) reported, and they were leaving domestic service in droves seeking other sources of work. The WEA had a long list of girls waiting to find employment in hotels only because, the girls said, hotel employees were paid and protected by an industrial award, and their wages were frequently supplemented by tips.[32] Work behind the bar also brought with it a chance to one day become a licensee and it carried low levels of unemployment because of the high demand.[33]

Hours could still be long: in 1912 in Tasmania they were reported to be up to seventy a week, similar to servants and waitresses, and there were no benefits or holidays.[34] Conditions in Australia were, however, better than they were in England where hours were also long (fifteen hours worked in broken shifts), with one afternoon off a week and no Sundays.[35] There skilled women in textiles earned between 29 and 36 pounds a year, semi-skilled workers – of whom shop assistants were the best paid – from 30 to 50 pounds, and unskilled workers from 20 pounds to 32 pounds.[36] As 'unskilled' workers, very few English barmaids received 50 pounds a year, the average wage was 33 pounds a year in London, while in the provinces only a top few earned as much as 24 pounds a year. Some publicans, especially those in London, provided clothes – 'two black dresses a year' – board and lodging, although this was crowded and uncomfortable. Australian barmaids had to provide their own clothes and also lived in. Hotel workers in Victoria went on strike in 1912 over the issue of their freedom to choose where they could sleep and eat.[37] Unionisation and the establishment of industrial tribunals, which are discussed in chapter 6, helped to improve the conditions of bar work in the Australian colonies at the turn of the century.

There were, therefore, undoubtedly economic attractions to working behind the bar. Perhaps though, what was more significant, was the way work behind the bar occurred in public space. Many young women seeking paid work were going into public workplaces (shops and factories and schools) rather than private homes. Pubs more than any of these other workplaces brought young women into contact with young men. Unlike domestic service, where there was virtually no time off for social pleasures away from the family, or retail shops where both the workers and the customers were largely other women, bars enabled young women to meet men in the course of their daily routines. 'Thousands of virtuous wives and faithful mothers give testimony to the fact that the bar may be a stepping-stone to the domestic hearth ... the bar is a very favoured place for courtships', an American journal reported. Barmaids frequently received offers of marriage and, although few were in real earnest, the anonymous conviviality of the bar facilitated contact for 'the bashful swain who would not make a call upon a "lady" acquaintance, who ... could not say two words to aid a conversation'. As a consequence, there were many barmaids now married 'high in the ranks of society'.[38] Even if young women were not seeking marriage partners, there were few other workplaces where men and women could mix together with this same freedom.

The similarities and differences between bar work and other women's work are what constitutes its particular definition as an occupation. Most barmaids were reasonably young. An 1893 study of English barmaids found they were predominantly 20 to 25 years old, with almost as many between 25 and 35, and about half as many aged between 15 and 20. The number of barmaids over the age of 35 decreased dramatically but there were some women employed who were over 65 and about four who were over 75. This was partly a result of employer preference. Some firms preferred older women, but only a few positions were available as 'head-barmaid' and the majority of advertisements were seeking young women. Statistics from the 1901 New South Wales census confirm that most barmaids in Australia, too, were aged between 20 and 45 years of age. The English study found that turnover among barmaids was frequent, supposedly because it was thought 'trade was stimulated by a new face in the bar' and employers sought a frequent change of staff. The study also saw the high demand whenever a position was advertised as evidence of 'overcrowding' rather than of women's desire for this kind of work.[39]

These characteristics were consistent with the female labour market in other industries.[40] Most of the female labour force was young, and turnover was high in most occupations. Young inexperienced labour was cheap and therefore economically attractive to employers. Attempts to suggest that youthful employment, high turnover, overcrowding and lack of promotion prospects were what distinguished the work does not really stand up to historical scrutiny. To that extent work behind the bar did have a lot of similarities with other forms of employment for women. But there were key differences and these are important to explore.

The workers

'There seems to be a kind of mystery attached to the name of barmaid', an article in an English magazine claimed.[41] Peter Bailey has taken up this point in his study of the glamour and sexuality of the barmaid. He placed the development of the gin palace/public house in the cultural history of the theatre and attributed the lavish trappings, the mirrors, the gas lighting, the sumptuous fittings to a 'theatrical aura' where the pub had 'the dramatic properties of the stage', which provided the barmaid with 'a framing effect' making her both 'conspicuous and seductive'. The theatricality of work behind the bar was captured by Melbourne journalist John Freeman who claimed there was a distinctive 'peculiarity about barmaids' that was apparent whether the barmaid was 'doing the block [of Collins Street] or adding brilliancy to the dress-circle of the theatre'.[42] Using racialised language – their uniqueness, 'independent of form, or height or complexion', nevertheless 'let them dress as they like ... the barmaid is seen through all' – Freeman presented a very unflattering image according to nineteenth-century ideals of womanhood. Barmaids lacked modesty in appearance, 'acquired a boldness of manner', 'became chatty and a trifle slangy' while at the same time maintaining a modest demeanour' in hopes of attracting a husband, 'some of them possess pretty faces and nice figures, though hardly', he hastened to add, 'such as a painter would choose as models for a Madonna'.

Freeman's choice of images casting 'the barmaid' as the antithesis of demure modest womanhood, and describing their physical attractiveness as deliberately unlike the Madonna, painted a picture of barmaids as un-respectable, which in late nineteenth-century terms meant tantamount to prostitutes. 'Prostitute' meant more than simply being paid for sexual services. It meant being abandoned to sensual indulgence, licentious or debased. Any woman not conforming to prevailing views of acceptable behaviour was at risk of being cast in these terms. The confusing element was that barmaids were paid workers but not prostitutes. They were engaged in legal if undesirable employment.

Barmaids were more like actresses in their status and Freeman's description indicated as much. He concentrated on their public display when outside the workplace. While at work 'they mostly affect black lustre dresses, some worn plain and some trimmed', but away from work they were 'showy in appearance', and being 'great in earrings' could 'usually flash a pair presented to them by some [male admirer]'. He also drew attention to their hair, a major signifier of femininity in the nine-teenth century. While some wore 'an exaggerated kind of head-dress' others wore their hair 'cropped close like a boy's, with a few frontal curls left to show the femininity of the wearers'. A defender claimed 'though they may affect a loudness of speech and fastness of manner' yet they were 'resistant to temptations where those on a higher level might sink'.[43]

Barmaids were challenging definitions of respectable employment and redefining conventional definitions of femininity. The Sydney barmaid who wrote her autobiography for an 1890s public presented herself as a woman who aspired to well-paid work and took pride in her intelligence and physical appearance. She was bold and forthright in her claims to superiority and there was no blushing modesty about her ability thereby to attract her due reward. Barmaids as workers were like actresses in their independence, freedoms, good wages – their ability to behave like men. The advantages of increased monetary gains and marriageability, which historian Tracy Davis says made acting more attractive to working-class girls than other varieties of female labour, were also true of work behind the bar.[44] However, bar work shared with acting many of the dis-advantages of overwork, exploitation, and vulnerability to dismissal that other female employments carried. But unlike acting, where work could be intermittent and unpredictable, the living that bar work afforded was considerably more than factory or domestic employment.

Barmaids were also like actresses in having to negotiate the boun-daries between their occupation and that of prostitution. Actresses shared with prostitutes the venue of theatres as the location of their work, and barmaids the venue of hotels. Similarly, bar work, acting and prostitution all provided entertainment commercially, not as a public service. That meant consumer demand shaped the production of the service.[45] Bar-maids' work was certainly theatrical in its display and performance, but it was also servant-like in its drudgery and its relationship to its clientele. A description of a heat wave in Melbourne, when all the hotels in both city and suburbs were inundated with hot, thirsty customers as the tem-perature soared above the century for days in a row, also gave some indication of what the work could be like. 'Perspiring bar-belles dashed hither and thither, yelling and demanding orders in voices that rose to shrieks, their hair becoming touselled and their tempers soured, because there was no time to take even a furtive glance in the mirror, and less time to resume their accustomed air of spick-and-span tidiness and unalloyed sweetness and coolness' as customers hung about under the fans idly talking as they tried to get cool.[46]

Bar work was in many ways another form of domestic service and it had many of the same attributes. It had, for example, the element of subservience to the customer; attention to his particular requirements; the domestic tasks of keeping the bar clean and inviting. The significant difference with domestic service was the location of the workplace: like the theatre, bars were in the public domain. Public drinking as opposed to private consumption was a growing social phenomenon in the nineteenth century, and a very different activity in being subject to scrutiny and legal regulation in a way that private habits were beyond. Public encounters between servants and customers were therefore of a qualitatively different kind in the public imagination simply because they were public. The sexual dynamic encoded in the performance of women's service to men was no longer invisible once it was outside the domestic sphere.

Once in the pub, therefore, the servant became the barmaid; in this situation the emphasis on the barmaid's personal attributes and the expectation she would provide a personalised service to her male customers made for a delicate balancing act. One barmaid complained the customers 'get on your nerves'. When the barmaid asked what they would have, the customer would reply 'Oh! I'll have you' or 'A beer with a smile in it' and other similar unfunny jokes that hindered and harassed the woman behind the bar.[47] The bar therefore made a theatrical performance of her sexuality. Like the actress she was there to be seen and admired, the space behind the bar becoming her stage where she performed her customer's desires. But unlike the actress the barmaid was not only there to be viewed 'while a particular desire was gratified'.[48] She was also there to perform specific household-like tasks. Acting, domestic service, and prostitution all blurred into one. The sexual difference between the workers and their customers meant their intermingling also deliberately obscured the boundaries between respectability and unrespectability and required that careful negotiation of the boundaries between 'prostitute' and 'barmaid' become an important and quite explicit skill in the exercise of the barmaid's work.

By the 1890s, when gold was discovered in Kalgoorlie, Western Australia, women seeking work on the goldfields had no trouble finding employment in the many pubs. 'The outstanding shortages were water and women', one author has claimed, and women were shipped in from the eastern colonies to work behind the bar where they could develop quite a following.[49] 'There was always gossip and speculation about the morals of barmaids, especially by other women who regarded them with suspicion', a historian of the Western Australian goldfields has written.[50] Norma King was keen to distinguish barmaids from the prostitutes who also worked in Kalgoorlie and on the western goldfields. She described 'a 1903 remembrance' of the pioneer barmaids and how much they contributed to brightening the lives of the men who 'paved the way': they were 'bricks', 'the right sort, the girls who came out West'. She pointed out 'there were no such eulogies for another class of woman ... Few serious poems were written about prostitutes, or dedicated to them. The men used the prostitutes and then spoke of them with amusement or contempt.' In contrast, 'the barmaids were generally very popular with their customers, even those who were plain' and 'the men usually accepted the standards set by the girls themselves and acted accordingly'. The careful dividing line is maintained even as the history is written.

'I remember ... I was dreadfully ashamed of her being a barmaid', one woman said of her mother who was one of those barmaids on the Western Australian goldfields in the early 1900s, 'but that was the way that women earned their living'. She believed women were barmaids if they had nothing else they could do, 'not every woman was educated to the extent they are now'. But being attractive was the most important characteristic: 'you had to have *some* ability because you had to count the drink out. But it was really being good-looking. You see, it was really a form of prostitution, the women were supposed to oblige the men.' Women had a better chance of keeping their jobs if they became 'willing victims' to the male customer's desires. Sometimes, she said, 'barmaids were sacked if they weren't obliging, not if they weren't efficient'.[51]

But barmaids did have skills specific to the job. 'Some hints to bar attendants' compiled by Western Australian hotelier R. C. Harrison in 1912 stressed the importance of efficiency for bar staff. His 'little series of don'ts' addressed to 'the young ladies behind the bar' came to thirty-six instructions, most of them about cleanliness. Some were about recognising quality in the liquor, maintaining stock, and practising economies; others about preventing accidents or roughness in the bar, and attending pleasantly and civilly to customers.[52] Being able to pour drinks correctly, particularly beer, in appropriate glassware, was crucial.

'Pretty or plain there was one skill their customers insisted upon', according to Norma King, 'and that was the ability to serve them a decent sized drink, and one that was neither flat nor too frothy on top.' Barmaids did depend on their popularity among customers, which exposed them to charges of prostitution, but they also provided a high degree of skill (most notably in the pouring of beer) in performing a service to the customers' expectations. In pleasing the clientele, the goal of service work, they brought trade to the licensee. But it put them in a vulnerable position. 'Obliging the customer' meant walking a thin line that exploitative employers could manipulate. The bar was public space, an environment of predominantly masculine recreation, where service was performed outside the conventions of polite society. The rules of conduct had to be negotiated, the boundaries of sexual difference to be maintained, and it was in these negotiations that one skill of the barmaid lay. It was not the only one. The others they shared with barmen in the trade.

Maintaining sexual difference

If women were thought to be employed for their sexuality then distinctions could be drawn between men and women working behind the bar. While women were supposedly employed to serve and attract custom, the real work was men's. The duties, except for the actual serving at the counter, 'mostly ... require muscular strength – cellar work, cleaning, maintaining order' an English report claimed. Licensees employing women to serve behind the bar therefore also had to employ men to do the other work, thereby 'having to maintain a double staff'.[53] Barmen were thought to be better servers where a large casual trade was done but they couldn't attract custom, they were 'never trade magnets', according to another.[54]

There is no evidence that barmen did have to handle the heavy barrels of beer; they were delivered to the cellars by the brewery workers. A suburban hotelkeeper gave another insight into the issue of sexual differentiation in employment behind the bar, and the reason why women

Figure 2.1 Post Office Hotel, Sydney, *c.* 1880s. Note the grouping of women on the balcony and men at street level. This representation does not change in over thirty years (see Figure 2.2 and discussion of it in the text). (Mitchell Library, State Library of New South Wales)

Figure 2.2 Crown Hotel, Charters Towers, Queensland, *c.* 1919, showing female staff on first-floor balcony. (Collection: John Oxley Library, Brisbane)

found employment easily. Small suburban hotels usually employed one or more assistants to divide their work between the bar and the house according to demand. Male employees 'cannot or will not do the house-work usually done by women' during the slow trading times in the bar, so they were of less value to the employer.[55] This comment prefigured claims made by barmaids seeking equal pay in the later twentieth century.

These skills were recognised by the barmaids themselves, and their employers and customers. They were only partially represented in pop-ular images of hotel work, particularly the growing number of photo-graphic images.

Figure 2.2 is a fairly typical photo of hotel staff, one which conveys conventional knowledge of sexual difference and a rather obvious representation of woman as domestic servant. Where the male proprietor of a pub was present for the photo, the men were grouped downstairs, on the verandah, spilling out on to the public space of the street, any passers-by were stopped and included. The women were relegated to the upstairs, the private domain. Downstairs was where the public bar was situated. Upstairs contained the private bars and accommodation rooms. This sort of positioning, which is more apparent in photos from the turn of the century than earlier decades, is thus creating knowledge of public and private spaces, of the spatial arrangements of pubs, and of sexual differentiation. This spatial arrangement is also conveyed in the dress. These women are dressed in white, perhaps frilly, uniforms that speak of light domestic (inside) duties rather than dirty heavy (outside) work. (Compare their aprons to those of the brewery workers in Figure 6.1.)

The camera was a powerful medium for generating popular knowledge that men 'worked' and women performed domestic and sexual service for them, which masked the real changes occurring in the labour market and obscured the reality of many women's experiences. A century after the first Europeans had arrived ideas of nationhood had begun to dominate the culture, and photographers working in Australia were constructing images of what was 'typically Australian' to publicly represent the colonies to the rest of the world. Professional photographers were active in creating knowledge about Australia in the same way that the census takers were, that women didn't 'work'. Photographers, as well as statisticians, portrayed wives and daughters working in family businesses, hotels, farms and shops not as workers but as 'relatives assisting', because it reflected a higher standard of living (appropriate to the Australian labour ideal) to have one breadwinner in a family.[56]

Contrasting photographs of women hotel workers in their feminine finery (e.g. Figures 2.1 and 2.2) with images of male brewery workers is instructive. There 'strong masculine labour' is the theme. Work is represented as masculine, and breweries were undoubtedly a masculine workplace. The men in Figure 2.3 are shown working with heavy equipment, positioned so the viewer can see it is strong, physical labour. Their bodies are muscular and very visible; their sleeves are rolled up or cut off at the elbow. They are focused on their tasks, not the camera.

Hotels, on the other hand, were equivocal. Hotels as workplaces blurred the boundary of sexual difference, the boundaries between masculine and feminine. On the one hand they provided domestic service, accommodation, food and refreshment for the traveller, tasks requiring housekeeping, cleaning and catering skills that women provided in private homes and institutions as domestic servants. So it was easy enough 'back of house', where the cleaning, cooking and domestic staff worked, to view hotel work as feminine and traditional women's work. On the other hand, hotels provided bars ('front of house') as public space for pleasure and recreation, which men claimed as theirs. It wasn't entirely theirs, however: women did drink in pubs in the nineteenth century and were doing so at an increasing rate.

Work behind the bar thus was problematic. According to Brian Harrison, English public houses were, as long ago as the late eighteenth century, places for male drinking rituals, for 'establishing one's virility by drinking deeply' and for 'being initiated into manhood'.[57] The bar, where male customers congregated in their leisure hours, was undisputed

Figure 2.3 Brewery workers moving bags of grain, Melbourne 1895–1905.
(#05586, Collection 709, Courtesy of the Museum of Victoria Council)

masculine space where the presence of women was unwanted. But, at
least by the end of the nineteenth century, women, 'respectable women',
were there as customers in English pubs. Sometimes they were accompanied by men, often not. They preferred small bars 'where their husbands could not see them' or sometimes bars 'for ladies only'. A typical
suburban London pub in 1907 was reported to have different bars for
different customers: 'omnibus drivers and conductors' in one, 'horny-
handed sons of toil and lady customers in the bar opposite, and more
women in the bottle and jug, as the publican refuses to allow children'.[58]
Similarly Chris McConville has claimed women were very much an active
and noisy part of local corner-pub clientele in inner-city Melbourne in
the mid-nineteenth century.[59] Certainly there is evidence that convict,
Aboriginal and working-class women in the colonies drank, although
how much of this was done on licensed premises and how much in the
street or at home is unclear. Women's drunkenness shows up in literature
on poverty and charitable relief. It seems more than likely that women
from artisanal and shopkeeping families would also have enjoyed their
beer, perhaps going to the pub. Beer, as we saw in chapter 1, had been
part of the family diet for centuries. Unfortunately Australian women's

drinking culture has not been subjected to historical enquiry.[60] However this mixing of the sexes socially and at work in pubs made gender boundaries difficult to sustain.

Actresses contravened 'men's rules for feminine behaviour' by choosing an occupation that was 'anti-domestic' and 'doing exactly what men did: turning outside the home for social intercourse, intellectual stimulation, and occupational fulfillment'.[61] Similarly barmaids transcended gender prescriptions, but they went even further than the women on the stage. As has already been pointed out, wages and conditions behind the bar were far superior to those of most other women's work and closely approximated the conditions of male workers. The young women seeking work behind the bar were deliberately turning their back on domestic service and other 'womanly occupations', as were other women. But in their power to attract custom and therefore command high wages they were singularly apart from most other women workers, except perhaps prostitutes. Economically active single wage-earning women posed a threat to notions of sexual difference as Joan Scott has shown in nineteenth-century France.[62]

More importantly, the barmaids' work was not performed only in the company of other women. Kathy Peiss has written of the young urban women in the United States at this time who sought the company of young men and commercial pleasures outside their working hours.[63] As a barmaid a young woman had access to the unchaperoned company of many men or of individual admirers. As their workplace was frequented by men both as customers and workers, it was not only economically that their work approximated many of the privileges of masculinity. In re-establishing the boundaries, the bar counter became a very significant physical symbol.

The workplace

The photograph in Figure 2.4 is of a superior bar from a well-known city hotel, Scott's Hotel, in Melbourne. Such hotels took great pride in the presentation of their bars, and fittings and materials along with the staff were chosen carefully to create the right atmosphere to attract the desired clientele. Brian Harrison has pointed to the similarities between churches and hotels in early nineteenth-century Britain, 'in the priest/publican; hymns/pub songs; stained glass/frosted glass; the altar rail/the bar; the bar handles/altar candles; the altar/the bar back ... each conceived as housing their congregations'. But where previously the church and the tavern had been complementary recreational outlets for working-class men, in the middle of the nineteenth century they came to be in

Figure 2.4 Interior, saloon bar of Scott's Hotel, Melbourne. A superior city establishment. (Royal Historical Society of Victoria)

competition. Temperance organisations directed their efforts at emptying the taverns of their congregations and magistrates closed them during church hours on Sunday mornings.[64] Peter Bailey, maintaining this analogy, has subsequently described the barmaid as 'the high priestess of the night amid the brilliant gas-lights of the temple of Bacchus'.[65]

Scott's was known as 'a man's pub'.[66] In this photograph of Scott's saloon bar the religious connotations of the design, artifacts and layout of the bar are visible in the stained glass and leadlighting, the high-arched window, the altar-like bar, the silver water jugs, high ceiling, the lighting, and the care and reverence with which it is presented. The atmosphere of the pub, as an all-male inner sanctum from which women were excluded, where rituals of initiation into masculinity might be conducted, and where daily habits of custom and tradition dictated ways of behaving, still carried the hallmarks of religious worship even in the twentieth century. This was not a bar for working-class men's rituals. The customers here were from the wealthy city clientele.

There are no tables and chairs; customers were expected to stand, leaning on the bar, engaging in conversation with those nearby or, in the absence of friends, with the bar staff serving. This was an economical use of space – many more customers could be served if they were standing rather than being waited on, and more people could be accommodated if space was not taken up by furniture. It also drew attention to the placement of the bar staff at the centre.

A sense of spaciousness was conveyed through the use of mirrors and high ceilings. This photograph conveys the importance of the polished wood counter, the large mirrors on the wall, the careful woodcarving. The most striking example of this showiness was probably the Marble Bar of George Adams' Tattersall's Hotel in Sydney. It was renowned throughout Australasia, 'not only for its pretty and respectable barmaids and purity of drinks, but for its elaborate furnishing, choice statuary and high class works of art on the walls ... all that money could procure in taste, elegance and business facilities'.[67] Country and suburban hotels were not so grand, but the basic structure of the bar remained the same.

The width of the bar was significant as a divider. It has loomed large in masculine depictions (including Bailey's) of sexualised encounters between barmaids and customers. These, we are told, 'were strictly controlled'. Bar staff were at the same time both accessible and inaccessible; they were always within verbal reach, but they were always physically separated by an insurmountable obstacle. When the bar attendant was female and the customer was male, this dynamic conveyed a sexually titillating message that could entice the male customers to return. 'It is the bar', Peter Bailey has pointed out, 'that constitutes the necessary material and symbolic distance that simultaneously heightens and contains the sexual attractiveness of the barmaid ...' The width of the bar counter created a distance that sustained and protected the allure of the barmaid as glamorous, but also heightened desire through the tension generated by separating 'the glamour object from the beholder'.[68]

The bar, however, also separated male bar staff from male customers (and perhaps even female customers). Homoeroticism is not considered in any of these discussions of bars and the workers behind them. Nor is the other major characteristic of the bar considered: its length. The length of the bar was as, if not more, significant, especially for the worker on the other side of it. It allowed many customers to be served almost at the same time, requiring the barmaid to do a lot of walking up and down in response to customer demands. It also, therefore, reinforced the contradictions of her role: her simultaneous responsiveness to individual needs and her unavailability to individual customers, the very line she had carefully to tread.

In the photo of Scott's saloon bar there is some indication of how the work was performed: bottles and glasses are stacked in full view. Being surrounded by the commodities the pub sold emphasised the commercial enterprise and could have the effect of suggesting that the barmaid herself was a commodity, 'an article for purchase and consumption' along with the drinks she dispensed.[69] This, however, was never suggested in relation to sales staff in other retailing establishments where the customers were largely women. On the other hand, the bottles and glasses are within easy reach, thus indicating both speed of service and the barmaid's need for knowledge of a wide range of drinks and her customers' preferences. Having a good memory was an important part of the skill of serving customers. Memorising was the hardest part of the job for some barmaids.[70] The workplace was designed for service, where the bar staff were contained within a prescribed space behind a large impenetrable counter to provide speedy, individualised service to customers drinking singly or in groups in an atmosphere of conviviality. The bar counter thus also separated workspace from playing space, masculine space from feminine space, the customer from the servant. Its presence was the key to constructing the sexual, class and power dynamic in which the occupation evolved. The bar counter allowed only the barmaid's upper body to be seen: her legs (i.e. constantly walking), shoes (appropriate for long periods of standing), and the beer slops could not be seen. The bar rendered invisible behind it the identity of the barmaid as worker as it heightened the intimacy of her contact with the customer.

Celebrated for her physical attributes and her sexual appeal to the male customers (even in male historian's accounts), barmaids were nevertheless employed for much the same reasons that other women were being employed as shop assistants and domestic servants, that is, to provide service that was, by its nature, domestic in character. Paradoxically bartending was a service occupation undertaken by *both* men and women, sometimes in separate establishments but often enough in the same workplace. The sexual division of labour was more clearly established in other occupations where men's work and women's work were categorised differently. Thus the gender boundaries within bar work itself were unclear, and they shifted. Barmen tried to differentiate their work from that of women by pointing out that barmaids could not get through as much work as they did, or that the work was heavy and physical rather than people-oriented.[71] At certain times, as the census figures show, women bar workers outnumbered men, at other times the figures were reversed, but always there were both men and women working in the industry. The presence of women workers in this space created anxieties about sexual differentiation – the masculinity of productive labour, the femininity of service (that 'not-really-work' kind of labour) – that caused reverberations well into the next century.

Being a barmaid became sex-specific by definition. Although men were also employed behind the bar they were called barmen, they could not be barmaids. Bar work was similar to prostitution, domestic service, retail sales, waiting on tables, nursing and many other service occupations that women and not men were taking up in the latter part of the nineteenth century. Yet it was also significantly different from these because men participated in it, and because of the nature of the workplace and the content of its trade. The contradictions contained in these similarities and differences with other female work were what defined bar work and 'the barmaid' as a new category of occupation. They were also what brought it a considerable amount of attention from the popular press and government authorities and subsequently significantly different treatment by legislatures. From the 1880s onwards, no other woman's occupation was targeted like women's work behind the bar.

As urban centres grew in size and population in the 1870s and 1880s, government attempts to have people consume beer not spirits began to bear fruit and beer consumption at last surpassed that of spirits. Although beer consumption in Australia was still only half that in the United Kingdom, from an almost equal consumption (of 1.8 gallons a head of beer and 1.9 gallons a head of spirits) in 1877, in less than a decade the figures were 1.2 gallons a head of spirits and 13.5 gallons a head of beer. The greatest increase was in Victoria (16 gallons beer to 1 gallon spirits) and the least in Queensland (11 gallons beer to 2 gallons spirits). The number of hotels multiplied. In 1885 there were over 4000 hotels in Victoria and over 3000 in New South Wales, more than 800 of these in metropolitan Sydney alone. Within a 200-yard radius of one city corner in Sydney there were 33 licensed premises.[72] In the metropolitan area of Melbourne the ratio was about 1 pub to every 260 persons, although in the city centre it was more like 1:174.[73]

As pubs proliferated, liquor trading became 'wild and unconfined' with both men and women engaging in riotous behaviour. Some critics complained that the increased competition for trade meant pubs had become places of entertainment, and the presence of a barmaid was intended to add to the attraction.[74] There was thus both an increase in the employment of barmaids and an upsurge of concern about it. As with so many occupations women were pursuing, work behind the bar was portrayed as a dangerous employment, if not synonymous with prostitution then one undoubtedly likely to lead girls down that path.

Thus colonial governments began taking action in relation to hotels, instituting inquiries into the liquor trade and looking closely at regulating the industry, actions that had serious implications for hotels as workplaces for women. The campaign against wage-earning women's employment in bars began, just as the poem about the photographer and the barmaid did, in the 1880s, with seeing the barmaid as the innocent victim of unscrupulous men and employers. But the trajectory of the debate over women bar workers developed a momentum and took a course that had ramifications for all Australian women for almost a century.

CHAPTER THREE

'The Problem of the Barmaids': Urbanisation and Legislative Reform

Increased liquor consumption in the late nineteenth century meant a proliferation of pubs, more licensed premises and, within existing establishments, additional bars. Urban pubs were now two- and three-storey buildings, inside which were carefully segregated and discrete parlour bars for the more decorous drinkers, while the public bar continued to be accessible from the street to cater for the more disreputable and rowdy clientele.[1] This necessarily stimulated a demand for bar workers that advantaged women seeking work. But their success came to be characterised as a 'problem': 'too many licensed premises' and 'insufficient legitimate trade' meant publicans were resorting to entertainments; they were providing 'meretricious attractions' like 'gambling and showy or flashy barmaids' as one South Australian Member of Parliament claimed.[2]

Most significantly publicans began leasing some of these private bars to barmaids, thereby enabling some women to pursue an independent income without the capital outlay required to run their own licensed premises.[3] It gave barmaids considerable autonomy. While some private bars were simply the former guests' precincts now opened to the wider public, others might well have been used for prostitution. Evidence for this is harder to find. Giving the women who ran them a means of an independent livelihood, they also blurred the distinctions between establishments at a time when 'respectable' and 'unrespectable' were terms deployed to mark out boundaries of social propriety.[4] At the very least private bars were spaces beyond public view where men and women drank together outside the constraints and conventions of polite middle-class society. Despite the existence of legislation restricting hotel opening hours and attempting to curb excesses, private bars were out of the reach of licensing provisions and could not be policed, thereby generating considerable nervousness among authorities about the limits of the law.

J. M. Freeland has called this 'the problem of the employment of women as barmaids'.[5] Women's employment behind the bar posed a challenge for the spatial arrangement of sexual difference. The presence of women as employees in public space, that space that was thought to be male, created a problem among those who believed women should be confined to the domestic sphere. This was fuelled in the public imagination by popular anxieties about the close correlation between urban prostitution and the expansion of public drinking places. The occupation of 'the barmaid', especially when she was the proprietor of a private bar, challenged the definitions of respectability. Whether there was really any connection between women working in bars, modern urban public drinking practices and prostitution was less significant than the meaning that was attached to public displays, unconventional 'gay' exhibitions of womanhood, and anxieties about pleasure, drinking and public courtship. Consequently, from the 1880s to the turn of the century, barmaids were to come under public scrutiny in a way that shaped the definition of the occupation itself.

This was a time when legislation shaping the female labour market was beginning to be introduced. Some colonial governments, beginning with South Australia in 1879, set up commissions of inquiry into liquor trading and passed new licensing laws. Others, led by Victoria, set out to investigate factories and workshops and began to pass labour laws. Government regulation of the liquor trade and attempts to legislate on women workers' conditions became fused. 'The problem of the barmaid' came into sharp focus; it highlighted issues about the role of law in curtailing women's new economic freedoms – 'the liberty of the subject' to pursue her individual economic interests. It also provided a space for a public discussion that, in defining gender boundaries, was also imagining sexuality.

The photo in Figure 3.1, taken in the bar of the Crown Cornwall Hotel, Ballarat, in the 1880s, is an example of Jonathan Bayer's point that 'a photograph may present an ordinary situation in such a way as to imply an enhanced meaning based on mutual knowledge about that object'.[6] The mutual knowledge of the 'object' of this photo was the discourse of sexuality surrounding barmaids. Nineteenth-century viewers of this photograph would recognise 'the barmaid' being represented here as synonymous with sensual indulgence, with 'prostitute'. This is not a 'lady' who didn't work: she is clearly a worker surrounded by the accoutrements of her trade. This photo is interesting as an early interior shot that, despite its poor lighting and unclear picture, reveals much about the atmosphere of the bar. In contrast to the earlier photographs of frontier pubs, here the emphasis is on luxurious comfort and theatrical embellishments. Notice the rich texture of the walls, the wallpaper, paintings and lamps. There are collections of bottles and glasses on display surrounding the barmaid with glittering reflections of light and colour. Prominent in the foreground is the beer pump, which some have seen as highlighting the sexual symbolism of the barmaid's role.

Figure 3.1 Interior, Crown Cornwall Hotel, Ballarat, *c.* 1880s, with the barmaid in the background. (#00682, Collection 0101, Courtesy of the Museum of Victoria Council)

But our gaze is directed down the bar to the subject of the barmaid. The mediation of the photographer is clear in the composition of this photograph. The photographer has stood behind the bar, rather than in the place of the customer, so the vision we are presented with is the workplace, but not from the perspective of the barmaid who is positioned half-facing the camera and half-facing her (invisible) customers. The viewer is thus invited in, behind the bar, but not to share the barmaid's perspective. The barrier of the bar has been removed in this positioning, indeed the bar is not really visible at all except in the foreground as the structure supporting other fixtures. We are aware of its presence by the way the barmaid is leaning on it, though we ourselves are protected from its inhibiting quality. The way the photographer has eliminated the bar as all but a suggestion from this image is in marked contrast to the significance of the bar in other photographs (see, for example, Figure 2.4). This barmaid is not the pretty young maiden of contemporary poems and paintings, but still the mood here is inviting, welcoming (as suggested by the big 'Welcome Duke and Duchess of Cornwall' sign prominent in the foreground), and her stance is suggestive, informal, seductive. Ladies, and 'respectable' women, comported themselves discreetly. Leaning in this suggestive manner resembled the stance of the bar's male patrons, and was sexually suggestive in its invitation to intimacy. Many drawings of barmaids in the 1880s and 1890s had them leaning suggestively on or over the counter.

Images like these, and the existence of private bars and drinking clubs flouting the licensing laws, brought civic and governmental attention to hotels that focused directly on the employment of women within them. The first government inquiry was held in South Australia in 1879. William Sandover's reference to 'showy or flashy barmaids' led to further questioning about whether the employment of barmaids was conducive to community well-being. He replied that wherever he saw 'a showy or flashy barmaid' in a hotel he thought the owner must be 'far from respectable and ... not a suitable man to have a license'.[7] He did not suggest that the woman employed should be removed, or that no barmaids should be employed, but that the licence perhaps ought to be revoked. Pinning blame on the licensee for unrespectable conduct concurred with the South Australian Commission's purpose in establishing the number and appropriateness of licensed premises according to public demand and social order. The issue of barmaids was not paramount for the South Australian commissioners at this time. Similarly, other evidence presented to the commission pointed to the appropriateness of existing provisions for public comfort: notably the difficulties created by the close proximity of public drinking bars to the hotel's accommodation for 'ladies' staying with their families and not wishing 'to be jostled about by a lot of men standing about the doors of the hotel'. Attention was also drawn to the prevalence of pubs, too close together to be really catering to the public's need for refreshment but easily frequented by the very lowest classes of men and women whose drinking, quarrelling, dancing and fighting constituted an annoyance and a nuisance to the passing public.

The South Australian inquiry followed hard on the heels of concerns about the prevalence of prostitution in the cities. In 1878 the Victorian Parliament's Select Committee on Contagious Diseases took evidence from the head of the Victorian police force about where prostitution occurred. He reported it was in houses operating as brothels, some 'apparently respectable public houses', and in shops, the back rooms of tobacconists, cigar and fruit shops. These shops, he said, were more of a problem than hotels. No licence was required to own or run a shop, whereas the police were able to oppose the licensing of hotels if they were known to be a cover for prostitution. Evidence was, however, always hard to find. He was in favour of legislation to control disease, and when asked did he think that a man ought to be allowed to break any social law against society and escape so long as he was not diseased but any poor woman who broke a social law was to suffer, he agreed 'women are the principal sufferers'. The head of the Victorian police force was not, however, in favour of interference by the state with prostitution. It would not be 'politic or wise to interfere ... apart from the public exhibition of it', nor did he think legislation would succeed in suppressing it.[8] This was both an experienced police officer's personal view of the limitations of legal machinery in dealing with the issue of prostitution as well as a statement of the classic view of the negative role of law in matters of morality. Prostitution was not, and he thought ought not to be, illegal, it was more appropriate to regulate its manifestations rather than outlaw its practice.

This discussion about prostitution, its public exhibition and the judiciousness of state intervention in private morality, set the boundaries of the debate about women's employment as barmaids in the 1880s. It coincided with the beginnings of state intervention in the workplace. The first Factories Act had been passed in Victoria in 1873 followed by Tasmania in 1874, and a public campaign against the prevalence of sweated labour in the garment and clothing trades led to the establishment of a royal commission in Victoria in 1882 and renewed legislative endeavours in regard to factory workplaces. The focus on women workers, their exploited working conditions and the possibility of intervention in the employment contract by the state, together with new concerns about the meaning of these for public morality, brought 'the problem of the barmaids' into being.

The Victorian Royal Commission, 1882–84

The first serious investigation of barmaids occurred in Victoria with the Royal Commission on Employés in Factories and Shops, which began sitting in 1882. While investigating many other workplaces, this focused on barmaids in a way that differentiated them from other workers. How it did so and why reveals the confusion over women in public spaces that bar work generated.

The commissioners submitted several progress reports before their final report in 1884. These progress reports addressed the general conditions of employment in shops and endorsed the aims of the Early

Closing movement.[9] They said nothing specific about hotels which were, as the Victorian head of police had pointed out, in a unique position legally compared with shops. The commissioners were convinced of the need for legislation to close shops and suspend business at a reasonable hour in the evening. Their recommendation for legislation said nothing about barmaids. Although included within the purview of the commission's investigations, barmaids were treated under a separate heading, as a different category of employee, not like women employed in factories and shops. In singling barmaids out for separate consideration in this way, the commission signalled a category of employment that called for special treatment.

Not surprisingly, then, barmaids' employment was pronounced to be 'the result of a system in every respect objectionable'. It was the working conditions of bars they objected to; they were detrimental to women's health. A lot of authority was placed in the evidence taken from medical practitioners: Dr Girdlestone, Health Officer, declared barmaids were 'shamefully overworked'; Dr Fisher claimed bar work made women 'pale, their digestive organs get deranged'; Dr Gilbee stated they endured 'evils ... no doubt prejudicial to their general health and ultimate safety through after life'; Dr Beaney was 'astonished at what became of barmaids who ... suddenly break down and are obliged to seek refuge in the hospital'; Dr Youl, City Coroner, Dr Fisher, and Dr Tudor Hora were also called on to give evidence and 'emphasised the opinions' of the other practitioners.

Consequently, in their progress report submitted to Parliament in 1883, the commissioners cited these medical opinions and emphasised the health and safety risks that would justify any subsequent arguments for legislative protections. All the (medical) evidence they had heard made it clear, they said, 'that, in regard to the hours of labour, this class of employes are subjected to hardships more severe and physically distressing than perhaps any other class in the community'. They characterised barmaids as 'fairly educated, of superior address, active, capable and trustworthy'. They pointed out they were employed for their superior personal qualities and their 'supposed power of inducing expenditure' by a trade that offered inducements more attractive to young women than either factories or domestic service. Yet according to the medical experts they were subsequently 'shamefully overworked', for long hours, 'often under extremely insanitary conditions'. Dr Girdlestone thought it was '"outrageous" that young women should be required to work the bars of hotels and public-houses for fourteen or sixteen hours a day', the commissioners reported. He had argued they should not have to work more than eight hours a day, and certainly not beyond ten o'clock at night. Another doctor argued they should follow the example of the English company of Spiers and Pond (which had brought the first barmaids to

Melbourne). They should rotate the barmaids in shifts 'like soldiers relieving the sentry'.

In this 1883 report, the commissioners couched their concerns in terms of regulating the industry. They made clear it was the employers they had in mind: 'Some licensees are no doubt thoughtful and considerate of the health and feelings of their employes.' They argued that 'the obligations of humanity are paramount to those of trade'. While persuasion could, indeed had, accomplished much in reducing the hours of workers, they believed that without a legal obligation to close some employers, out of their own self-interest, would 'not be bound by any moral obligation to close early'. In 1883, then, the commissioners put aside consideration of 'the moral aspects' of womanly virtue while conceding that they saw women working in bars as 'in every respect objectionable' and leading to the 'demoralization of the youth of both sexes' because bars increased the property values and profits for the liquor interests.

Yet a year later, when the final report was submitted, and submitted separately from the main report, morality surfaced more intrusively in the recommendations.[10] Now they complained of 'fresh, pretty, worthy girls' whose 'health, morals and appearance' of respectability declined with the immorality of working behind the bar, and the argument for limiting the hours and conditions under which women in shops were to be employed had stretched to recommending banning barmaids' work altogether. In 1884 the commissioners urged that amendment to the licensing law was needed to deal effectively with the employment of barmaids whose presence in pubs was 'non-essential to public convenience' and whose employment involved social consequences thought to be 'most disastrous'. No details were provided in the recommendations as to what these consequences might be, but they probably referred to one witness's imaginings of the inevitable fall of barmaids into drunkenness, prostitution, going 'amongst the Chinamen' and, thence, from the gutter to the grave.

Supporting their case, the commissioners pointed out that several of the principal hotels in Melbourne did not employ barmaids and yet they transacted a more extensive and legitimate business 'conducted in accordance with the regulations and restrictions imposed by law'. Working conditions – long hours and relative wages, the fatigues barmaids endured – were discussed, but more attention was paid to the temptations that women faced and to which they were thought to 'fall victim': the language and manners of the customers, and the persons with whom they were compelled to associate, which induced 'habits of intemperance, with their inevitable consequences'. The medical evidence afforded 'emphatic condemnation' of the practice of employing young girls to work as barmaids. The only effectual means of remedying the many abuses that existed was 'absolute prohibition'. While it 'may seem a drastic mode of dealing with the difficulty', the commissioners said, 'it appears to be imperative'. They then quoted the evidence of one witness, 'Visitor at the City Court, but more generally known as the City Missionary', George Hill, who believed that simply closing pubs earlier, and thereby restricting the hours of women's employment in bars, would merely enable the bar to become 'a sort of assignation place'. He maintained this would give the barmaid time to go with a young fellow to 'some house of accommodation' and still be home at an hour that would make her 'appear to be a very respectable young woman'.

This imaginary fear – that sexually active young women might some-how be able to masquerade as 'respectable' if pubs were allowed to continue employing barmaids for shorter hours – was thought to be such an undesirable outcome that, on the strength of Hill's speculations, the commissioners proposed that legislation should ban barmaids. Hill's anecdotal evidence that many of the city's prostitutes had been barmaids clearly carried great weight in the commission and was subsumed into the medical evidence of the dangers of long hours, improper eating and overwork on female constitutions – 'their systems as women' – so that the work itself became unacceptable. Between the South Australian Inquiry of 1879 and this final report of the Victorian Royal Commission in 1884, a significant shift in thinking had occurred on 'the problem of the barmaids' and how to solve it.

Certainly there was some supporting evidence from women within the trade that working conditions of hotel servants who had to live in could be appalling, and that hotel workers were indeed 'sweated labour'.[11] Compared with ordinary factory hands who did 'not have to camp on the premises' and who at least could breathe fresh air going to and from their work, 'the unhappy hotel assistant' had to work 'exceedingly long hours and then rest in small stuffy rooms reeking with the stench arising from the grog-soaked bodies of dirty drunkards' where five women were crowded into 'space for [only] one person to dress at a time'. Instead of being exempted from the provisions of factory legislation, this writer thought hotels required strict regulation. 'Many of Sydney's "genial hosts" would be prosecuted for cruelty to animals were they to confine a brace of pigs all night' in the way they lodged both customers and their staff. 'No noxious-trade factory could produce a more hideous stench than that of the vast accumulation of all the various breaths ...'[12] Similarly long hours and overcrowded accommodation in small rooms, often under cor-rugated iron roofs where the heat was impossible in summer, was also the lot of Queensland bar workers. And the work could be dangerous – shattered glass from exploding bottles was a hazard one barmaid referred to. For those alone in private bars robbery and violence were also risks.[13]

But hotels, as individually or family-owned businesses, varied greatly in their size, location and standards. Accordingly, there was much diversity in working conditions that state regulation could certainly standardise. Standardisation of industrial workplaces was the goal of much industrial legislation. There were indeed real threats to workers' health in the exploitative working conditions of the nineteenth century, which is why male unionists were agitating for, and achieving, the eight-hour day. In recognition of the importance of the trade unions' success in reducing the hours of labour, the Victorian Parliament passed an Eight Hours Legalization Act in 1885.[14] In those industries where competition was fierce (as was the case in hotels in the 1880s) exploitation was greater, but hotels as workplaces were of uncertain legal status. They were already covered by licensing laws which, in stipulating the hours of opening and the conditions under which the trade was to be conducted, also set some boundaries on employment; for example, there was supposed to be no trading on Sunday. Bar staff had, however, to work on most Sundays, because trade continued illegally and the premises had to be cleaned.[15]

The Victorian Royal Commission of 1882–84, in exposing the hardships of working conditions behind the bar, was attempting by implication to bring public houses into the definition of factories and shops on which legislation protective of workers was based. But instead of treating bars as workplaces requiring the same safeguards as other (usually manufacturing) workplaces, when it came to advocating legislative interference, they concentrated on the morality of the purpose for which pubs existed and of the women who worked in them. The commissioners had clearly chosen their witnesses selectively. They could not see pubs in any terms other than the moral language of evangelical Protestantism. They could not distinguish objective economic factors that created trade, employment and exploitative working conditions from the 'evil' and sinful effects of drunkenness. And they could not equate 'woman' and 'respectability' with public drinking practices. They therefore sought to cast barmaids out of their workplaces and, by doing so, suggested they were indeed in the category of prostitute. Why and how barmaids were singled out for such concern when other women workers were not probably had a lot more to do with the reasons women were attracted to the work than the commissioners were prepared to admit.

Policing the boundaries between respectable and unrespectable women was becoming harder as urbanisation, commercialised retailing and public transportation systems drew women onto the streets, thoroughfares and public spaces of major cities.[16] It was always difficult, the Victorian head of police had said in 1878, to draw 'a distinction between the woman who is known to be only a little gay and the professional prostitute'. Finery was part of the way prostitutes were marked out.[17] The theatricality of the barmaids' appearance and public display confused these distinctions and therefore rendered barmaids' work illegitimate in the eyes of the self-appointed guardians of public morality. To the question of whether the abolition of barmaids' work would deprive respectable women of their livelihood, George Hill had replied, 'There is plenty of employment for young women in a respectable way of life, without either prostituting themselves or becoming barmaids.'[18]

Although Hill was apparently separating 'barmaids' from women 'prostituting themselves', he was simultaneously collapsing them into one. 'Respectability' and 'work' were the key terms here, and they were set up as oppositional to 'barmaids' and 'prostitution'. Throughout the nineteenth century, 'ladies' didn't 'work'; 'women' did 'women's work'. 'Women' worked in their own homes and in other people's homes, or in laundries. Attempts to reform prostitutes always involved them doing laundry work. Any work that took them away from these employments risked their respectability and therefore, in nineteenth-century language, made them 'prostitutes'. The 'plenty of employment' George Hill saw as available to young women was obviously neither bar work nor prostitution; nor was it necessarily the work that young women were seeking as they contested their restriction to domestic employment.

Working behind the bar had become increasingly popular as an occupation available to women, but it wasn't sufficiently domesticated to be appropriate 'women's work'. And it was performed in a mixed workplace, associated with pleasure and recreation. It was a service and a retail trade in what temperance advocates believed were undesirable goods. Thus it was to many, like George Hill, synonymous with prostitution, even if it didn't lead young women down that path when their ability to find employment faded. The *Australian Brewers' Journal* responded that 'respectability' seemed to be confined to those girls 'scrubbing pots in a sixpenny restaurant, or wheeling somebody's twins out in the family go-cart'.[19] This was a reference to the labour market that was unmistaken in its inference. It was no coincidence that comparisons were being drawn in some sectors between the respectability associated with traditional 'women's work' in domestic service and the immorality of barmaids' work with its superior wages and freedom. At the time middle-class employers were beginning to find it increasingly difficult to find domestic labour for their homes as increasing numbers of women moved into factories, workshops and commercial enterprises. The royal commissioner's report went to the heart of what 'work' was and who did it.

Pubs as workplaces were also anomalous in already being regulated by legislation. Hotels were controlled by licensing laws rather than industrial legislation, and had been since the first licence was issued in the colony. Therefore perhaps it was not so much surprising that the royal commission separated barmaids out, but rather that they were included at all. Indeed, the legislation that followed the royal commission's report, which sought to regulate working conditions for most other female employees in Victoria, did not include barmaids or pubs within its provisions. It was left again to the Licensing Act, introduced that same year, to address the problem of the employment of barmaids and to include the provision recommended by the commissioners.

Victoria was the leading manufacturing colony and attempts there to regulate industrial working conditions preceded those in other colonies. The 1884 Victorian Royal Commission's efforts to apply principles about dangerous workplaces and hazardous industries to barmaids' work was clumsy because it confused industrial issues with the morality arguments being promoted by temperance advocates. What the Victorian royal commissioners exposed were exploitative working conditions, what they then tried to do was to turn these into examples of the immorality of the trade in perpetuating drunkenness and intemperance. Like the more manufacturing-dependent states, Queensland also held a Royal Commission into Factories and Shops (in 1891) and subsequently (in 1896) passed legislation requiring factories to be registered and inspected. The 1891 royal commission took evidence from a barman who verified the extensive hours and difficult conditions hotel workers experienced behind the bar, which applied equally to barmen and to barmaids, and, when asked, said he thought it was not suitable work for women.[20] But the Queensland Factories Act that followed this inquiry made no mention of not employing women behind the bar. New South Wales approached 'the problem of the barmaids' differently.

The New South Wales Inquiry, 1887

In 1887 the New South Wales government set up an inquiry into the 'intoxicating drinks' trade. The report submitted to Parliament the next year made no specific reference to barmaids but did expound at length on private bars.[21] There were at least ninety-four such bars in Sydney, the vast majority of which were on the ground floor, and at least three-quarters of which the commissioners thought were conducted disreputably. These bars were not the private bars of respectable hotels and restaurants but were those that were 'a fraudulent extension ... of the publican's license'. They were not under the direct control of the licensee, no stock of liquor was kept in them, and the people working in them were not in the licensee's employment. There could be as many as three such private bars in any one establishment distinct from the areas of legitimate trading. They were sub-let by two sometimes three women, they were furnished with a sofa, a table and a few chairs, and any liquor was obtained by the bottle from the landlord and then dispensed in glasses as required. There could be 'no question that these bars are not frequented for the purposes of legitimate refreshment', the commissioners reported. 'The chief attraction of them would appear to be the women by whom they are kept ... persons of gay appearance and doubtful character', though they were not known prostitutes. Men of all ages and classes were the customers but the majority of them were young and they were frequently joined by young women from the ballet and neighbouring theatres.

Despite the fact that their habitués were not known prostitutes, the commissioners thought private bars were very little more than houses of assignation, which, if they were run by men, would quickly lose their appeal. 'Their real attraction [wa]s one which should not be permitted to co-exist with a license to sell liquor'; they were an 'evil influence'. The problem was the authorities could not prove the relationship between the proprietor and the women running the private bars because their payment of rent was covered up by a receipt for wages which they then gave the proprietor who passed them off as servants. The commissioners recommended that the abolition of all upstairs bars would be the best way to remove the problem because they provided opportunities that ground-floor bars didn't. They also recommended that the principle of single bars only be adopted; a second bar 'fenced by proper safeguards and conditions' would be a privilege only allowed in 'cases of proved exceptional need'.

There was no recommendation in this report on the occupation of barmaid, although the report's silence on any categorical distinctions between women working in bars as genuine employees and those sub-letting private premises but passing as employees could effectively place them all in the same group. Although the report did not refer to barmaids, several of the police witnesses did. Inspector Anderson claimed that the women in bars were not always of the best character and he 'would not object to them if there were no barmaids'. Sub-Inspector Atwill did not object to two bars on the ground floor or elsewhere 'as long as gay women are not allowed to keep them'; Sub-Inspector Lenthall stated that he had never seen women other than the barmaids in these bars, that they had a fast appearance but were not known as prostitutes to the police, and that the bars when kept by women were decidedly objectionable; Inspector Camphin said the girls conducting them had a gay appearance but he had never seen women of loose character in them, he thought those run by women ought to be abolished and that the women running them were not of the best character. He did not call them barmaids. Nor did he claim they were prostitutes.

Of the other witnesses, mainly magistrates and clergy, only one spoke against barmaids as such: Stipendiary Magistrate Johnson said he was 'decidedly opposed to the practice of employing women to serve in bars'. The others all spoke against the practice of sub-letting, the undesirability of upstairs bars, the difficulties of inspection available to the police, the need for bars to be open to public scrutiny, or objected to upstairs bars presided over by women. Others, usually hotelkeepers themselves, favoured the provision of two bars for convenience or the need to serve different clienteles. Two cab drivers spoke from personal experience: one claimed he had never proved that anything wrong occurred in these bars, that no women besides the barmaids were allowed in there, and that the women did not live on the premises; the other had a bad opinion of them but went there for a good glass of liquor. Other witnesses spoke from hearsay evidence that respectable citizens had been shocked, they had been told there were women with whom 'arrangements might [be] made', 'that the dresses were unbecoming; and that some of the girls sat on the men's knees, and threw their arms round their necks'. This was rumour and speculation rather than concrete evidence. Only the temperance advocate, Mr Knapp, Secretary to the Local Option League, claimed that 'young men and girls could be seen ... going into dormitories together; [and] the head bar-woman was a known prostitute'.

Specific questions were asked about the employment of barmaids. Only the employers were wholly in favour of their continuing employment; the clergy, the magistrates who granted the licences, and the police were divided in their opinions for or against them. The clergy and other temperance advocates were against them for the usual sorts of reasons. Mr Powell, the Collector of Customs, was against the employment of barmaids but did not think it a proper subject for legislation. The Governor of the Gaol knew of former barmaids in gaol for drunkenness; one magistrate distinguished between the employment of barmaids in first-class hotels and low-class establishments; another, while not approving of barmaids, did not think it prudent to interfere with their employment; another thought it would be interfering with the liberty of the subject to prohibit women being barmaids if they so chose, that it was a dangerous occupation that should only be allowed to married and matured women, certainly not young ones. 'Witnesses from the artisan classes' were, according to the report, 'against the employment of barmaids' with two exceptions. Once again the temperance advocates, one from the Victorian Alliance, one from the Local Option League and one identified as a Sailors' Missionary, charged barmaids with effectively being prostitutes: '50 per cent of the women of ill-fame [in Melbourne] had been barmaids', in Sydney they were 'employed to visit the men-of-war and other steamers', 'they wait about the Macquarie-steps ... when the leave-boats are expected ... in port'. One temperance advocate claimed that he 'went into a bar where there were more barmaids than necessary, and saw ... young men going into ... rooms with their arms around women's waists'.

Queensland did not hold a Royal Commission of Inquiry into Intoxicating Liquors until 1901, but when it did the royal commissioners took evidence from publicans, as well as from the police, clergy, doctors and licensing magistrates. In order to ensure 'that the rights of the people as a whole may be protected', the Queensland commissioners were careful to position themselves as independent of both 'those who espouse the Temperance cause' and what they termed 'the Publican party', both of whom they said were guilty of indiscretion or single-minded self-interest. The commissioners saw themselves as acting in an unbiased way, and they saw the adulteration of liquor as of the utmost importance to their deliberations. Although, once again, no one asked barmaids about their employment, the commission explored the working conditions in hotels extensively and took much evidence from other witnesses about 'girls who serve in the bars'. On the question of women's employment as barmaids, a word not actually used by the commissioners, who discreetly referred to them as 'one class of servants in hotels, in whose well-being many estimable persons are greatly interested', the commissioners do not seem to have even considered the possibility of prohibiting them. 'The questions we have specially taken into consideration are the minimum age at which they ought to be allowed to serve in a bar, and the hours of service', they reported. 'With respect to the first, we *recommend* that no girl under eighteen years of age to be employed or serve as a barmaid. The hours of labour have been dealt with under a recent statute.'[22] Thus Queensland dealt with 'the problem of women's employment as barmaids'. No legislation came before the Queensland Parliament and after a brief allusion in 1886 there was no parliamentary discussion about the propriety of women's employment in bars. Women's work behind the bar was treated as no more than another form of employment.

Parliaments debate the issues

There were attempts to restrict women's employment behind the bar in New South Wales in the Licensing Bill brought before Parliament in 1883. That bill was defeated as was another, the Barmaids Employment Restriction Bill introduced into the Legislative Council in June 1884. A bill following the 1887 royal commission was subsequently presented to the New South Wales Parliament in 1890 but it did not get passed before Parliament was prorogued. That bill sought to regulate private bars by providing for only one bar on the ground floor of each hotel and the abolition of all female labour in hotels except the licensee's wife, sister or daughter.[23] The object of the bill, according to its supporters, was 'to preserve the purity of our female population', to its opponents it was 'to destroy the fair and legitimate occupation of many women'. One said that he would oppose any measure seeking 'to limit the employment of labour, and particularly of female labour' and he 'refused to believe that the manliness and intelligence of the House would ever sanction [such] a measure'. Another pointed out 'Even at a Sunday School picnic people of undesirable character could be found.' One supporter of the proposal spoke of the 'mischief' that was done in country areas where there were young men with 'nothing to do but simper at the barmaids'. Both sides alluded to the American experience where only men were employed, proponents pointing out that this was a desirable path to follow, opponents pointing out that America was vastly different, there bars were open twenty-four hours a day.[24] Two months later Premier Sir Henry Parkes introduced another bill to amend the Licensing Act and a subsequent 1898 Liquor Act was unsuccessful in attempting to regulate women's employment behind the bar.

Victoria meanwhile was grappling with the recommendations of the royal commission. In 1885, with the strong backing of the *Age* newspaper, legislation to abolish 'the sweating evil' and address employment conditions in manufacturing workplaces – the Factories and Shops Act – was introduced into the Victorian Parliament. Significantly, no mention was made of barmaids or of hotels. The Licensing Act of that year, on the other hand, did attempt to prohibit women's employment behind the bar. Section 86 read

> No female shall be permitted to attend or be employed in attending customers at the bar of the premises of any licensed victualler, saving and excepting the wife and daughter of the licensee, and saving and excepting the licensee if a female, and saving and excepting females employed as barmaids in Victoria at the time of the commencement of this Act[.]

The burden of proof rested with the licensee, who would be liable for a fine for committing the offence.[25] In rejecting the clause, opponents disputed the facts acquired in evidence by the 1884 royal commission and the grounds on which the measure was justified. They argued that over-work was a reason for restraining the employers not abolishing the workers; that many of them were 'young persons striving to act honestly and decently', breadwinners 'supporting mothers and younger sisters', women scarcely fitted for any other occupation, unable to take up factory work or domestic service. Furthermore, to stigmatise barmaids in this way was shameful and ridiculous.

In introducing this bill, the Colonial Secretary Graham Berry pointed out there were about 346 barmaids employed in the colony. If that were so, as barmaids were only employed where population was dense, there couldn't be too many up the country 'where the Bishop had complained of hearing bad language in the pub' one opponent of the measure, David Gaunson, jeered. Gaunson, a solicitor who had been engaged as defence counsel for Ned Kelly, was now the legal adviser to the Licensed Victuallers Association and Melbourne's best known brothel-owner, Madame Brussell. Not surprisingly he opposed the temperance purpose of the bill to reduce the number of licensed premises, and he exploited the absurdity of the reasoning in relation to barmaids to full effect. He pointed out that it was inconsistent to discriminate between hired barmaids and the wives and daughters of publicans, for if it was not indecent for the licensee's family, why was it for other young women? If it was not therefore indecent, he wanted to know why they were preventing females from adopting it. But concomitantly, if it was unfit for women, why did the Bill allow those presently employed to continue? If it was unfit in the future, he said, it was unfit now. He also pointed out that higher licence fees would not ensure respectability: indeed the Act would bring hardship on the many married women, especially in country districts, who held licences and who had taken out protection orders against their husbands or who were living apart from them without benefit of protection orders. These women ran their establishments in a 'highly creditable manner' but risked having their means of living taken from them with the provisions in the current bill. Gaunson pointed out that in saying the occupation was not fit for a young woman to be in, the legislation was also saying the publican was pursuing an improper calling.

Thomas Bent, land speculator and later premier, concurred in opposing the abolition of barmaids and attacked the royal commission's report as 'disgraceful', 'not founded upon the evidence', 'misleading and untrue'. It had omitted to mention that barmaids were employed by two leading Melbourne hotels, and had mistakenly claimed that the doctors were against the employment of barmaids when in fact they had been against the long hours they worked. Bent asked how the doctors' humane concern could have been so distorted. Instead of slandering respectable women the commission should have recommended the enactment of a law, limiting their hours of labour, against the slave-driving publicans. Proclaiming his independence of both publicans and teetotallers, he continued his derision:

> There are some women who are not able, as are women in India, to carry a load of metal on their heads; there are some women who are not strong enough to go into factories, or to wash the shirts of the Minister for Railways; there are some who would not have been able to dance with the Chief Secretary when he went on that embassy to London; still there are many who are sufficiently qualified to hand over liquors even to the honourable member for Moira.

George Coppin, well-known actor, theatre entrepreneur and some time hotelier, pointed out that barmaids were being targeted because they contravened the government's intentions regarding public morality, but he also argued that the provision stipulating a single bar was unwarranted. It would eliminate the custom of retiring to the dining-room bar after lunch at one of the grand luncheon houses, like Scott's Hotel. Furthermore, every licensed victualler was to be held responsible for the presence of prostitutes and thieves on their premises, while being prevented by another provision from refusing service either in the public bar (now to be the only bar) or of lodging and accommodation to any member of the public. The bill would allow prostitutes and thieves to enter any bar they chose to patronise and no exceptions were available to any 'family' hotel. As a theatre owner he had considerable knowledge of and interest in the implications of the bill's provisions. Theatres too were going to be confined to one bar instead of being able to provide a bar for each section of the audience, causing Coppin to delight in the image of the members of the government, whom he had seen enjoying taking their coffee 'from the very handsome barmaids there', now having to fight their way through a lot of thieves and prostitutes at intermission to get a cup of coffee from the counter, 'only to find no barmaid there but a nasty hairy-faced man'. Yet at the same time brothels were allowed to flourish in Lonsdale Street. Coppin shared the aim of reducing the number of licensed houses but thought proper enforcement of the existing Act plus experimenting with a few hours trading on Sunday would achieve the same result.

The debate continued for several months. The Licensing Bill, 'full ... of strange crude, and extraordinary provisions' was an attempt to please both the teetotallers on the one side and the publicans on the other, one opponent claimed. Another spoke of the 'absurd nonsense ... embodied in the report of the Shops Commission', and the way the bill appeared to have been drafted upon principles furnished solely by someone's imagination, with no knowledge of the facts at all. He thought avenues of employment were limited enough for women, and that the government had indeed tried to expand them, so was very surprised to find that now they weren't seeking to protect them but to annihilate their business. It was 'monstrous' for Members of Parliament to be led away by 'fanciful stories'. A barmaid could hold her own better than almost any young woman her own age; they were better able to protect themselves from the dangers that beset girls, and if their occupation was being abolished why weren't women being prevented from working in factories and other employments? He couldn't see the difference and was 'thoroughly disgusted with the report of the Shops Commission. It might just as well be said that young ladies who "do the Block" [i.e. promenaded around

Collins Street] have in view the same purpose as that ... be[ing] imputed
to barmaids.' Considering the large number of barmaids who were
supporting their families he also worried that driving them elsewhere for
employment might in fact do more to recruit them to the ranks of
prostitution than the present situation.

J. Gavan Duffy, a member of the Catholic group in Parliament and the
man responsible for carrying a bill to enable women to take university
degrees, thought the provision 'curious'. Although he was sorry indeed to
see a girl employed behind the bar because of what she would see and
hear, were they not, he asked, 'straining at a gnat and swallowing a
camel?' They were being hypocritical if ballets were allowed – 'in the
dress or rather undress in which they were acted' – yet girls were
prevented from serving as barmaids. He would approve it if force of
public opinion were to keep women out of bars, but he did not endorse
the legislation and he thought that allowing barmaids at present employed to continue while not allowing any future ones to take up the
work was 'too grotesque to be seriously discussed'. William Shiels, who
was to make his parliamentary career as a proponent of women's rights,
pointed out that there was a mixture of grounds contained in the royal
commission 'for this extraordinary crusade which has been got up and
waged against 340 women', and he told the government 'you are stamp-
ing the occupation as a degrading occupation', saying to the women 'we
are reserving your right to remain behind the bar; nevertheless, we say
that you are where you ought not to be'.

There was, according to Shiels, also a practical difficulty in enforcing
the provision, for in the country districts there were a great number of
women who combined the work of barmaid, housemaid and waitress
according to demand at different times of the day. Prohibiting barmaids
meant prohibiting housemaids in small country hotels from going into the
bar to serve liquor. Indeed, Shiels thought housemaids were in far more
danger than barmaids, for they were frequently to be met with in bed-
rooms and hallways and were far more open to sin. Barmaids were better
able to preserve their virtue, were more capable of judging philanderers;
there was 'no class of women who are really so secure, who are better
judges of men's character, than these despised barmaids – those degraded
women who are following an occupation which we propose to abolish
by Act of Parliament'.

William Collard Smith, Chairman of the Royal Commission, was a
wealthy employer who had brought in the first Factory Act in 1873. He
claimed he felt extremely reluctant to do anything to restrict the field of
occupation open to females in this country but they had to deal with the
evidence presented. William Anderson, who had also served on the
commission, was Scottish born and an ardent Presbyterian. He thought it

'a monstrous thing', 'an outrage on humanity', to have 'young ladies ... who are of respectable parentage, and who must have a certain ladylike manner and appearance to render them good barmaids', working, standing, sixteen hours a day. When challenged to provide the eight-hour day for them, he replied that the employers would just give them domestic tasks to do for the rest of the time. A publican could employ his wife and daughter because he had supervision over them but it was objectionable to employ 'a girl with, perhaps, very few friends'.

The opposition to the provision repeatedly stressed that the appropriate way to deal with the working conditions of barmaids was through legislative restriction on their hours. Another speaker pointed out that just as young men liked to be served in bars by young ladies, so ladies in shops liked to be served by young gentlemen selling buttons and tapes, and if they attempted to turn young men out of that employment they would be petitioned by women. Another claimed it would be better to punish those who misbehaved themselves in bars 'instead of punishing the unoffending barmaids' who were often supporting 'widowed mothers and orphaned brothers and sisters'. Charles Pearson, historian, university lecturer, and long-time advocate of women's full and equal education, 'the outstanding intellectual in the Australian colonies', was opposed. He would never put on the statute book a law that 'depressed the other sex rather than elevate them, or which cast a slur on a particular class of female workers which would not only harm their means of employment but their position and prospects in life'. He thought it imperative to get the principle of eight hours work written into all new legislation. The only point that had been proved was that barmaids were overworked, so he suggested that the eight-hours principle should be applied to barmen as well as barmaids – to whomever was employed in the bar, which would overcome any problems in relation to barmaids and would simultaneously be a very important addition to the eight hours legislation. As the government was going to deal with it in the Factories Bill, they were perfectly justified in proposing it be applied to barmaids. His argument fell on deaf ears.

The Victorian debate continued just as strongly when the Licensing Bill was in committee and each clause was being discussed separately. At this juncture Bent moved an amendment to the effect that no female under 18 years of age should be allowed to serve in a bar. He had promised his constituents he would not be a 'party to reducing the field of female labour for he believed that a woman had the same faculties and the same ability as a man, and was perfectly able to take care of herself in every position in life' – a belief he seemed conveniently to forget when it came to woman suffrage – but he believed that she should be of a minimum age before going to serve in a bar. At least one Member of Parliament thought they were treading very dangerous ground interfering with 'the liberty of the subject'. For the first time they were proposing to mark out a line of prohibition with regard to employment, he said, and there was no way of predicting how far the principle might be carried. Logically if public morality required that women not be employed as barmaids, the prohibition should be absolute because wives and daughters of licensees would be exposed to the same temptations and risks as other barmaids. The proposal was too great an interference with the liberty of the subject. And there were other occupations where women were equally exposed to temptation; in coffee palaces, for example, waitresses were talked to in the same way that barmaids were. Pearson thought if Bent's amendment as to the age at which barmaids could be employed was accepted, the way was also clear for them to add an amendment that barmaids were not to be employed for more than nine hours a day, 'the only point on which it was necessary to interfere with the liberty of the subject', which would not involve a prohibition on their employment. Debate continued but the final result was a compromise: Bent's amendment on the minimum age of barmaids, now raised to 21, was passed, but the amendment limiting their total hours of work to nine a day was lost by one vote.

Arguments about 'the liberty of the subject' were compromised because the English Parliament had previously legislated against women's employment in coal mines, thus undermining the principle of non-interference at least for dangerous or hazardous occupations. Bars were being classified as dangerous workplaces for women but of course the definition of danger was particular. Women were held to be in *moral* danger and even the medical arguments about the physical dangers of unrestricted hours of labour were turned into moral dangers. Injury to a woman's health, in this line of reasoning, would inevitably lead to her moral demise. In the report of the Victorian Royal Commission the two were conflated and in the process of legislation through Parliament the dangers became perceived as being specific to very young women. The moralists would have liked the story to have been for all women, but on this occasion the opposition, and some logic, prevailed.

The debate did, however, allow the attribution of gender and constructions of sexual difference to be delineated. For example, one speaker pointed out that drinking habits were much more deplorable in Great Britain than they were in Australia because there it was not uncommon for a woman to go into a pub to drink, or for men and their wives to sit drinking together on a Saturday night, the wives sometimes with children in their arms, or on holidays for a cluster of men and women to sit together on the ground passing a jug of beer around to each other. Here, he was happy to say, things were very different. In pointing out that 'the native born Australian was, as a rule, sober, modest and industrious and

Figure 3.2 'Free lunch at Greaves's Australian Hotel, Brisbane, 11 a.m. daily. View of the public bar.' Drawing from (Queensland) *Figaro*, 11 August 1888. (Collection: John Oxley Library, Brisbane)

even on public holidays like St Patrick's Day there was almost a complete absence of drunkenness', he simultaneously drew attention to the dangers of mixed drinking that occurred in Britain.[26] Barmaids should go; it was an unfair occupation to put a young woman into because he shared the American idea that work of that kind properly belonged to a man and it was unfair to have a woman standing behind a bar for very long hours. The Americans thought it was the work of a man to be among men, and to hear the language of men in the bar of a hotel, he said, and he too thought it was not fair to expose a woman to that sort of work. It was incumbent upon men, an attribution of their masculinity and their right as citizens, to protect women. Though 'it may be called grandmotherly legislation, on the same principle that we protect woman from the degradation of working in a mine, we have a right to protect her from this kind of work'.

In full oratorial flourish, arguing the opposite position, Shiels went even further in chivalrous defence of barmaids: 'What have these barmaids done,' he asked, 'what high crimes and misdemeanours have they committed' that they should be so treated. But then he went on to appeal to the parliamentarians' masculinity as he denounced the measure. 'Why should we [men] declare in an Act of Parliament that they are past all redemption – that whether they are pretty or plain, married or single, "the stale virgin with the winter face" or one with charms to captivate the Minister of Railways into drinking on Sunday, their occupation is so heinous and so wicked that for the sake of public morality and for the sake of themselves, they must go ...?'

Shiels thought the work was gender-specific: 'I think no occupation is more fitted for the delicate hands of woman than that of passing you a cup of tea at a coffee palace, or a good jorum of whisky punch at an hotel.' Shiels' attack on the barmaids provision was to endorse women's right to an occupation. The legislature 'should seriously pause before shutting up any avenue to the honest employment of any woman in this country', should indeed 'desire to see every possible career opened for the exercise of woman's talents, or for the employment of her energies'. He was also concerned to reorient men's prerogatives. 'What right have we men to say to women – "This occupation is unfit for you ...?" We should allow woman to select her own occupation. Why should our prejudices or prepossessions be the guide to a woman's life? If a woman enters upon an occupation which suits her let her continue it. It is a great mistake to think that a woman should have only one career, and that marriage. One of the greatest evils women have suffered from is that they have always been taught to look to marriage as the be-all and end-all of their existence. I say that a woman's dignity is best consulted when she is left to gain her independence in any occupation for which she feels fitted. If you are going to abolish the occupation of barmaid, you will have to go very much further, and I don't know where you will stop.'

The claim that 'the barmaid' induced men to drink was just 'the old miserable and cowardly plea which Adam urged', he said, which even if it were true would hardly be a justification for passing this legislation. He believed less drinking occurred in a bar where there was a woman employed, not more. Respect was paid to women and they could exercise 'an honest influence' toward sobriety, an argument frequently put by others in support of barmaids. As to the issue of women's morality being endangered, he said 'if we are to legislate in such a way as to hedge women, under all circumstances, with inducements to chastity and restraints against immorality, I don't know where we shall stop'. Wherever women met men, even at church, there were the same necessities for being virtuous as there were when a woman was behind the bar. He even thought there was no place where a woman was more secure, her virtue more above temptation, than behind the bar. The bars of Victoria had 'sent far more recruits to the altar than to the brothel', he said, and it was 'utterly unmanly for the Legislature to ... brand the employment of barmaids as degrading'.

It was clearly against any nineteenth-century notions of chivalrous masculinity to smear a woman's reputation in public, 'a thing, of course, which no man would like to do'. So arguments went to a defence of the character of the women taking up the work: they were quite 'as reputable, as honest, and as virtuous as those who speak about them in Parliament'. Preventing them earning an honest living was 'a scandal upon our manhood, a reflection upon ourselves and our families, and a slander upon women generally', according to Shiels. Bent spoke of the barmaids 'as my sisters'. Similarly when legislation was put before the New South Wales Parliament in 1902 one member called on his fellow parliamentarians: 'If we are going to deal with the barmaid question at all, let us deal with it as men', he said. 'Do not let us try to traduce unfortunate women behind their backs' or do 'a dishonourable or mean thing towards those who are not in a position to defend themselves'. He attacked the opponents of barmaids for not 'having the manhood' to tackle 'the crime and shame … of the city' rather than slander 'the purity and decency' of respectable women.[27]

While some men therefore used the theatrical venue of Parliament to pronounce their chivalrous masculinity, others used it to prescribe feminine behaviour. Coppin opposed licensed grocers because it introduced drinking into families without the knowledge of the head of the household, it encouraged not only females in the family to drink, but female servants to drink in a way that, he claimed, if they had to do it openly they would be ashamed to do. Gaunson blatantly pointed to the class dimensions of masculinity when he suggested the barmaids were an attraction not to the working man but rather to the well-paid and educated classes, like the clerks in banks and the members of the mercantile community, men who without the presence of barmaids in pubs would otherwise go to worse places.

On the other hand some Members of Parliament saw the larger implications. Gaunson likened the legislation to similar legislation passed by James I 'who also passed Acts of Parliament to punish … – to impale and burn poor lunatic women under the name of witches'. Former police commissioner Sir Charles McMahon went even further: in denouncing the clause he also pronounced on the gender of citizenship. He said the legislation involved much more than the employment of barmaids for it opened up the question of whether women were entitled to as great a voice in government as men. He personally believed they should have the same power in politics, indeed more, because of their responsibility for the next generation.[28] He knew many barmaids married respectably and thought the clause was calculated to cast a very unfair stigma on them. If men didn't treat women as they should be treated then the men should be punished not the 'girls'.

The opponents of the provisions against barmaids had a clear view of the implications for women's economic and political equality. In 1883

New South Wales Premier Sir Henry Parkes, a temperance sympathiser, claimed 'it was not so easy a question to settle as some would suppose' and he went on to argue that it was 'our duty to teach women to be independent and self-respecting and there ought to be as many avenues of respectable employment as possible'. Parkes acknowledged that women earned more as barmaids than they did in any other occupation but he couldn't agree to exclude women from their employment in pubs and nor did he see why respectable women couldn't retain their respectability in that employment.[29] In Victoria Bent's amendment satisfied both sides for the time being, and barmaids over 21 years of age were allowed to keep working.

In New South Wales and Queensland there was no apparent legislative confusion about hotels as shops, factories or workplaces. Women's employment as barmaids was unambiguously considered as part of their investigations into the liquor trade. South Australia had begun with this approach in 1879, but by the 1890s had followed Victoria and first attempted to legislate against barmaids at the time factories legislation was introduced in 1896.

The story of these royal commissions and the parliamentary debates that followed them is important to consider in detail. They throw light on the meaning of women's work behind the bar in a decade when sufficient numbers of people thought paid work for women was a desirable eventuality. They also mark the moment when this view began to face sustained challenge. Parliamentary arguments against women's employment as barmaids fell into three categories: the dangers of the public workplace for respectable women; the immorality of employing women to sell men drink; and the hazards to women's health of unlimited hours and unregulated conditions. Those in favour were the defence of the barmaid's character and reputation; the right and necessity for women to have paid employment; and the inappropriateness of employing a legislative remedy to moral or industrial problems. This last was drawn from the liberal jurisprudential belief that 'the liberty of the subject' was free from state intervention. But a new liberalism thought the state had a role to play in regulating the marketplace, especially in protecting women workers. Thus the period saw the beginnings of much industrial legislation on minimum hours and standard wages. The governmental inquiries and legislative provisions against barmaids' work were part of this industrial legislation movement. Neither the 'liberty of the subject' nor the idea that women had a right and need to have paid employment was to survive over following decades.

Although in the 1880s great attention was paid to the probable deleterious effects of bar work on both the health and morals of respectable young women who were thought to be at risk, 'the problem of the barmaids' did not secure legislative restrictions at that time. Barmaids' work and hotel workplaces escaped regulation under the various Factories and Shops Acts passed in the Australian colonies from 1873 onwards. Hotelkeepers, licensees and publicans were not required to conform to the stipulations of the Factories Act on hours and conditions. Arguments proposing that the occupation of barmaid be abolished were met with counter-arguments about 'the liberty of the subject' and women's right to work at an occupation that was not illegal. This did not prevent the passage of legislation controlling conditions for women workers in many other workplaces. However, none of this factories legislation included pubs: they were controlled by separate legislation. Licensing laws stipulated the terms under which liquor could be traded, and it was these laws that were used to specify the means by which staff could be employed. But it took some time before the legislation limiting the hours of trading and therefore employment in pubs succeeded in being passed.[30]

Legislative moves against barmaids, however, provided moments for men to assert their masculinity. Virtually every Member of Parliament who spoke on the issue addressed the slurs and aspersions being cast on the reputation of women currently working behind the bar. The defenders of the barmaids used such smearing as a reason for opposing the measure. The advocates of the restrictions rushed to disclaim any lack of chivalry in their intentions. Only outside Parliament were women able to join the debate and be heard on issues affecting womanhood. They did so as the temperance organisations took up the 'problem of the barmaids'.

CHAPTER FOUR

'Wanted, a Beautiful Barmaid':
Temperance and the Language of Desire

The strongest, most vocal opponents of women working as barmaids were the temperance organisations. A temperance movement had been operating in the colonies since the 1830s, having been established almost simultaneously with settlement in South Australia and Victoria.[1] After a number of Scottish and American temperance missionaries visited Australia, the number of members increased. Temperance as a social movement began to gather strength in both the Church of England and other Protestant denominations, and by the mid-1870s temperance advocates were being elected to public office. In 1880 an International Temperance Conference was held in Melbourne and an umbrella organisation, the Victorian Temperance Alliance, was formed. A parallel organisation existed in Sydney. By the end of the decade branches of the Woman's Christian Temperance Union (WCTU) had also been established in all colonies: these will be dealt with in chapter 5. From then on there was a concerted campaign to convert the population to temperance principles.[2]

Temperance views were clearly evident in the final report and subsequent legislative proposals of the Victorian Royal Commission on Employés in Factories and Shops in 1884. The *Age* reported in January 1884 that the percentage of Melbourne's population who were temperance supporters had grown in ten years from less than 16 to 28 per cent. In the previous six months, forty-five meetings had been held, 80 000 copies of pamphlets distributed, and membership stood at 1500. The royal commission had apparently also succumbed in that time.

Temperance had come increasingly to mean teetotalism. Temperance campaigners' real goal was prohibition. If that was unattainable, then local option – the procedure whereby local communities decided if and how many licensed premises could be built – was the next best thing. Temperance organisations waged a very long campaign for a reduction in the number of liquor licences and, wherever possible, for local option. They sought both to reduce the number of licensed premises and to 'clean up' those they couldn't remove.[3] In their concerns about drunkenness and their efforts to regulate the drink trade, temperance advocates focused their campaign on the attractions of pubs. In doing so they discovered and created 'the barmaid'. As the royal commissioners of the 1880s were, in the words of one historian, 'obsessed with sex',[4] so, too, were the advocates of temperance.

'Wanted, a Beautiful Barmaid' was a temperance poem, published first in a Victorian temperance paper and reprinted subsequently in other temperance publications. Parodying the advertisements found in the press for bar staff, it became the paradigmatic temperance view of the place women had in the trade: 'the barmaid', with her alluring beauty, was the source of the evils of the trade in drink. In temperance literature 'the barmaid' became a metaphor for the consumption of alcohol on licensed premises. Her sex became the issue around which the debate over liquor reform was conducted. Men's desire for alcohol was conflated into male desire for the person serving the alcohol because of her sex, which became her sexuality. Male staff behind the bar were not seen in the same terms. Her presence was intended to lure male customers: 'the barmaid' was the unequivocal object of men's desire. Seeking to control men's desires for drink in the interests of a social good, they highlighted the symbol of men's desire; not men as the desiring subjects but 'the barmaid' as the object of the desire. Alcohol consumption, public drinking, women, sexuality and licensing were then blurred together into a single symptomatic evil of the liquor trade.

The 'beautiful barmaid' was as much a creation of the temperance organisations' desire that she be so, and therefore the cause of men's drinking practices, as she was a result of the labour market outcomes of a competitive retail liquor trade. As the temperance movement increasingly turned towards legislation to achieve their goals and sought to influence legislatures on liquor reform, they created 'the barmaid' as a 'seductive lure' and represented her as symbolising the glamour of the pub. Removing barmaids thus became a symbolic campaign against the evil attractions of alcohol and the activities of the drink traders.

For a time the removal of barmaids became the centrepiece of the temperance campaign. This was a strategic move. Taking the case labour reformers were making for factory legislation, advocates of temperance argued for legally removing 'the barmaid', for her own good, the customer's good and society's good. The need for legislation against the employment of barmaids was offered as a simple solution to what was perceived to be the increasing social disease of drunkenness. 'If we are justified in preventing persons from injuring themselves or others, we are justified in legislating against barmaids.'[5] The drink trade was regulated by licensing laws and temperance campaigners focused their energies on changing them. Their influence was not unimportant although it took twenty-five years before they could claim significant success.

Temperance was an attack on the evils of drink but its targets were the liquor *trade*, not the victims (the drunks who were to be saved), not even the brewers who made it, but the retail outlets who distributed it. Thus hotels and other outlets like licensed grocers were the direct focus of temperance advocates. Their literature was full of attacks on hotel-keepers, and contains many references to America where the saloon was targeted by prohibitionists: 'only in the lowest class of saloon were women employed in America, and they belonged to the most disreputable class'.[6] The idea for targeting barmaids in order to achieve the Temperance Alliance's greater goal of local option came not, however, from their American counterparts but from the liberal press, the Melbourne newspaper, the *Age*.

In the December 1882 issue of the *Alliance Record*, under the heading 'Pity the Poor Barmaids', the journal printed verbatim a report from the *Age* on 'the hardships endured by difference between romance and reality' that existed in 'the apparent and real condition of young females of prepossessing appearance who deal out nobblers to the community.' Describing the medical evidence given to the Victorian Royal Commission on Employés in Factories and Shops on the ill-effects of working very long hours as 'bearing testimony to the terrible hardships to which barmaids were subjected' by their employers, the article had gone on to say that 'Few perhaps, who see and admire the elegantly got up young person who serves the drinks in those magnificant bars, ever thinks of the hardships, the temptations, and the dangers to which she is subjected, or associate with her genial presence the sad fate which may await her.' This was a standard argument in pushing for industrial legislation and the *Age* was a leader in that movement in the colony. But the interests of the barmaids as workers (in removing the hardships and improving their working conditions) was not the point. The temptations and the dangers the barmaid supposedly faced were also the ones she herself embodied.

It was this article in the *Age* that first suggested that lobbying to ban barmaids would be a sensible strategy for temperance advocates to adopt. The barmaid herself deserved 'consideration and sympathy instead of reproach' but nothing could be done for her because too many people were against 'interfering with vested rights and recognised institutions'. To the *Age*, then, the 'one true remedy for the admitted evil rising from the employment of pretty girls in hotel bars', which would probably be more effective in furthering temperance objectives than pushing for either local option or the Maine Liquor Law (statewide prohibition on the manufacture and sale of liquor), would be the legislative prohibition on women serving behind the bar. 'Remove the young ladies of prepossessing appearance from all connection with the liquor traffic, and in a short time 50 per cent of the establishments now in existence would disappear', the

Age declared. Not only would the number of licensed establishments decrease but 'on the principle of survival of the fittest, only those that sell wholesome and unadulterated drink will be enabled to carry on business'.

This last point revealed the strategic concerns of the temperance forces. In the decade before, when their strategy had been to increase police surveillance of proper trading, they had failed in their efforts to eradicate the traders who adulterated the liquor and that campaign had come 'to a disastrous halt'.[7] A new strategy was called for. A licensee having difficulty attracting customers and making ends meet was more likely to water down the alcohol, and to offer other entertainments to induce custom, than was one who traded in liquor of superior quality. It was 'a general axiom that where there are pretty barmaids there is vile drink', said the *Age*. 'People like good liquor and will avoid a place that has got a name for selling "bad stuff". The failing business is bolstered up, and the house made attractive by the presence of handsome girls' who always had 'a contingent of followers to bring custom to the business'. 'The barmaid' thus had another significance for temperance organisations: her presence assisted the unscrupulous traders in the business.

To the *Age* the barmaid was akin to the counter lunch, 'a thorough piece of illegitimate trade trickery'. Only as an afterthought were her wages an issue: by 1912 the paper acknowledged that the fact that she was 'cheap, doing a man's work at less than a man's cost', was 'one of her chief attractions' to the hotelkeeper.[8] Where custom was assured by the reputation of the establishment for its fine liquors, older women and men could be employed, 'otherwise a pretty young woman was essential ... Wines and spirits of indifferent brands may be sold freely with the helping glamor of a pretty face ... getting a man "of equal capabilities" was much more expensive for the employer'.[9] It was obviously easier for the licensee of a less profitable public house to employ cheaper labour. In an increasingly competitive market where the number of pubs was growing daily, if the house was not a salubrious one and margins for profit were tight, selling cheaper liquor as well as cutting labour costs was probably competitive business sense. Employing a barmaid and emphasising her glamour covered up the cheap liquor, attracted customers looking for some entertainment, and saved the employer's wage bill. This economic reasoning, however, became transposed in temperance literature into a sexual rationale. Rather than campaigning to increase women's wages, they chose instead to focus on the apparent (non-economic) reasons women were being employed.

In a subsequent article the *Age* went on to describe barmaids as the real victims of the greed of hotel proprietors. It chronicled their progress into physical, social and moral decline as youthful charms diminished and 'like an aged spinster' the barmaid began to find her hold on professed admirers gradually relaxing, and more desperate attempts were needed 'to conceal from prying eyes the actual state of things'.

While temperance advocates professed concern that the young women who were 'caught in' the evils of the liquor trade often fell victim to the temptations that pubs offered, historian Ann Mitchell has pointed out 'there was a dreadful fascination in considering the iniquity of these miniature hells-on-earth'.[10] In elaborating what Mitchell called 'the spectre of intemperance', temperance advocates were also articulating their own beliefs about sexual difference. They held the language and manners of the customers were 'offensive at times to every sense of womanly modesty and self-respect', as were the working conditions: 'the fatigues which they endure, the class of persons [with] whom they are compelled to associate'. Barmaids were also more likely to be insulted in the course of their work than other workers. Although the life had its attractions and was recognised to be preferable to 'the drudgery of a domestic servant', and women in bars themselves were very often 'good and respectable', it was also 'unhappily a fact that the reverse was too often the case'. The work induced 'habits of intemperance, with their inevitable consequences' and the medical testimony presented to the Victorian Royal Commission 'afforded an emphatic condemnation of the system of employing young girls as barmaids'. Society could not continue to condone 'the physical and moral debasement of womanhood under the present barmaid system'. 'The employment of barmaids is an aggravation of that evil since to the existing desire for alcohol, is also added the desire for female society, which desire, under different circumstances, might prove a corrective of the other.'

Women were therefore responsible for men's intemperance: as good women they prevented men drinking, as bad women they encouraged it. Barmaids were therefore by definition bad women. 'The name of barmaid has always been, if not a term of reproach, at least associated with less respect than the names of other occupations.'[11] One description also conveyed the impression that barmaids were too uppity, and insufficiently deferential to their male customers. The barmaid was 'young, plump and fair ... exceedingly active, and is inclined to be very curt with the customers she does not know. They are always very civilly spoken to and addressed as "Miss".'[12] A term of address that was taken by barmaids to be respectful – an indicator of their respectability – was being reinterpreted here as being somehow unseemly because it broke down barriers of class and womanly modesty.

As work behind the bar jeopardised womanly virtue and was represented as undermining the sexual ignorance on which femininity was premised, the Victorian Temperance Alliance held that it was inappropriate work for women to take up.[13] The alliance hoped that the legislature would prohibit the employment of barmaids altogether and return women to 'less pernicious vocations'. The likelihood that young women would be deprived of an important means of earning a living, and therefore many would go on the street, was a danger temperance advocates dismissed: there were 'hundreds of other ways of earning bread' and reasonable notice could be given 'with ordinary barmaids' to allow them to find other work. Those in private bars should get no such consideration.[14]

Temperance arguments against barmaids therefore also defined what work was and who did it. In a very revealing piece, published while the 1885 Licensing (Public Houses) Law Amendment Bill was being debated in the Victorian Parliament, the *Alliance Record* asked if there was anything special about work behind the bar, which they trivialised as 'the filling of pots and glasses', that men could not do. They recognised that women who were employed as barmaids were educated, and had the tact and knowledge needed for business. Demonstrating the anxiety that bar work created because of its blurring of the boundaries of sexual difference, the *Alliance Record* claimed there were businesses where a woman was indispensable because the customers were women. The majority of the customers in the pub were, however, men. While the hotel business needed women to take care of the many domestic details involved, the barmaid's work was nothing to do with these. Clearly if a woman was not performing 'womanly', that is domestic, tasks, she could have no skills: 'she doesn't have to cook, neither does she make beds; she does nothing else but fill and wash glasses, &c., take money, and make herself agreeable'. She could therefore have no place as a worker in the paid workforce: 'Why is she there?' they asked provocatively. Without skills or purpose, '... then she is simply a decoy'. If her work wasn't motherly or wifely tasks, cooking and making beds, then it must be sexual. 'No matter how respectable the house may be, no matter how irreproachable in manner she may be, she is fulfilling no good or useful purpose, but is rather an accomplice of whatever evil agencies may be at work in the hearts of the customers' for the very way they were attracted to her had 'its origins in a sentiment which is debasing in itself and degrading to her'.[15] Ostensibly the temperance movement sought to protect young women from the evils of the pub workplace where they were both in danger and were themselves endangering young men by enticing them to frequent pubs. They were both the source of evil and danger and in need of protection from evil and danger. It is in arguments like these, associating the presence of women in the bar with men's sexual pleasure, that we see 'the barmaid' as 'prostitute' being created.

Other temperance advocates appealed for the abolition of barmaids to restore the boundaries of sexual difference, 'in the interests of young men, and in the interests of married men as well'.[16] Although couched in the language of the protection of female virtue – 'the sights and language often heard must have an injurious effect upon the character' – ultimately temperance leaders were concerned about the effect of alcohol on young men. It was unacceptable to employ a pretty girl 'to attract soft young men and keep them hanging about the bar'. This concern for the idleness of 'soft young men' evilly tempted by these modern manifestations of Eve in the garden of Eden meant a public-house bar was 'not a fit place for any young woman'. From 'the employment of women to sell and deliver drinks', but not from the employment of young men, 'much social impurity follows'.[17] There was no similar argument about removing young men because they were not, in nineteenth-century language, 'the sex'.

Archdeacon Francis Bertie Boyce was a leading temperance campaigner, and for twenty-four years president of the New South Wales Temperance Alliance. He found the existence of private bars in Sydney to be more serious than simply the idea of women working as barmaids or the fact of barmaids *per se*. His target was the women who ran them for they were the main source of attraction. It was clear, he said, they could not pay the high rents and simultaneously 'maintain virtuous or right conduct in the rooms ... There dissolute men met dissolute women'. His oblique, cautious language stopped short of actually labelling them as brothels but he said they existed only 'for making money by means of improper conduct'. J. M. Freeland when he came to write his history of pubs was less coy: the licensing laws he said, by requiring accommodation facilities and allowing long trading hours, had effectively created the colonial public house as 'no more than a tavern with a brothel on top'.[18]

Highlighting the barmaid's sexual allure was also titillating. Boyce spoke of girls 'gilding the wine cup or beer glass with her attractive, and, alas! her most dangerous presence'. His language expressed a fantasy about the sexuality of women in pubs, a fantasy that was reiterated in illustrations, poems and cartoons of the period, both by defenders and opponents of barmaids. Another spoke of 'the beauty, grace and tenderness of a woman – not to mention a girl ...'[19] Proclaiming publicly about the barmaid's licentiousness and the danger she faced in the pub workplace also kept alive an excitement about sexual risks that were otherwise forbidden or not spoken about publicly. Debating 'the barmaid' licensed a public discourse about sexuality. It also, however, created 'the barmaid' as sexualised object. It associated barmaids with sexual licentiousness in the public imagination in a way that became difficult to shift. It remained long after temperance as a movement had dissipated.

In the 1880s the Victorian Temperance Alliance's attitude towards the necessity for legislation firmed.[20] The temperance forces always timed their pronouncements about barmaids to coincide with legislation that was before the Parliament. In 1883, 8 000 women in New South Wales signed a petition to Parliament seeking the abolition of barmaids and another petition was presented in 1888.[21] When the new Licensing Bill was introduced into the Victorian Parliament in 1885, the temperance press sought to exert pressure on the legislature as it reiterated the recommendations of the Victorian Royal Commission. In including hotels within the coverage of 'factories and shops' and pointing out in great detail the poor working conditions most women laboured under, the Victorian Royal Commission was a real boon to temperance forces. By the middle of the 1890s, as a new Factories Act was under consideration, the temperance campaign against barmaids once again gathered momentum. At the Temperance Alliance conference in 1895, Reverend A. R. Edgar opened up discussion of the employment of barmaids with extensive extracts from the 1884 commission's report, and a statement of belief that conditions had since grown worse. Edgar strongly supported the recommendation that barmaids should be prohibited claiming that 'in his own experience amongst the girls who roam the streets, he had been astonished to see how many had been connected with hotels'.[22] Boyce, too, quoted the Victorian Royal Commission at great length in his 1893 book, and then said although 'some of the statements in the report and evidence have been denied', he still believed that 'even a modicum of truth leaves good ground for demanding a thorough reform'. Truth and evidence were less important than his belief that 'We should have no barmaids in Australia.'

Clearly the temperance campaigners' arguments against barmaids were not based on much factual evidence. Even the Victorian Royal Commission of 1882–84, which was their constant reference point, had based its report on anecdote and supposition. Visual representations of barmaids perpetuated these myths as they portrayed barmaids in alluring fantasies associating men's desire for pleasure at the pub with the sexual attractiveness of the pub workforce, 'a pretty face, a buxom figure, and a coquettish dress are added to the allurements of the "balmy"'.[23] 'The barmaid' symbolised men's desire for alcohol but she was also a creation of the wish that she be alluring, a fantasy that temperance advocates, journalists and *Bulletin* cartoonists alike all conjured up.

Barmaids had their defenders. These included the Sydney radical paper, the *Bulletin*, and, among the employers, the Licensed Victuallers Association and the Australian Brewers Association. 'For a respectable body of women … the barmaids are receiving too great a dose of invidious attention in the colonies', the *Australian Brewers' Journal* claimed when South Australia made its first move against barmaids in 1896. Their defences of barmaids constructed them as 'workers' – real women who were working at the occupation, who might have been breadwinners. The brewers also perceived the ironies and contradictions inherent in the measure stating that 'the virtue, the chastity, and general respectability of Hebe is to be preserved at the cost of Hebe's livelihood', and they pointed out that 'real harm ... [was] being done to honest, respectable, well-educated, and practical young women acting as barmaids'. They highlighted the implications for the labour market, the irony of pushing barmaids into 'women's work' in a sexually divided labour market. 'On every side we hear the cry of sweated women who cannot earn more than what procures the barest substance for life, because the woman-labour market is overstocked,' the *Australian Brewers' Journal* said, 'and to improve the position the rabid teetotaller would throw a few thousand of unfortunate women out of work to increase the glut on the market.' This was 'Woman's Rights with a vengeance'.[24]

The brewers defended the work as appropriate, women were well suited to it, and could 'hold their own – with flattering and admiring "Johnnies"'. Indeed, their presence improved the tone of the bar by refining and restraining men's behaviour. Their skills in 'making everybody feel at home, and creating respect from everybody' added immeasurably to the attractions of a pub. This was of course precisely the problem their opponents were worried about, but the brewers were casting the barmaids as homely rather than sexual. 'Everyone who frequents a bar knows that the presence of women in it is conducive to morality and invariably "softens manners".' But primarily it was unjust to deprive them of an occupation at which they could earn an honest and respectable living while no efforts were being made to open up any other employment for them. They also drew attention to the class differences between the women working as barmaids and the women in the temperance movement, who were 'mostly blessed with a little income of their own, which relieves them from the necessity of toil'.[25]

Yet the brewers were also enjoying the pleasures the presence of a barmaid promised when they spoke of how the abolition of barmaids would 'take away all the poetry from the bar', although there was 'little poetry in South Australia', it was 'too holy'. And they were drawing distinctions among bar workers when they spoke of 'decent barmaids' – women they said were seldom seen in 'rough bars'. Proposals contained in the 1898 Victorian Licensing Act – to abolish the occupation of barmaid, to close all licensed premises on election days, to abolish grocers' licences and grant local option, to raise the drinking age, reduce the hours of sale, abolish temporary licences for sports meetings et cetera –

really brought the ire of the brewers down on the Victorian Temperance Alliance. They were 'too fanatical and unreasonable to be regarded with anything approaching serious thought by common-sense people'.[26]

'The men who are desirous of relegating Flossie to the wash-tub or the sewing machine are cranks' they said. The truth was the average man wouldn't care if his drink 'were dished up by a toothless hag with a hump ... the fact that some men could pass a counterfeit coin easier than they could pass a corner pub was not the fault of the bar-belle'. After all, pretty girls in restaurants were not responsible for implanting in young men 'a passion for black coffee ... or a craving for pale-blue milk or dyspeptic buns'. Purists who would force these girls to earn their bread in occupations beyond temptation and immorality would be hard put to provide openings: servant girls were at risk of bad masters and villains pursued young girls in all walks of life. Barmaids were usually very knowledgeable 'of men and things', had commonsense and were the least likely 'to put too much faith in the vows of fickle men'.[27] Even restricting the age at which barmaids could be employed was imposing a hardship, and hard to justify. If houses employing barmaids were indeed engaged in immoral practices it was the duty of the police authorities to stop it rather than deprive young girls of the means of earning a living.

In 1906 a petition signed by 30 000 people in Victoria was presented to the Parliament. In response the brewers tried to demonstrate that barmaids were no different from other women in the paid workforce: all workshops presented temptations usually with less safeguard than the public observation afforded in bars. It was 'just another interference with the liberty of the subject, and a stupid ignorance of human nature ... If a girl wants to be a barmaid instead of a kitchen slavey or a soap-sud toiler, that is her business'. Facetiously they suggested that a better reform might be for the temperance advocates to become publicans and run the business on the strictest lines of propriety, 'whose barmaids would be all daughters of temperance'. There were 'barmaids and barmaids', more 'good' barmaids than barmen in the trade: a good deal depended on the landlord.[28]

The *Australian Brewers' Journal* continually represented the antibarmaid crusaders in misogynistic terms, as aged, unattractive women: 'Puritanic meddlers', 'a concourse of angular, vinegar-visaged crocks', 'this attenuated morsel of narrow-minded womanhood', 'the hysterical woman', 'poor frumps; they cannot fascinate the gentlemen themselves, so they are jealous of [those] who can'. Yet many of the deputations and petitions to Parliament were from the men in the Temperance Alliance.[29] Gendering the temperance movement in this way made support for barmaids manly, consistent with the parliamentary attacks on the proponents of anti-barmaids legislation as 'unmanly'.

The *Bulletin*, too, supported women working as barmaids. When the Licensing (Public Houses) Law Amendment Bill was before the Victorian Parliament in 1885, they pointed out 'people will not be made virtuous by Act of Parliament' and the statistics on unwed mothers from the lying-in hospitals of both Melbourne and Sydney showed that barmaids came off exceptionally well. Domestic servants were more at risk. 'The fact is,' argued the *Bulletin*, 'any occupation which brings a girl into contact with men is morally dangerous.' As that was the truth motivating the crusade against women working behind the bar, they asked why barmaids were being singled out for abolition on moral grounds. 'If barmaids must go, factory girls should go, girls employed in various kinds of shops should go, and away, most solemnly and certainly, should female cooks go.' However, the logical consequence of abolishing women workers in this way was their replacement by 'the almond-eyed son of Confucius' and 'that black kanaka from the isles of the sympathetic cocoa-nut'. The idea that the 'moral times' required such measures was 'humbug'.[30]

The *Bulletin*'s racist support of Australian workers was usually restricted to men. Their support of barmaids as workers was at odds with this, but they obviously did not see them as being in competition with men, consistent with their masculine desire to have young women serving behind the bar. The *Bulletin* celebrated a kind of masculinity that eschewed all hints of the respectability and domesticity represented by the Temperance Alliance or the WCTU and, while endorsing the attainment of woman suffrage, it opposed and mocked the women of the WCTU and the ideas of respectable morality their campaigns contained. The *Bulletin*'s opposition to the Victorian legislation in 1885 was to the moral grounds on which it was being justified: there were no labour market reasons for such a legislative intrusion into the employment contract. Meanwhile the *Bulletin* created its own fantasies about 'the barmaid': 'red-dimpled cheeks, little rosebud mouth with pistils of pearly teeth, arched brows pencilled and pointed, and eyes laughing like the merriest of twinkling stars'. 'Because she lights up his desert wastes we want her to stay.' And they mocked Graham Berry, the Colonial Secretary in Victoria who had introduced the legislation: 'He is old now. He doesn't care. He is full up. But time was – aye, time was.'[31]

There was an element of playfulness in the *Bulletin*'s reporting of serious concerns about protecting the Australian labour market. The year before the *Bulletin* had reported that 'the mantle of the barmaid extinguisher' had 'fallen on the editor of the Sydney *Liberal*' for a report that barmaids in Australia soon got married and 'the bad ante-natal influences exercised over the children of such mothers cannot be too deeply deplored.' The report had been reprinted in the London press where, the *Bulletin* claimed, barmaids' wages were much lower (indeed half) than they were in Australia. Having been told by 'lots of fellows – "squattahs" from Australia – ... wondrous stories of the wealth and beauty of the land of the kangaroo', and now having it confirmed in print that not only were wages high but husbands easy to get, the *Bulletin* fully expected Australia to be inundated with a 'forthcoming invasion ... by London barmaids' all, they mischievously added, carrying personal letters of introduction to the editor of the *Liberal*.[32]

The *Bulletin* also frequently published poems and drawings representing barmaids in the language of sexual lure that temperance campaigners used. There was, however, a contradiction in their representations. When the subject was 'The Barmaid' herself, the drawing was highly sexualised, a fantasy that reiterated the drawings found in English magazines (see, for example, Figure 4.1). But when the subject was men – for example male workers at leisure in the bar – and the barmaid was merely part of the background, then the representation was of woman as worker, often older and more matronly looking, and with a drying cloth in her hand (see, for example, Figure 4.2).

On another occasion, when legislation was before the New South Wales Parliament, the *Bulletin* published a lengthy letter from someone who clearly thought the measure was absurd: if man was 'such an offensive animal that he has to chain woman up lest she should hear him and be demoralised', wasn't it 'rather humorous' that he should be passing laws for preserving female purity? And they argued that if women couldn't listen to men's bad language then perhaps marriage should be abolished for, however bad it was listening to men swearing in a pub for an hour or so at a stretch, 'the idea of marrying that same individual and hearing his language continuously for perhaps half a century ... is infinitely worse'. Facetiously, the letter concluded, 'shouldn't men be abolished altogether?'[33]

Despite the wit, factory girls, shop girls and cooks didn't, in the *Bulletin*'s words, 'go'. Nor was there any suggestion they should. Indeed there was no discussion about abolishing other occupations for women although increasingly limits were being set on the ages and conditions under which women could work. Only barmaids were to be forbidden by law to work at their chosen occupation. In the next chapter we see how licensing laws became a way of intervening in the labour market through the restrictions imposed on women employed as barmaids.

In his drawing *The real 'strength' of the anti-barmaid movement – the struggle for the man* (Figure 4.3), published in the *Bulletin* in 1902, Norman Lindsay represented 'the barmaid' as young and glamorous, sexualised and desirable under an archway of pleasure, where images of Bacchus and naked cherubs cavorted with glee. She was coaxing the man to come with her into the precincts of pleasure; he was being pulled back

"MANY A TRUE WORD," &c.—(Old Proverb.)

FIRST MASHER: "WHAT AN OUTWAGE, BAJOVE! THE DIRECTORS OF THE A.J.S. BANK HAVE FORBIDDEN THEIR CLERKS, WITH AN INCOME UNDER TWO HUNDRED, TO GET MARRIED, BAJOIVE."
SECOND MASHER: "AN OUTWAGE! I SHOULD SAY SO. HOW DO THEY EXPECT A FELLAH TO LIVE, I WONDAH, IF HE CAWN'T MAWY A WICH GIRL, BAJOVE?"

Figure 4.1 'Many a true word', *Bulletin*, 29 August 1885, cartoon commenting on the class status of bar patrons. (La Trobe Collection, State Library of Victoria)

by the unglamorous spoilers – an aged, asexual woman and an equally dried up old prune of a clergyman, standing under an archway whose sign reads 'Abandon joy all ye who enter here.'

Undoubtedly the spoiler image was Lindsay's perception of the 'wowsers' (a term for a prudish teetotaller or killjoy): the men and women campaigning for temperance and other legislation thought to be about public morality. In Lindsay's drawing, the issues about the liquor traffic were characterised in the individualised simplistic terms of wowsers and spoilers of men's fun, specifically men's sexual desire. 'The barmaid' was represented as the object of this desire, both by Lindsay and the Temperance Alliance. She was the cause of men's drinking habits. But to

Lindsay, temperance was buttressed only by evangelical Protestantism; wowsers had the institution of the church behind them, not families, not dependent women and children. The issue of men's drunkenness was not portrayed in the structural terms of the devastation that a bread-winner's irresponsible drinking could wreak on dependent families. Instead Lindsay saw the wowsers as aged, unpleasant matrons spoiling a man's fun, much as the *Australian Brewers' Journal* did. This reveals

A MINING ITEM.

PUBLICAN : " *Don't give any more 'tick' to any of the miners working at the White Elephant.*"

BARMAID: " *Why ?* "

PUBLICAN : " *Because she's going to start crushing on Monday.*"

Figure 4.2 'A mining item', *Bulletin*, 13 November 1897, cartoon depicting the barmaid as domestic worker. (La Trobe Collection, State Library of Victoria)

Figure 4.3 'The real "strength" of the anti-barmaid movement – the struggle for the man.' Cartoon by Norman Lindsay for the *Bulletin*, 1902. (Courtesy of Mrs J. Glad, New South Wales)

more to us about (Lindsay's and others') masculine anxieties than it does about the truth of the meaning that the temperance movement had for women. For that reason it is worth examining the position of the WCTU separately and at some length. Yet Lindsay's drawing is perspicacious and therefore more interesting than in its surface representation of the harridan wowser. In 'the struggle for the man' he saw that in 1902 the balance was clearly tipping towards the forces of temperance.

PART II
The Twentieth Century

CHAPTER FIVE

'White Slaves Behind the Bar': Women Citizens, the WCTU and the Laws against Barmaids

In 1887 a group of women, deeply troubled by the proliferation of pubs and alcohol consumption in the city where many husbands went to work each day, formed the Victorian Woman's Christian Temperance Union. Identical organisations were formed in other states. Although similarly committed to the principles of evangelical Protestant Christianity, the WCTU organised separately from the men's temperance organisations.[1] The WCTU was not tied to the churches as the Temperance Alliance was, it was avowedly non-sectarian and remained an independent women's only organisation committed to advancing women's interests on many fronts not always promoted by other temperance organisations or the churches. Feminist histories have pointed out the feminist goals of the WCTU, in simultaneously demanding woman suffrage, and the appointment of female factory inspectors and female prison guards, in addition to their demand to curb the consumption of alcohol because of the detrimental impact on women and children economically dependent on a drunken male breadwinner.[2] The WCTU's position on 'the barmaid' and women's employment as barmaids differed from the male temperance lobby.

The WCTU strongly endorsed the Temperance Alliance view that the employment of barmaids was intended to lure young men into bars and as such was an undesirable occupation for women to take up. 'The W.C.T.U. has always opposed the barmaid', Mrs W. McLean, President of the Victorian WCTU, said in 1902, '... we cannot be uninterested in what concerns a large class of our sisters who earn their daily bread by this occupation'. The WCTU's campaign against barmaids was part of their purity crusade: their evangelism stressed the dangers of evil and sin and they developed a set of beliefs against practices that obscured the clarity of the division between evil and good.[3] But they also wanted to support women earning a living. McLean was sure there was no reason to fear what the barmaids might do once their occupation was abolished; it was easier for girls to find work than it was for boys and she did not think that barmaids would be very long out of employment. She also added,

'I would not instantaneously oust them from their present positions, and I am sure they would very soon be drafted into much more womanly and suitable work.'[4]

It was clear the WCTU pursued the issue of barmaids with less vigour and somewhat more ambivalence than the rest of the temperance advocates. At their annual convention in 1893 not one of the twenty resolutions passed primarily addressed the employment of barmaids. Resolutions were passed regarding smoking on railway platforms, serving beer to children, the churches setting aside a Sunday for peace, the sale of unfermented wine, encouraging the consumption of fresh and dried fruits, the discountenancing of any theatrical performance as dangerous to young people, encouraging members to boycott licensed grocers, against the sale of tobacco to minors, opposing the spread of gambling, protesting the exhibition of 'immodest pictures and trade marks and advertisements', and several more about educating the young and spreading the influence of the WCTU. An expression of opposition to barmaids was certainly there, but it was as an addition to the resolution urging the WCTU to petition Parliament to amend the Licensing Act to make it an offence to serve liquor to children under 16 years of age. To this was added, 'Also, that a clause be inserted prohibiting the employment of barmaids.'[5] It is reasonable to deduce from this cursory treatment of the issue that it did not rate highly as a priority. Nor did it receive any further elaboration as did most of the other resolutions.

The WCTU was, however, agitated about the sweating of women workers, 'this social cancer' they called it, and the general status of women. They called for a syndicate to be formed to stamp goods with a guarantee to the public buying them that fair wages had been paid to the workers. The formation of this syndicate would be 'a splendid opportunity for women of brains and means to develop their talents'. The WCTU felt that women in Australia were in a sort of intermediate state, 'we are no longer treated as dolls; the term breadwinner does not necessarily mean a man. But we are not yet accepted as equals; although we are taxed and controlled by the same laws, we are not yet privileged to help make them.' The work of the WCTU was to 'hasten the ... time when oppression and injustice will be things of the past'.[6]

The WCTU supported the formation of women's trade unions, for 'mutual help and protection', to help raise wages, shorten hours, exchange information about the availability of work and provide assistance to sick or out-of-work members.[7] It advocated equal pay, and the appointment of women factory inspectors and prison officers. This made its support of the abolition of barmaids inconsistent and equivocal. In 1896 the Committee of the Victorian Temperance Alliance resolved to persuade the government to restrict barmaids' hours to eight a day in the

Factory Act then under consideration. The WCTU supported the move. Until it was illegal to employ women as barmaids, the WCTU thought that at least their hours should be restricted as barmaids were greatly overworked, and if they were not allowed to serve in a bar after 7.00 p.m. the bar would lose some its attractiveness for the young men of the colony.[8]

The WCTU supported women's right to work and recognised the importance of state intervention in limiting exploitation by employers. But barmaids were employed in a workplace that the WCTU was determined to abolish. The public house was an alternative to the home and women's employment was predicated on their attractions as women, both domestic and sexual. All the popular representations of 'the barmaid' emphasised her sexual charms, and the government inquiries emphasised the overlap with prostitution, both actual and imagined. The laws insisting on the accommodation provisions reinforced the domestic, homely nature of pubs.

The equality of citizenship the WCTU sought was more unreachable when women were employed in exploitation of their sexual difference, only for their sexual ability to attract custom and thereby bolster a trade that the WCTU women opposed because of its detrimental effects on the home. Furthermore, in placing themselves in such a workplace women were exposed to a culture of masculine behaviour that did not elevate women or improve relations between the sexes. It locked women into reinforcing the very conditions of inequality between the sexes that the WCTU was struggling to combat. This was not just an issue of narrow-minded morality. Excessive drinking was a real issue for economically dependent wives and children, and struggling for equal citizenship status both politically and economically a major commitment of the WCTU and other women's organisations in the 1890s.

'If women are ever to rise in the social scale they must change their tactics' one article warned. Merely living by labour was not enough; as money was the article of exchange, women must strive to become capitalists before they could get justice. If women could get control of the clothing industry all women would benefit. Women would run the factories, arrange their own labour market, become universal labour agencies for all female workers, and then the legislators would take notice of them. Women would recognise their own power, 'shake themselves from present dependence and raise them[selves] to honest self-esteem' while bonding in sympathy with other women. In 1896 a bill enfranchising women had been passed in the lower house of the Victorian Parliament but had failed to pass through the upper chamber. This stirred up the WCTU: 'Agitate, agitate, agitate must be the rule of women ... indomitable activity must be a distinguishing feature.'[9]

However while the woman suffrage bill failed, a new Factories Act was passed in Victoria in 1896. This new law was welcomed by the WCTU for its appointment of two more women as factory inspectors, although they also thought it would be ineffectual in ending sweating. The sweating system would flourish 'till men will take up woman's cause as their own. Men will not allow men to work at lower wages than the fixed standard, but they allow women, and employers find women can do equal work with men for less pay.' The result was that men looked upon working women 'as their enemies forgetting that women must live, and sometimes sustain families and relatives as well as themselves. Men have not yet recognised women's right to labour in the great industries.' Prohibiting women from working was not the answer, this lay in helping women to demand equal pay for equal work. 'It is said that drink causes poverty, but poverty sometimes causes drink'; the fallacy that alcohol was a food was still current and many workers who had insufficient money for fuel and food turned to drink instead. The WCTU argued that the wages question directly affected the home, in several ways, and they sought to get public houses to observe the trading hours other business houses observed, to get wages paid at the beginning of the week not the end, to get women equal pay so all workers were paid a living wage and men's wages were not reduced – all advocated as better ways of protecting the home.[10]

While the 1896 Victorian Factories Act also sparked off renewed discussion about barmaids' work and whether the law should intervene, no resolutions on barmaids were reported as passed at the 1897 WCTU Convention. A resolution to petition the government to bring pubs and wine shops within the Early Closing Act, and one to prohibit the sale of tobacco to children under 16, as well as one declaring the WCTU's 'uncompromising hostility to every form of State regulation of immorality', such as embodied in the Contagious Diseases Acts, were passed, but there was no specific reference to barmaids.[11]

Something of the ambivalent position the WCTU adopted was captured in their stand on women's right to work. Thousands of women must work or perish, one article argued, 'and so the question is not whether women should work, but what is woman's work?' They believed the answer was different according to national cultures. 'We claim perfect right to enter every field of honourable labour of which our physical condition is capable, and we go farther, and claim also our right to receive equal pay for equal work done ... A strong reason for woman to fit herself for commercial life is that it makes her independent and prevents her' marrying just for economic comfort. 'While claiming the right to enter on any line of honest labour, there are some employments where women are superior to men, such as inspectors of factories and shops where women are employed.'[12] 'The basis of all oppression is economic dependence on the oppressor', another declared, 'Until there is political equality, until men and women possess equal educational advantages, until there is a common code of morals for all, and until a standard of remuneration for labour be established, which shall apply equally to both sexes, there can be no permanent adjustment of grievances.'

This article argued 'women have been an oppressed sex. They have been an article of merchandise. They have been, and are, severely punished for the slightest moral dereliction, while their husbands might, unremarked, be as unfaithful as they pleased; and their very immorality has been questioned.'[13] In keeping with their demand for women's economic independence, the WCTU journal frequently published information on working women. In 1893 it reported 41 per cent of all women in Victoria were without husbands to support them, 20 000 of these had never married (they were virgins over 30 years of age); more than 21 per cent of the whole female population were breadwinners, an increase from 17 per cent in 1871 and compared with less than 15 per cent of New Zealand women. There were more women earning their own living in Victoria than in any other Australian colony, of those women aged between 15 and 20 years of age, 47 per cent were breadwinners, of those between 20 and 25 years of age, 43 per cent were breadwinners.[14]

The WCTU's concern with the economic status and independence of women – their right to work and their need for financial independence for self-respect – should have made the WCTU support the barmaids' right to employment. But the pub drew men from the home, encouraged their drinking, and exploited the women working there as a commodity, treating them 'as merchandise' in perpetuation of an undesirable trade. Only by characterising them as suffering victims was the WCTU able to fit barmaids into their world view. Attention was drawn to the fact that the barmaids themselves were encouraged to drink as part of their work, in company with the customers or to keep themselves going, 'smiling, chaffing, flirting, mad with pain, wild with want of rest, half delirious with the riot and the glare and the jingle of the glasses, only conscious of the hot throbbing at her temples, and living in a state of agonised fear lest she serve gin for ginger beer and port for porter. Spirit may relieve her, and for a moment spirit does.'[15] Categorised as drinkers, barmaids would have been targets of the WCTU's temperance campaign even without the other attributes of the work.

Nevertheless the campaign against hotel trading and barmaids' work was also part of a campaign for early closing of shops from which pubs were being excluded. From the mid-1890s the WCTU's attitude to banning barmaids strengthened as colonial governments increasingly intervened in areas previously thought to be beyond legal regulation and the movement for woman suffrage and economic independence gained in power and strength. A more fervent evangelistic note entered their campaign. 'Honest labour in no wise impairs womanly dignity, nor need it detract from purity of character', Mrs Phillips, State Superintendent of Evangelistic Work, told the WCTU convention delegates in 1897. 'But what is needed is for our young women to discriminate between positions in business life where womanly dignity can be maintained, and where there is no risk of character being sullied, and those employments where dignity and character are alike at stake.' Why young women needed to find employment in commerce was irrelevant, what was at issue was whether the employment of women as barmaids was 'conducive to the maintenance of womanly dignity and purity'. Evidence, drawn once again from the Victorian Royal Commission of 1882–84, demonstrated that employing barmaids was 'in every way detrimental to womanly dignity and reputation'. Barmaids were being used to induce excessive drinking. Phillips concluded by urging a scheme of approaching barmaids directly and circulating literature to them on 'the evils of barmaid life'.[16] An item reprinted from a London daily paper presented a similar picture of degrading and unhealthy working conditions.[17]

One WCTU member tried to raise similar concerns about the lot of domestic servants, especially their lack of leisure time. Pointing out that shop and factory employees, while hard worked and poorly paid, had clearly delineated hours outside of which their time was their own, the writer said the domestic servant had no freedom. 'Every week is one round of monotonous toil, among people who take no interest in her.' While some thought this restraint on a girl of 15 was wholesome, keeping her out of mischief, the woman who wrote the letter thought that a girl's very natural and to be expected desire for society and amusement would be more likely to lead to trouble if kept in check. Besides, she asked, 'what moral right has anyone to appropriate the whole time of a young girl leaving her no chance for mental or physical recreation?' If eight hours was a sufficient day's work for a man, it was hardly fair to expect up to sixteen hours a day from women and young girls. She argued that more girls would enter domestic service if they could claim their liberty for certain hours each day as a matter of right. With an astute eye to her audience as employers of domestic labour, she supposed 'the remedy must lie in an enlightened conscience on the part of the mistress ... No doubt a great deal of injustice results from mere thoughtlessness, but this is one of the evils which, as White Ribboners, we are bound to fight against.'[18]

The WCTU also wanted to stop young girls selling newspapers and other periodicals in the streets, asserting that such trading tended to degradation.[19] They continued, however, to concentrate on barmaids. The major strategy employed by the WCTU was to present petitions containing thousands of signatures in a personal deputation to the governments of the day. In 1885, while the new Licensing Bill was being debated in the Victorian Parliament, the Victorian WCTU presented a petition with 45 000 signatures on it to the Colonial Secretary and in 1902 a similar deputation was made by the South Australian WCTU to the South Australian Premier.[20] By 1899 the Victorian WCTU had set up a Public House Visitation Department which undertook to go around the pubs in order to distribute temperance literature to the customers and enlighten bar staff on the evils of their occupation.

For the women in the WCTU, as it was for the men in the Temperance Alliance, the pub was a mysterious place redolent of the dangers of uncontained sexuality.[21] Undoubtedly drunkenness and men's unpoliced sexual practices created very real social problems, especially for women and girls, and the WCTU's 'social purity' crusade was important in bridling men's freedom for indulgence and exploitation. At the same time, in opposing women's work behind the bar, WCTU women were also visiting pubs, walking the streets and engaging in a public discourse about sexuality that 'respectable' women were otherwise denied. There was an element of pleasure for them in doing this. One woman wrote of confronting drinkers in a pub and being challenged by them to answer difficult theological questions ('What I want to know is, who was Eve's mother?'). Her tone was ironic, her depictions of the characters she encountered almost humorous. At the end of her day she felt 'bright as a polished button'.[22] The women of the WCTU were claiming their right to speak on matters affecting women – their work, employment, wages, sexuality, relations with men – and to join with other women, including barmaids, in doing so.

After the turn of the century, as women's citizenship status improved with enfranchisement and their unchaperoned negotiation of public spaces was less novel, the WCTU's fervour declined. At their convention in 1900 the Victorian organisation resolved that the WCTU 'again strongly protest the employment of barmaids' but a report of the Hotel Visitation Department was very brief because only three unions had reported in. Hawthorn hotels were visited regularly and a Saturday night concert for young men set up, and the one and only hotel in Lancaster was also visited regularly. No mention was made of reaching the barmaids.[23] This was not a very dedicated or powerful strategy. By 1902 the Superintendent of the Public House Visitation Department reported that it was a very unpopular department with members, and most local unions could not get people to take on the work. There was a reluctance among some to interfere with pubs because the WCTU could not then go about its work so quietly. But the Superintendent responded that 'as soon as we become aggressive the enemy rages'. Indeed it was 'not a healthy sign when all men speak well of us', and the need for this work was 'simply tremendous'. It was 'the foundation work' of the organisation. The Irish WCTU stood outside pubs to prevent men going in, she reported, but their method did not reach the women working inside and barmaids also had to be included. As they rarely had a chance to speak to the barmaids, the superintendent suggested they have a nicely written letter warning each barmaid of her danger enclosed in an envelope which they could then hand to her. This attempt to work with women for women, in a united front that reached across the divides of class and respectability, was the key difference between the WCTU and the Temperance Alliance.

A year later, at the 1903 Victorian WCTU Convention, State Superintendent Roper could report more activity in the now-entitled 'Public House Visitation and Employment of Women as Barmaids' Department. In addition to the usual work, letters had been written 'to girls advertising for situations as barmaids warning them of their danger, also copies of the "Age" report sent to registry office keepers who advertise for barmaids'. She was hoping that the Barmaids Restriction Bill to be brought before Parliament that session would prove successful. The convention carried the resolution that the WCTU fully endorsed the bill's restriction on the employment of barmaids and was working also for the abolition of grocers' and club licences.[24] That year another deputation delivering a petition with thousands of signatures called on a state premier, this time in New South Wales. The next year the WCTU applauded the fact that Tasmanian women had, and Queensland women were about to get, the vote, thus leaving only Victorian women unenfranchised, and once again it lamented the lack of enthusiasm among members for the hotel visitation work. Once again they resolved 'to continue to work in every possible way against the continuance of the employment of women in the sale of strong drink'.[25] The next year they presented barmaids with Christmas cards enclosed with a little white-ribbon bow in an envelope and in 1906 they reported increased activity and that about 30 000 signatures had been secured for a petition for the abolition of barmaids.[26] In 1908 Victorian women finally were enfranchised and the WCTU made no further mention of barmaids until a resolution was passed in 1910 reiterating that the WCTU continue working to abolish the employment of barmaids, a resolution that was repeated once more in 1914 and again rather limply in 1916, when they urged, 'as in the past 15 years, that women be not employed as barmaids'.[27]

During the course of those fifteen years, however, the fire and evangelistic fervour had gone out of the campaign. Between 1906 and

1916 there were only those three token mentions of the Victorian WCTU's continuing commitment to the abolition of barmaids.

The WCTU wanted to put a stop to the exploitation of women's sexuality both because it was inappropriate and demeaning to woman-hood, and because it perpetuated the double standard of morality. Nevertheless, while the debates about the work were undoubtedly conducted in terms of the 'respectability' of women working behind the bar and the morality or immorality of the system, it was also an anxiety that pubs were attractive to young women, and not just as workplaces. Pubs had become places for public drinking and leisure activities associated with urban culture at a time when courtship practices were increasingly being conducted in public spaces. There is some suggestion that young women were also seeking to drink in them.[28] Barmaids could well have been employed to attract young women. Women were more likely to enter a public space where other women were already present. English drinking practices were condemned by Australian temperance advocates: 'if women have vanished from behind the bar, they are now rarely seen in front of it: in this respect Australian public opinion is happily in advance of that in the Homeland' wrote one keen observer of moral reform after the provision against barmaids' employment had succeeded in South Australia.[29]

Other women speak on barmaids

It was not only WCTU women who found it hard to accommodate 'the barmaid'. Neither, it seems, did other women's organisations. 'I have waited anxiously for some lady to take up this scandalous attack on her sex, and not leave it to a mere man to write in the barmaid's defence', one letter writer said.[30] Louisa Lawson's paper the *Dawn*, while publish-ing articles condemning drunkenness, and supporting women's work in other occupations, was singularly silent on the question of women's employment behind the bar. Women calling for early closing of shops, age-of-consent laws, and prohibitions on women's employment behind the bar, were also calling for an elevation in women's citizenship status. Barmaids were, like shop assistants, mainly young and female but unlike shop assistants they had no feminist defenders of their employment. Sydney feminist Rose Scott was a regular speaker for the Early Closing Association of New South Wales and campaigned for improved working conditions for shop assistants.[31] Nevertheless, while feminists like Rose Scott supported early closing of shops as a way to improve the working conditions of their mainly female workforce, and with other feminists like Alice Henry and Louisa Lawson endorsed young working women in their efforts to gain economic independence and support for themselves, they did not openly and specifically speak up to condone their work as barmaids.

Journalist Beatrix Tracy thought there was much that 'a considerate employer of barmaids – and a wise one' could do to improve their lot: provide a cash register so the barmaids didn't have the burden of responsibility in handling money; establish a 'tone' by always employing women of indisputable respectability so that others were not tarnished; inhibit drinking while on duty, a hazard encouraged by customers wishing the barmaid to drink with them. But 'the barmaid is a working woman whom I approach with diffidence', she wrote in 1908. Tracy herself 'had been brought up to be more than just marriageable' and her mother ran a glass factory in the city.[32] She had undertaken a series of studies of working women's occupations and, after finding employment at each occupation studied, wrote from first-hand experience.

Of shop assistants she wrote approvingly.[33] But she had difficulties writing about barmaids' work. 'Alternately represented as a sore upon the back of society and a victim of its Sabbath frame of mind', Tracy conceded the barmaid 'presents a minor problem – more sociological than industrial'. 'Allowing that a woman can make an honest and adequate living as a barmaid, I don't hesitate to say that it is unworthy work', Tracy argued. Tracy thought 'few barkeepers consider it necessary to appoint themselves the guardians of their girl workers'. She believed no woman in any occupation should be allowed to work continuously more than eight, indeed even six, hours per day, and she alluded to the evidence given to the Victorian Royal Commission in 1882–84 as to 'the peculiar dangers of bar-service ... the physical results of their work ... so shocking that it has no place outside a medical text-book'.[34]

It was an occupation in which 'there was less than a 50 per cent chance of desirable livelihood' and the barmaid's matrimonial chances were depleted by her 'sordid associations'. While she probably received many offers of marriage, and might even make 'a good match', men who sought wives from behind the bar were not 'a good catch', were not 'the highest specimens of good sense and solidity'. 'In amorous affairs the bar is a bridge rather than a barrier between unprincipled men and foolish women', Tracy wrote. Many women seeking work had an aversion to working in contact with other women, women patrons of restaurants were thought to be rude and supercilious in their patronage. But Tracy thought men were more affronting. 'Women customers never showed any inclination to chuck their female attendants under the chin', she said. The real problem was that 'since time began it has been a natural thing for a woman to wait on a man, in the way of either love or cheerful service. And so the instinct comes to prefer serving a man to serving a woman.

Then, too, ... a woman measures most things by their possible relation to matrimony. To wait on men means "chances"...'

This was a different argument from that put forward by the WCTU. The danger as far as Tracy was concerned for women working as barmaids was that 'Woman's destiny for good or evil was usually built upon the initiative of other people. It is a man, not a circumstance, that strikes the keynote of her virtue or her criminality.' While 'really bad women' were rare, women in the middle range of virtue, 'mediocrities', could be turned to extremes not only by their own actions but by their associations. A woman's reputation was still obviously her primary virtue but Tracy's position was not that simplistic. She was more concerned about women's lack of power in their relationships with men. 'In a bar a woman is exposed to the eyes and tongue of every man who cares to approach her', Tracy pointed out. 'The barmaid is an attempt to pander to the sensuous – or worse – sides of a man's mind', she said.

Tracy's experience of the work, although brief, was illuminating. She was acutely aware of the class differences between customers. 'The poorer and older men who drank there were not offensive in any respect, so long as they were sober,' she reported, 'but vapid young men [of her own class] who imagined that their clothes and their pretensions were letters patent of superiority, were hard to bear with.' The labourer drank solitarily, without frivolity, or with companions with only slight acknow-ledgement – prompted by courtesy – to the barmaid present. 'The better-clothed youth ... was actively rude', she reported. 'He and his kind seemed to find it incumbent upon them to show condescension to the girl behind the bar' a condescension that manifested itself as 'impudent familiarity'. Her observations of these matters are very close to the comments bar attendants make today about customers.

Feminist reformers were most exercised about women selling, par-ticularly women selling to men, and the wage nexus – where cash was paid for services rendered – was where the danger lay. As a service occupation, retail selling continued the power relationship inherent in the master–servant relationship of domestic service.[35] 'The barmaid', like the shop assistant, was another category of servant but unlike servants employed in private homes their work was performed in public, the bar-maid's for male customers. Her relationship with male masters who could legitimately make demands of her was now occurring in public space and the public sphere, by definition, required legal regulation.[36]

The customers of shops whom the young female shop assistants were serving were mainly women but the customers of pubs were men and Beatrix Tracy's most illuminating comments alluded to the relationship between the male customers and the barmaids. 'Conversation in a bar is an affliction. Men talked to me about racing, theatres, politics, mining,

Figure 5.1 The liquor industry's representation of the barmaid: 'Who said Beggs?' An advertisement for Beggs whisky, *Bulletin*, 15 November 1906. (La Trobe Collection, State Library of Victoria)

shipping, without any thought of my ignorance or interest', she said. 'Some essayed humour; some were sentimental', and, she said, 'I felt like a target at which any marksman aimed a shot.' She went on, 'They were civil, foolish, noisy or quiet, as their inclinations dictated (my attitude affected them hardly at all) or as the number of drinks they had consumed prompted them.' Superbly she recounted, 'They held orgies of egotism to which I was sacrificed.' It wasn't that they were 'censurable' in either their conversation or their behaviour but 'No woman should voluntarily risk the sullying of her dignity', she said.

Tracy's description of the men's indifference to her is the most revealing comment she made about the work of women behind the bar and its manifestations of gender relations. She found the bar a 'strictly improper' place for the presence of a woman because, she claimed, of the possibility of misbehaviour, 'one blackguard – or the mere chance of one' was too great a risk, even though the men she encountered were not blackguards. But she clearly was deeply affronted by her own inconsequence to these men in the pursuit of their own pleasure, except for what she could give them when they wanted it. This put them in a position of power over her which 'the better-clothed youth' recognised and Tracy herself felt demeaned by. She believed that morals depended on individual character rather than on the environment: 'A woman, self-contained and sturdy in character, could spend her life in a bar and be impeccable', while another, 'a moral weakling would, more than probably, sink ... down, down, till she reached the gutter'. But her own personal experience, observations and enquiries induced her to say 'no matter what provisions are made for the maid's comfort, no matter how superior it may be, a bar is not a fit place for a woman'. And it was the presence of men and their 'orgies of egotism' that made it so.

Nevertheless Tracy was not in favour of women working in most of the occupations she tried. Only nursing got her unqualified approval. The barmaid 'invited abolition'. She was 'a sinister substitute for the man-server ... cheaper than he would be, and ... a much more profitable servant by attracting custom'. Barmaids 'offend against many rules of womanly pride and self-preservation' and it was 'no part of woman's right destiny to be an attractive drink-server'. The shop assistant invited sweating by her own 'submission to it ... she condones it by her anxiety to enter this "genteel" employment. She deserves it for her spinelessness.' Still, along with waiting on tables and domestic service, shop work was 'one of the most suitable employments for women'. Domestic labour was the ideal employment for women of all classes. Some of this was Tracy's own intellectual arrogance: 'If I had a daughter who was incapable of earning her bread in intellectual pursuits, I would train her in common-sense and the kitchen, and bid her to be a cook or maid of all work until she became a matron.'[37]

In contrast to Australian women, New Zealand women were not so unanimous on the subject of the abolition of barmaids. The New Zealand WCTU was opposed to barmaids whom they called, following the English temperance organisations, 'white slaves behind the bar',[38] a reference to organised prostitution. But the National Council of Women said all avenues of work should be open to women, and they should have equal pay. The Waiapu Council of Women said it was the bar not the barmaids that should be abolished: outlawing the job was discriminatory and would add to the disabilities under which women suffered.[39]

Only barmaids' voices were absent from the discussion. A hint of their position came at the Victorian Licensed Victuallers Picnic in 1904, when Mr G. H. Bennett, MLA, proposed the toast of the Licensed Victuallers Association (LVA) saying it would be 'a lasting disgrace' should the Barmaids' Abolition Bill pass, 'whereupon a shrill shriek of approval rose up from 50 female voices'.[40] In Tasmania in 1908 a meeting of barmaids demanded that a Tasmanian Member of Parliament retract or prove his 'disgraceful statement about defenceless women' that 'the average barmaid was not such a good woman when she left her profession as she was when she entered it'. A deputation of barmaids called on him and spoke 'in no uncertain terms' about the insult they felt.[41] And there's evidence from South Australia that barmaids there petitioned Parliament on their own behalf.[42] A barmaid interviewed by a New Zealand paper just wanted to be allowed to get on with her job and live her life without continual public and official scrutiny. She complained she 'could not go to supper with a man in case anyone should speak about it' and she was 'heartily sick of all the spying and restrictions'. Bar work and barmaids were no better, no worse than anyone else, she said. It was a good job with good pay that enabled her to support her mother and younger sisters. One 'Barmaid from the Bush' wrote that she hoped that when the women in New South Wales were enfranchised, a strong domestic union might be formed 'to exercise sufficient pressure to compel the gang of selfish talkers, called "our legislators", to transform the present system of household slavery and slow murder called "domestic service" '.[43]

While the WCTU fought for enfranchisement and otherwise supported women's economic independence, it never found these compatible with women's employment as barmaids. The WCTU sought to defend the home. The pub and the barmaid represented the extent of the liquor trades' threat to that: even parodied it.[44] Indeed the pub made homely by a woman's presence, in the way the *Australian Brewers' Journal* described, was a bigger threat than alcohol itself.

In 1902, the year Norman Lindsay drew his now famous caricature of wowsers, the WCTU president pointed out that the Victorian Trades Hall Council were now on side and were 'determined to put the liquor question before Parliament'. That year the Victorian WCTU Convention resolved to follow 'the excellent example set us by the authorities of the City of Glasgow'.[45] After two decades of campaigning success seemed to be within reach.

The context changes

After 1900 state governments began enacting the very provisions the temperance organisations had been seeking. Between 1902 and 1908 all the Australian states introduced legislation limiting or restricting barmaids' employment, and by 1916 two states and New Zealand had succeeded in passing prohibitory laws. The legislatures that passed these laws have been characterised as 'wowser governments'. Usually a coalition of liberal and labour politicians, they subscribed to the new liberal philosophy of state intervention in the workplace and sought measures to protect the working class from the ravages of poverty and destitution that had prevailed in the 1890s Depression, while also implementing many measures that circumscribed activities – like drinking on Sundays – they thought caused poverty.

They also had particular views about women as citizens and workers that brought contradictory measures. On the one hand, they enfranchised women as voters, reduced their working hours and gave them minimum wages; on the other, they forbade them to gamble, decried the reduction of the birthrate, and decided what work was or was not appropriate for women to do. So, while women were gaining political citizenship, they were simultaneously being denied economic citizenship. The legislation against barmaids was part of a process constructing women's citizenship status. These measures appeared to arise from ideas of morality, and 'the barmaid' had long been held to signify immorality. Similar arguments about the unsuitability of the work behind the bar were being used as had been used in the 1880s, and the Victorian Royal Commission of 1882–84 was still called on to provide evidence and argument. Nevertheless, although it is reasonable to suppose that the temperance campaigners' long-running educational and political campaign might finally have been bearing fruit, it is not that clear-cut. The same people and organisations continued to be for and against 'the barmaid', yet no new morality arguments were forthcoming: the Temperance Alliance was still recycling the arguments from the Victorian Royal Commission. In fact it is clear from reading the temperance press that by the time the last anti-barmaid provision was passed (in Victoria in 1916) the heat had gone out of the temperance campaign. Barmaids were merely part of a larger picture and, after 1907, 'the barmaid' was increasingly less important symbolically. Neither the Australian nor the New Zealand WCTU gave the legislation much of a mention when it was finally passed. Indeed there were equally powerful pressure groups, in the Liquor Trades Union, the Trades Hall Council, the brewing corporations who owned many public houses, and the employer organisation of hotelkeepers (the LVA), all of whom were exercising pressure on the governments. And the legislation wasn't passed in all states.

At the turn of the century there were other factors contributing to the pressure for legislation. The first of these was the establishment of nationhood. Where before arguments about legislating against barmaids had been located in a discourse about occupational health and the dangers and immorality of the public workplace for women, now they were located in a discourse about racial purity, nationalism and sexuality. The main protagonists in the debate were still the forces for temperance, but the influence of nationalism and eugenics in shaping perceptions of appropriate woman citizens now had greater currency. Economic changes in the labour market and in the structure of the industry also affected the timing and outcome of the legislation. What had disappeared were the arguments for women's entitlement to paid employment, and for 'the liberty of the subject', which had been deployed to preserve women's employment prospects and oppose the abolition of barmaids in the 1880s. After 1900 women's liberties as subjects were adjusted as citizenship and subjects were being redefined within a nationalist liberal political discourse. 'The Barmaid', long a symbol of the evil liquor trade, was now the antithesis of the desirable woman citizen subject.

One factor shaping arguments against the employment of barmaids after 1900 were eugenicist arguments for a White Australia. As other historians have demonstrated, a large component of the industrial and immigration policy of the new nation was the protection of the wages and living standards of *white* male workers; but 'White Australia' also meant Anglo-Protestant monarchist Australia, not Irish-Catholic republican Australia. Sectarianism, which had been rife in the nineteenth century, now resurfaced as national destiny. As one historian described it, 'to descendants of English and Scottish Christianity the Catholic minority seemed improperly big; it seemed bigger and more offensive because it was Irish ... sectarianism, became endemic in Australian public life'. Protestants, he said, 'stood in formidable array ... in a long struggle for liquor reform'.[46] After 1900 arguments against barmaids were very much about appropriate womanhood within the new nation. There were concerns about its proximity to prostitution and immorality and the risks to 'our girls' of the attractions of bar work (which were not inconsiderable as women's occupations went). 'Our girls' – 'often the brightest and smartest in the neighbourhood, also fairly well-educated, ... able to talk well and play a piano', who were being 'enticed by a good wage and ... light employment'[47] into this corrupting and demoralising 'unwomanly' situation, were the daughters of the new nation, perhaps even of the Protestant Anglo-Scottish majority, attempting to define Australia in their own ethnic terms. Significantly, many hotel licences were held by Irish families, and they employed Irish barmaids.[48] Anti-barmaid agitation after 1900 was often couched in the language of race, racialism and national identity. Nevertheless, while the Irish have a long history of mistreatment by the English, it would be a mistake to exaggerate the anti-Catholicism of the anti-barmaid movement and thereby to obscure the sex-specificity of the legislation. Anti-Catholic sentiments were never expressed explicitly in the campaigns to abolish barmaids. More often the issues were couched in gender rather than explicitly racial terms.

'Our girls' were also future mothers, the nation's Mother of future citizens. Women symbolically represented the quality of the nation, how a nation or people treated its women supposedly indicated that nation's worth (one of the ways the hierarchy of race was determined). Simultaneously women were expected to carry the burden of (re)producing the next generation of citizens. This was their national duty, for which they were to keep themselves, and their children, pure and healthy.[49] Thus, the formation of the Australian nation in 1901 led to a spate of racist legislation and pro-natalist policies at the federal and state level, all aimed at keeping Australia white and British.[50]

However it also led to a shift in thinking about the importance of controlling the liquor trade (in the national Anglo-Protestant interest) and of symbolically 'protecting' womanhood and women's true role as Mothers of (racially-pure) Citizens. The threat hotels posed to White Australia was argued by temperance campaigners and pointed out by the Victorian WCTU President in 1902: 'We have heard the cry for a White Australia; well I think ... it is far more unsuitable for our women to be employed selling intoxicants in a bar room to the kind of company usually found there than for the kanakas to be employed in the sugar plantations. There is no question as to which would be for the bettering of Australia; as to which would be better for a white Australia', she said.[51] 'If we are going to progress as a nation we must wipe the [drink] traffic out of Australia completely', Victorian MLA A. G. C. Ramsay argued in 1903. 'Undoubtedly, to check the drink traffic increases, we should abolish the employment of barmaids. It would be better for the State and the nation.' And comparisons were drawn with the United States: 'Americans had too great a respect for their women' to let them work in saloons, one temperance advocate told an assembled gathering, 'Was it not time Australians thought more of their women?' Another pointed out 'As the women of a nation are, so will that nation be. The love of our country and our homes, and the belief that Righteousness exalteth a nation ... should inspire and unite us to put an end to this unhallowed occupation.'[52] While this was perhaps no more than contemporary rhetoric, pitched at a particular moment of a debate to achieve an old end, it does highlight the issue of racial exclusiveness that was built into the very concept of the Australian nation at this time. It was to be a White Australia, proud of its Anglophile heritage.

While drunkenness, especially among men, was considered to be the problem in the nineteenth century, in the twentieth century the concern shifted onto women. As eugenicist arguments generally gained strength and ideas about fit mothers gathered momentum, concerns about the deleterious effects of alcohol, pub life, and bar work, not only on society as a whole but on women in particular, were more effectively argued. Hesitations about legislative intervention in the labour market and of denying wage-earning women access to an occupation gave way to concerns about appropriate womanhood. This was summed up by the New South Wales Inquiry into Factories and Shops in 1911, which held the state had the power to prohibit the employment of male workers under 16 on dangerous machinery (but not, they noted specifically, in dangerous trades) but it had the power to do so for all women, whatever their age, at 'undesirable employment'.

'The barmaid' had, since the Victorian Royal Commission of 1882–84, been held to symbolise 'undesirable employment'. What was striking about this statement was the unequivocal authority the New South Wales Inquiry took upon itself to declare what was or was not appropriate for women. It is in that statement that we see the change that had occurred by 1900 that enabled legislative prohibitions on the work of barmaids to succeed. In 1885 the Victorian proponents of the legislative provision against barmaids had tried to characterise hotelkeeping as a dangerous trade for women, because of the long hours as well as the moral dangers. By 1911 in New South Wales, 'dangerous' had given way to 'undesirable'.

The laws against barmaids

In 1902, just a year after the colonies federated into the Commonwealth of Australia, licensing magistrates in the city of Glasgow forbade publicans there to employ barmaids, although barmaids were practically unknown in Scotland and there were only about one hundred barmaids in Glasgow at the time.[53] In November that year the New South Wales government introduced proposed amendments to the Liquor Bill that included a provision against women working as barmaids, but the debate in the Legislative Assembly was so sustained the government was forced into retreat.[54] The opposition to the proposed bill was both to the provisions and to the procedures taken in bringing them in. Delaying its introduction lessened the chance of it becoming law that session. Feelings ran so high that members ignored requests to leave speeches until the debate on the second reading and the matter had to be re-introduced on a subsequent day. As in Victoria in 1885 a minimum age of employment was not opposed, as the Member for Denison and President of the LVA said, 21 years was 'an age of discretion, when a young woman should have her mind fairly well balanced'.

The gist of the arguments against the bill were, as they had been elsewhere, about interference with a perfectly respectable occupation. Several of the New South Wales parliamentarians were hotelkeepers and they welcomed measures leading to 'greater respectability' that would end 'little bedroom bars, and little parlour-bars', but they did not want barmaids attacked.[55] It was clearly in the interests of hotelkeepers to promote their establishments as solid, respectable business enterprises. The LVAs had been formed to ensure such an outcome, and many of their members were Members of Parliament, or otherwise leaders in the community. To be tainted as unrespectable, as tantamount to brothel-keepers, would not enhance their political or economic power. They therefore supported any measure that ensured the respectability and free running of their business and made clear the boundaries between brothels and pubs. They were, however, also keen not to have their business interfered with and much of the opposition to women working as barmaids was intended to do just that by dictating whom they could (not) employ. Particularly damaging was the slur cast on barmaids' reputations because it then reflected back on their employers. 'No-one but a stupid Scotch Presbyterian would dream of attempting to do such a thing', claimed one member.[56] Only one Member of Parliament pointed out that barmaids worked too hard and in this respect 'the law must interfere'.

New South Wales resolved these concerns by following the Victorian solution of restricting only the age at which women could first be employed, and by placing the responsibility for compliance on the employer. In the face of the procedural difficulties the opponents of the amendments raised in 1902, the clause referring to barmaids was withdrawn at that time and not reintroduced in the life of that government. Three years later, the law subsequently passed, the 1905 Liquor Amendment Act, contained a clause making it an offence if 'any licensee allows any female under the age of twenty-one years, other than his wife and daughter, to sell, supply, or serve liquor ...' This clause remained in force until 1954 when the words 'or any near relative or connection' were added to those allowed to serve behind the bar. The attempt to have them inserted in 1905 had failed on the grounds that doing so would be 'opening the door' to even more exemptions ('a sister, an aunt or a cousin').

In 1904 when Victoria amended the existing Licensing Act no mention was made of barmaids; two years later, in 1906, a new Licensing Act stipulated that women under 25 years of age could not hold a licence (s. 53) and it repeated the 1885 provision that women under 21 who were not the wife or daughter of the licensee could not work as barmaids (ss. 87 and 99). In 1905 the Western Australian Parliament also debated a licensing law, one which introduced the possibility of local option but said nothing about barmaids. The government lost office before it could be passed, and no subsequent legislation was introduced.

At the same time an anti-barmaid movement was gaining force in England. Efforts to remove barmaids there had been unsuccessfully introduced into the House of Commons since the 1890s. Already there were laws against barmaids in nine states and one territory of the United States, France, 'as long ago as 1887', and in Scandinavia, 'where spirit shops were owned by public authorities', women were forbidden by law to sell spiritous liquors. The employment of barmaids was prohibited in the Transvaal in 1902, in Bengal in 1903, in Burma in 1904, and unsuccessful efforts were made to ban them in Cape Colony in 1904 and New Zealand in 1903. Now efforts were being made in Australia, which, after England, was 'the country where the employment of barmaids is most common'.[57]

The opponents of barmaids in England argued against the 'half-measures' of merely reducing the hours, imposing shifts, limiting the age, et cetera, because these were 'unwieldy and unworkable' and required constant policing. As the evening hours were the busiest in the pub trade it was impossible to impose any regulation of hours as was done for factories. 'Protective legislation ... would leave untouched the chief danger incurred by women serving in the bar.' The danger barmaids posed to men quickly became transposed into a danger for women.[58] These arguments were also used in the Australian states although there wasn't the same exhaustive investigation of barmaids' working conditions as was undertaken by the Labour Commission in the United Kingdom in 1893. Information from it was condensed and reissued in a small pamphlet for wide distribution by the Joint Committee on the Employment of Barmaids, a temperance organisation consisting mainly of women.[59]

The House of Commons did not pass the bill on the employment of barmaids in 1906 and after 1908 no more were introduced. The next Australian attempts to legislate on barmaids came that year, and they were successful. In 1908 Tasmania and South Australia brought in measures that went significantly further than any other state. The South Australian legislation was aimed not just at restricting the ages at which women could start work as barmaids, but at 'disqualify[ing] women generally'. The purpose of the South Australian bill was to prohibit wage-earning women undertaking the work at all. Exceptions were, as always, made for the licensee's wife and daughters, but the special conditions imposed for those women already employed were meant 'to restrict the employment of females in bar rooms to those already engaged as such'.[60] Most significantly, and reminiscent of Contagious Diseases legislation, a register was to be kept in each licensing district as a means of ensuring the law was followed. Only those barmaids who had been employed in a district for three months during the previous twelve would be entitled to register in that district, although they could have their registration extended to other districts. No one else except those so registered could work in that particular district. Thus 'the barmaid' was a category established in law as separate and distinct from other women and other workers. She was registered, labelled, identified. And now, significantly, if a barmaid worked outside these provisions, both she and her employer were punishable. The South Australian legislature succeeded in not only preventing women working behind the bar, but also in making the barmaid, as well as the licensee, responsible for the offence.

One opponent of the provision described it as 'wicked' because it stipulated that barmaids could not be employed beyond 9 o'clock at night, 'too early to go to bed', too late to go to any amusement, just early enough to tempt them 'to loiter about the premises ... drinking with a lot of young fellows'. He thought the only honest clause in the bill was that preventing any single woman holding a licence. The South Australian legislation was undoubtedly brought forward as a temperance measure but the provisions on barmaids and women licensees were supported and advocated for quite different reasons. F. S. Wallis, for example, pointed out that the LVA thought it was a weakness of the licensing system that so many women were allowed to hold licences. Over one-quarter of the 700 licences in the state were held by women: 'it would be in the interests of the trade if licensing benches exercised more discrimination than they do when young single women are the applicants', reported Wallis. He therefore found it satisfactory that the bill made it harder for women to obtain a licence.[61]

Tasmania followed New South Wales in relation to barmaids by making it an offence 'if any licensee allows any female under the age of twenty-one years, other than his wife, daughter, or sister, to sell, supply, or serve liquor in any bar on his licensed premises' (s. 33). Tasmania had, in 1889, stipulated that women could not sell liquor after 10 p.m. (s. 88). Despite moves towards Married Women's Property Acts, New South Wales (in 1897) and Tasmania (in 1889 and again in 1902) stipulated that no married woman was to hold a licence unless she was legally or geographically separated from her husband, and no single woman under the age of 45 could be granted a licence. Two years later, in 1910, New Zealand followed South Australia's model. An attempt to introduce a similar clause into Western Australian legislation was opposed by the government there on grounds that 'it was a modern tendency to allow every freedom of action to women as well as to men'.[62] Of all the Australian states, only Queensland made no efforts to restrict barmaids or women licensees. Indeed the Queensland Liquor Act 1912, s. 22(5) stated 'The mere fact that an applicant is a married woman shall not operate as a bar to such applicant becoming the holder of any license under this Act.' They did not even consider restricting barmaids. Western Australia's attempts had failed and in 1911 the Western Australian Industrial Commission gave barmaids equal pay. It was not until 1916, when it was curtailing the hours of liquor trading during wartime, that Victoria took action on barmaids.

This progressive shutdown on women's work behind the bar occurred, apart from Victoria, all in one brief period between 1902 and 1908. While the provisions covered by these different laws were changing and becoming progressively more severe, the arguments for and against didn't alter. And, given the rising tide of sentiment against barmaids, it is worth noting that some states avoided the restrictive provisions. Victoria, the state where the agitation against barmaids first began in the early 1880s, was, nevertheless, the last state to introduce legislation specifically targeting barmaids. When it did so, in the Licensing Act 1916, it merely followed the precedent set by South Australia and followed in New Zealand, of prohibiting any new barmaids being employed and requiring the registration of those currently in employment.

The actual provision in the Victorian legislation was exactly the same as that initially introduced but subsequently amended in 1885: it limited the future employment of women behind the bar to the wives and daughters of licensees, and only those who had already been working as barmaids for three months. These women could continue working but they had to be registered by the Department of Labour. No new barmaids were to be employed. By these means the legislators hoped that 'the barmaid' would disappear as those barmaids currently employed left the workforce or died. The Act was renewed in 1919 and they had until 1920 to register.

This time, however, when the clause was introduced, there was no debate within the Parliament. There was no pro-feminist defence from the men in Parliament, no contest about the justice or injustice of the provision to women workers; indeed, there was no discussion of the clause at all. Removal of barmaids was no longer an issue of dispute: it was already a *fait accompli*. In 1916 Victoria, the last Australian state to give women the vote, the state where the temperance movement was most powerful, and where anti-barmaid agitation had begun first in the 1880s, became the last jurisdiction to pass a law against women working behind the bar.

The significance of the legislation

Such a success for the temperance campaign went almost unremarked; it didn't even raise a mention in the WCTU press. Similarly in New Zealand, where a numerically strong deputation of the WCTU had petitioned the government about barmaids in 1902, there was barely a mention in the WCTU journal when the provision was brought in.[63] The disparity between the moments of greatest agitation and visibility in the temperance campaign and their reaction at the moment of the law's passage therefore suggest that factors other than the strength of the temperance campaign were influencing the legislatures. Indeed, after 1907 the provision against barmaids was not a major goal of the Victorian Temperance Alliance nor of the WCTU. It had become a formulaic demand recycled every time the legislation was under revision but otherwise no effort was made to secure the provision, and certainly the WCTU put no effort into it after their big petition and deputation to the Premier in 1902.

In 1907 Victoria had amended the licensing law and deferred local option for ten years, the really big goal of the temperance campaigners. Instead it established the Licenses Reduction Board. It thus took much of the heat out of the temperance campaign against barmaids: new strategies were looked to. By 1914 this board had closed over seven hundred hotels.[64] The 1907 Act was to remain in force for eight years, at the end of which time temperance campaigners knew a new licensing statute would be brought in. When it was, it brought both the restriction on women's employment as barmaids and 6 o'clock closing of hotels. While the provision against the barmaids was a temperance measure, the success of 6 o'clock closing was a victory for the Early Closing Movement, only some of whom were temperance supporters.[65] It brought hotels into line with other retail traders. Hotels had at last become shops and their trading hours and their employees were now subject to similar provisions. The special position hotels had enjoyed compared with shops, which was a factor in the 1870s and 1880s, was no longer maintained, and once that distinction went, so too did that special category of shop assistant, the barmaid. Anti-barmaid laws need to be placed more firmly in the history and changes of shop work. While the WCTU presented a petition to Parliament on early closing in 1914, they actually preferred to see the accommodation and liquor selling provisions of hotels separated so that 'mere drink shops' could no longer disguise themselves as 'respectable' businesses.[66]

Legislation on barmaids' work was passed at that moment when young women were moving not into factories but increasingly into shops. Hotels as a form of retail trading also benefited from this movement. Conditions for employees in shops were arduous and uncomfortable but it was not until the turn of the century that retail shops began to come under the ambit of industrial legislation.[67]

While laws regulating hotel trading did bring them into line with other retail traders in the hours they kept, those laws were not the early closing laws that applied to shops, but separate licensing laws that kept hotels in a distinct category of retail trader. The simple fact remained that hotels were required to be licensed by the state in order to engage in the retail trade of liquor and they were therefore distinct in the treatment they received. So too was their workforce. The significant feature of work behind the bar was that it was a selling occupation which thus carried all the characteristics of seduction and persuasion that other sales jobs carried.[68] But it differed in the goods it traded, and in the clientele it served. Not only were they men, but they were more often now middle-class men. The consequences of these differences were felt by the workers. Shop assistants and other independent working women who came within the purview of legislation did not, like barmaids in South Australia, New Zealand and subsequently Victoria, have their occupations abolished.

Australian licensing laws required hotels to provide accommodation which meant housekeeping skills were part of running the business. Legislators frequently pointed out that women's labour was needed for these housekeeping services and it would be unfair to punish a hotelkeeper for sending his family into the bar when their labour was also required there for the successful running of his business. Thus the legislation prohibiting the employment of women as barmaids specifically excluded the wives and daughters of the licensees. The presence of wives and daughters, a 'natural' corollary to the accommodation provisions in the licensing laws, removed only independent wage-earning women from the bar. The category of barmaid was now left only for 'relatives assisting' a male breadwinner. This was important more for its symbolism, for the knowledge it created about 'woman' and 'worker', than it was for the actual practice of bar employment. The majority of women working behind the bar were members of the family running the pub. Women did continue working, even a small minority of those who were employees. The provisions may not have been rigorously policed, registration certificates were also passed on illicitly. Over time, however, the numbers did decline, and the age of the barmaid increased as young women were no longer recruited.[69]

It was in keeping with the familial ideal – that '"natural" organisation within which people lived and that determined such economic phenomena as the law of wages'[70] – that underwrote so much other social policy in this period. The South Australian legislation that abolished barmaids also prohibited single women from obtaining and holding a licence to run a hotel on the assumption that widows and wives were needed to carry on their husbands' financial interests, a provision ex-pressly wanted by the LVA. Independent wage-earning women living outside the confines of a family created anxiety.[71] Not only was 'the barmaid' an independent wage-earning woman but many barmaids lived on the premises of the pub.[72]

It was a singular departure for Australian labour legislation to forbid anyone to work at a particular occupation. Only in coal mining did legislation specify an occupation that was off-limits to women, but that English legislation was never enacted in Australia.[73] Colonial Factories Acts stipulated minimum ages and maximum hours of employment, and placed limits on weights that could be lifted, which effectively debarred women from working at certain occupations. They therefore segregated the workforce on lines of sexual difference, a principle upheld in the Conciliation and Arbitration Court in the decade after 1900. Nevertheless it was these industrial tribunals and their compulsory awards that maintained the sexual division of labour within the Australian labour market, not prohibitory legislation. Except, that is, in hotel workplaces where the presence of young wage-earning women working behind the bar challenged ideas of sexual differentiation.

In addition to the temperance campaign significant economic changes also contributed to the introduction of anti-barmaid legislation. At the turn of the century beer manufacturing was undergoing change as breweries amalgamated into corporations. These brewing corporations owned hotels (tied houses) and leased them out to approved licensees who purchased supplies only from that brewery. Government attention to the implications of the tied house system meant 'the brewing trade would have to be careful', the *Australian Brewers' Journal* reported in 1902, the labours of the New South Wales Committee 'may turn out to be very serious'. They deplored the lack of a representative body in Sydney such as existed in South Australia, Queensland and Victoria, that could safeguard the interests of the trade.[74]

Several state governments undertook inquiries into the system of tied houses at the turn of the century. By 1905 'things were going very wrong for the brewers' of New South Wales as the public discovered the extent to which they controlled the liquor trade and they were forced into defending themselves. It had been in response to the temperance movement's success at achieving local option that tied-house agreements, which had first been mooted in 1839, had become more stringent and widespread. When the full extent of the ties was made known, public opinion accelerated in support of the temperance objectives of local option. The revelations about the tied house system were the catalyst in 'provoking a complete turnabout in reasoning about the drink problem in New South Wales'. The publicans, who had been the focus of the temperance attacks before 1900, were now considered the 'unfortunate pawns' of the big wealthy brewers who forced adulterated liquor onto the market and whose power over the publicans prompted breaches of the licensing laws.[75] Significantly, although it was the licensee who employed the bar staff, it was the brewers joined with the LVA who were the most strident public defenders of the continuing employment of young wage-earning women as barmaids. As they lost the battle for public and parliamentary support, so, too, did the barmaids.

'The barmaid' as wage-earning woman was inconsistent with the familial ideal of men as breadwinners, but this she shared with all those other women seeking paid employment. What was significant at the turn of the century was the increasing presence of *young* women desiring paid work in pubs. The overwhelming characteristic of the growing female labour force at the turn of the century was its youth. The significant transformation in women shop assistants and clerical workers after 1880 was their decreasing age, a trend that intensified after 1900. Between 1891 and 1911 the proportion of men under 25 years of age employed in commerce remained relatively stable at less than one-third, but the proportion of women under 25 rose dramatically to be nearly half. Employers spoke of an 'oversupply' of women seeking commercial employment and a 'dearth' of juveniles seeking manufacturing employment.[76] The youthfulness of barmaids was first addressed in legislation in 1885 when a minimum age was set for their employment. As increasing numbers of young women chose to move into shops employment, laws on early closing followed. Even states that stopped short of prohibiting barmaids imposed some restriction on their age.

In having their occupation targeted in this way barmaids were finally a different category of employee, as the Victorian Royal Commission had indicated and tried to establish over two decades before. 'The Barmaid' was not only a symbol of men's desires for drink: she was also symptomatic of women's desires – for independence, glamour, work, mixed company, freedom, sexual experience, indeed, even alcohol.[77] And, as a perceptive hotelkeeper wrote when the Victorian legislation was passed in 1916, all the arguments against women in bars failed with 6 o'clock closing as there was 'no time for philandering between drinks'. On the other hand, the hotelkeeper stated, abolishing barmaids widened the avenue of employment 'to young and active men'.[78] The significance of the legislation lay in the knowledge it created that pubs were the domain of men. This was true even for those states where barmaids were allowed to keep working. Women's association with pubs was 'unrespectable': barmaids were respectable only in providing assistance as the wife or daughter. In the twentieth century 'the barmaid' became the pub(lican)'s wife.

CHAPTER SIX

'When Men Wore Hats':
Gender, Unions and Equal Pay

While legislatures were busy trying to prevent women working behind the bar, barmaids themselves were organising into unions and getting their occupation acknowledged and legitimated in the industrial arbitration system. They did so by attaching themselves to workers from the manufacturing side of the industry rather than to the other hotel employees, the back-of-house domestic and catering staff who were predominantly female, and they thereby put themselves in a better position to negotiate in the newly instituted industrial tribunals.

There are three significant periods for bar workers and their union history: the first is that of initial organising, from approximately the mid-1880s to 1914. This was when a national Liquor Trades Union was formed and the breweries merged into big corporations, for example Tooths, Tooheys and Resch's in New South Wales, and Carlton and United Breweries in Victoria. They subsequently became the major hotel owners through the tied-house system. Various state industrial tribunals and the federal Court of Conciliation and Arbitration were established, and key decisions affecting women workers were implemented: the 1907 Harvester judgment which institutionalised 'the family wage' for male workers and set women's wages at 54 per cent of the male wage; and the 1912 federal Rural Workers Case which legitimated the sexual division of the labour force into 'men's work' and 'women's work'. Women doing 'men's work' were to be paid male rates. These early judgments were to have a long-lasting effect on women workers.[1] For bar workers in hotels this initial period saw the first determination brought down by the Victorian Hotel Wages Board in 1912; the first equal pay decision to barmaids in Western Australia in 1911; and it culminated in the granting of the first Liquor Trades Award (1914) by the federal arbitration court (see Table 1).

The second significant period (discussed here and in chapter 7), at least for bar workers, occurred between 1910 – when bar staff were first brought into the newly formed Liquor Trades Union to be consequently covered by award wages and conditions – and 1949, when the

Table 1   Comparative wages for the Melbourne hotel and liquor industry, 1903 and 1914

	Average weekly wage	
	1903	1914
Adult male (factory hands)		
Brewing	44s (48 hrs)	51s (48 hrs)
Aerated Water and Cordial	30–40s (50 hrs)	43s 6d–50s (48 hrs)
Hotel workers		
Barmen	25s (60–80 hrs)*	50s (58 hrs)†
Barmaids	20s (60–80 hrs)*	37s 6d (56 hrs)†
Waiters	25s (60–80 hrs)*	45–50s (58 hrs)†
Waitresses	12s 6d (60–80 hrs)*	26–30s (56 hrs)†

* Board and/or lodging supplied by employer.
† Employers now charge their employees 10s for board and 5s for lodging.

Table compiled by Louise Walker from *Victorian Yearbooks* 1903 and 1914.

Liquor Trades Union successfully argued for, and won, equal pay and employment for barmaids in those states that had sought to drum them out of the industry altogether. This period covered the infamous '6 o'clock swill' of early closing, the time when barmaids were prevented from working in public bars, the Depression when even their fellow unionists saw advantages in preventing them from working, and the two world wars when shortages of male labour in the industry made possible positive advances for women workers.

The third and final period is that from the 1960s (discussed in chapter 8) when women hotel workers, first barmaids then cooks and other domestic staff, finally won 'equal pay' in their federal award and therefore in those states where they still lagged behind. In this period 'the brewery workers thought it was their union and didn't encourage bar attendants to attend their meetings', a female unionist later claimed, 'the Union always gave us a harder time than the customers did'.[2] That was to change in the 1980s.

Forming a union, 1880–1910

The process of union formation that began in the late nineteenth century was significant for women working behind the bar, for unionisation differentiated barmaids from those other women workers in service occupations for whom union organisation did not eventuate. Unlike domestic servants, actors and prostitutes, union representation made significant advances possible for barmaids when real changes began to take place in the industry after 1900. The first step was taken when male workers began to organise.

The story of the formation of a union of employees in the hotel and liquor trades has been told by Alleyn Best.[3] Imagining a meeting that occurred in Melbourne in October 1902, Best reconstructed the amalgamation of brewery, maltsters and aerated waters workers which became, eighteen months later, in February 1904, the Liquor Trades Union

Figure 6.1 Cascade Brewery workers in their hats and aprons, Tasmania, *c.* 1924. (Courtesy of Woodstock Museum and Cascade Reception Centre, Hobart)

in Victoria. Best has traced the earliest organisation in the hotel industry in Victoria back to the Cooks and Confectioners Mutual Provident Society, a trade benefit association formed in 1859. This was followed by a Waiters Union in 1874, a Brewery Employees Association in 1884, and a Maltsters Society and an Aerated Waters and Cordial Makers Employes Union in 1885. These were all male unions. There were some women working in the aerated waters industry but far and away the majority of workers were men. Hotel workers (including 'waiters, barmen, hotelkeepers and caterers' employees') were first covered by the Victorian Hotelkeepers Union, incorporating the previous Waiters Union. Formed in July 1890, a few months later it became the Hotel and Restaurant Employes Association and subsequently the Hotel and Caterers Employes Association. Although female employees in the same occupations were excluded from membership – the union's rules made the Hotel and Restaurant Employes Association an exclusively male union – the way was open for later mergers.

Women employees had a slightly different history of unionisation. Concentrated in domestic service or 'unskilled' factory work, women workers were often unorganised and there was little chance of their being so while unions organised around the craft-skill interests of male workers. The big shift in union history for women workers was the development of industrial rather than craft unionism. Throughout the 1880s workers were forming industry-based unions, a move that was boosted in Victoria by the passage of a Trade Union Act in 1884 which meant unions could become 'legal bodies'. Thus there were attempts to form women's unions in the 1880s–90s: for example, the Tailoresses Union formed in Victoria in 1882 and ran a very successful strike, a domestic service union was formed in Victoria in 1886 and struggled on until 1912 when it amalgamated with the female branch of the Hotel and Restaurant Employes Association. Similar attempts were made to organise domestic servants in New South Wales, although they were unsuccessful. While hotel staff had established the Hotel and Caterers' Union in New South Wales, this, like its Victorian counterpart, was largely comprised of male employees and women working behind the bar were excluded from membership. Initial organisations of barmaids in New South Wales, which began in the 1890s, were short-lived as, with other women's unions of Tailoresses and Laundresses, they failed to survive the economic crisis of the 1890s depression.[4]

Clearly the threat of cheaper female wages was an incentive for male unionists to organise women workers as well as men, but it could also lead male unionists to oppose such organisation. In New South Wales initiative for the organisation of barmaids first came from the Trades

and Labour Council when, early in 1890, they called on the Hotel and
Caterers Employees Union to organise barmaids and waitresses. The
union forestalled: they were opposed to the organisation of female labour
but were willing to receive a deputation on the matter from the Trades
and Labour Council. They subsequently conceded the need for
organisation of women workers, but thought it should be separate from
the men's union. In 1891 they (obviously reluctantly) established the
Barmaids and Waitresses Union with a male organiser, Mr Morling, as the
Acting-Secretary. By May they reported a membership of forty. However,
while these women workers in the hotel trades were separated off as
different from their fellow male workers, attempts by women organisers
to enlist them into the distinctive Female Employees Union, which was
established a few months later, were stubbornly resisted by Morling.
When called on, the Trades and Labour Council referred the dispute to
the Hotel and Caterers Employees Union for consideration.[5] To be treated
separately and differently as 'workers' in the same industry, because they
were women, was one thing; to be organised with other women by other
women as separate and distinctly 'women' (workers) was obviously
something the male hierarchy would not tolerate.

Women workers were, in the 1890s, acutely aware of the masculine
domination of work and unionism, and the extent to which this inhibited
women's negotiation of their working conditions. One woman worker
said, of the kind of central organising body for women workers that the
Female Employees Union represented, the idea was 'a good one', for
unions 'have been monopolised by the lords of creation until very
recently'.[6] The issue of organising women workers was continually
contested. It worked itself out differently in different industries. In
manufacturing trades, like printing, clothing and bookbinding, which
were increasingly employing women, male unionists saw women
workers as 'invaders' taking jobs that were rightfully theirs. Unions were
a protection against such incursions and insisting on the employment of
only union labour while not organising the women workers was one way
male workers could protect their employment. Wendy Brady found that
in Western Australia unions were much more likely to encourage women
to join than in the eastern states.[7] When Louisa Lawson wanted to employ
only female labour to print her newspaper, the *Dawn*, male printers
protested not, supposedly, because she was employing women but
because she was employing non-union labour. She took no notice. 'The
lords of creation' made it difficult for women workers but one solution
that some men saw was to organise the women as well and ensure their
wages did not undercut men's. This was an argument also put by women
workers keen to achieve equal pay.

Industrial tribunals: From wages boards to arbitration

By the turn of the century, union formation throughout Australia was further boosted by the establishment of state industrial tribunals under the various Factories Acts, culminating in 1896 in the Factories Act in Victoria, which established the principle of industrial mediation through wages boards. In the early years of the twentieth century, other states followed. Some, like Victoria, set up wages boards (South Australia in 1906 and Queensland in 1912) while others (Western Australia and New South Wales in 1901) set up boards of conciliation and arbitration. The Commonwealth adopted the model of compulsory arbitration after the colonies federated in 1901. Now workers could be covered either by state awards laid down by industrial tribunals in the various states, or they could be covered by a federal award. The overlapping of awards was one of the nightmares of the Australian system of wage fixation, but it was a crucial factor in defining workplace conditions and wage and skill relativities, especially between male and female workers. To get their industry covered by an award, workers had first to have a union.[8]

Male workers were quick to see the advantages afforded by the new tribunals and to act on them. The first moves towards amalgamation of the brewery, maltsters and aerated workers' unions in Victoria were prompted by the establishment in 1900 of a combined Brewery and Malt Wages Board. This was a spur to further recognition of the unity of their interests for male workers in the manufacturing side of the liquor industry. Expansion into the service side of the industry came after 1900, but it took until 1912 for Victorian barmaids and waitresses to be covered by a wages board.[9] A push for union organisation came with the establishment of a federal system of compulsory arbitration.

In 1904, to overcome the problem of industrial disputes that, 'like bushfires and rabbits in search of food', could cross state boundaries, the new Commonwealth government passed legislation establishing the federal Conciliation and Arbitration Court. It was the existence of this federal tribunal that provided the stimulus for the formation of a federal union of brewery and other employees out of the existing state unions.[10] Significantly, though, this union covered all employees engaged in the liquor trade. In South Australia in February 1907, a 'mass meeting of all employees, male and female,' employed in the liquor trade was called, 'aerated water, hotel, wine and spirit employees specially invited', out of which a combined Liquor Trades Union was formed. In March they sought to amalgamate with the Restaurant and Hotel Employees Union of that state (this was done in May) and in April to have the union placed under a state wages board.[11] A year later, in 1908, the Victorian and New South Wales unions federated to form the Federated Brewery Employees

Association of the Commonwealth of Australia and, at the suggestion of the South Australian Union that there should be a national organisation of all employees from both sides of the industry, in 1910 Victoria and New South Wales were joined by South Australia and Queensland to become the Federated Liquor Trade Employees Union of Australasia. No doubt, given the success of the local option provisions in the licensing laws passed in Victoria in 1907 and pending in South Australia in 1908, this was a defensive measure in response to the temperance movement, for temperance was an attack on liquor and its retail distribution. All engaged in the liquor trades were at financial risk should the Temperance Alliance achieve its goals of prohibiting liquor sales. Industry workers thus also joined with their employers in the Liquor Defence Leagues set up in different states.

Industrial tribunals generated union formation among those workers who desired to be covered by awards. Simultaneously, therefore, a change was occurring within the service side of the industry – in the hotels – where beer and aerated waters were sold in the dining rooms and bars. In the same year as the federal union was formed, barmen in Victoria sought to disassociate themselves from other 'hotel workers' and opted to join the Liquor Trades Union when their Hotel and Caterers Employees Association sought a Hotel Wages Board. They clearly perceived their interests were better served by joining, as their South Australian workmates were doing, an organisation according to the product they served (liquor) not according to their workplace (hotels). From then on, hotel staff 'back of house' were organised in the hotel, club and caterers' unions, and staff serving alcoholic and non-alcoholic beverages 'front of house' (including dining room waiters) were covered by the Liquor Trades Union. Soon, in 1911, Victorian barmaids followed the barmen in demanding to join with workers in the Liquor Trades Union rather than those in the Hotel and Caterers. In Western Australia bar workers went even further and in 1910 formed a separate Barmaids and Barmens Union. In Queensland the Liquor Trades Union resolved in September 1916 'to take immediate steps to organise the Barmaids into the Union'.[12]

The significance of these developments was profound. Firstly, the infant Liquor Trades Union took as its title the product (liquor) its workers manufactured, rather than the craft, occupation or workshop in which they manufactured it and on which their old associations had been formed. Thus it followed that organisation could, and no doubt would, subsequently pick up other non-manufacturing workers from the distribution side of the industry who also handled the product. This gave the union greater scope for organisation, the possibility of greater strength in numbers, and unlimited capacity to organise as an industrial, not occupational or craft, union. It thus gave bar workers some added protection because of the industrial strength they could muster, not only against their employers, but also against the threats to their work from outside the industry. The union gave them an organisational base, industrial awards gave them legitimacy. And women saw the advantages of being covered by industrial awards.[13]

Nevertheless the union was indisputably masculine in leadership, membership and orientation. The union was originally formed in the interests, and around the work, of male workers engaged in manufacturing beer. This identity remained for a long time; even with the introduction of mechanical bottling women were not employed by Australian breweries. So the change of orientation signalled by the new union's title, 'liquor trades', rather than 'beer or aerated waters' [manufacturing] employees', opened up membership to not only enable the inclusion of 'workers' serving liquor behind the bar of hotels, but also enabled the inclusion of women as those workers, and women as barmaids became members of the Liquor Trades Union.

The meaning of unionism

Beginning in the early twentieth century as a largely manufacturing-based union of brewery employees, the expansion of the Liquor Trades Union into the service side of the industry was one of the most important developments in the history of bar work for women, and it had long-term ramifications. Work behind the bar was now protected by union organisation and defined in an industrial award. This did not mean legislatures could not pass laws prohibiting barmaids from working. Nevertheless it did differentiate them from prostitutes, which is what the legislation had imputed they were, a category that was itself being constructed in criminal legislation in this period.

There were not many women's unions, and male workers' attempts at organisation were usually motivated, as already pointed out, by their desire to protect their right to work. Organising the women in the industry was beneficial to the women, but to the union hierarchy the women's rights to work and full wages were incidental to the main game of protecting men's conditions. Nevertheless, to be included within a union where the majority of the members were male, alongside male workers doing pretty much the same work, placed barmaids in a position of relative strength (compared with other female workers) from which to negotiate their pay and conditions. That did not make their struggle easy. It merely meant barmaids were in a better position to campaign, and they got equal pay before their fellow hotel workers back of house. But the achievement of equal pay was a problematic victory because of the sex-specificity of the occupation, and because of the legalistic nature of the award system of tribunals which relied on historical precedent when setting award wages for women workers.

'The acceptance of a lower wage is an admission of inferiority', an anonymous correspondent wrote to the *Labor Call* in October 1907. That year the federal Court of Conciliation and Arbitration had set women's wages at 54 per cent of the male rate in other industries, despite demands for equal pay that women workers and feminist organisations like the WCTU had been making for two decades. As industrial tribunals became the primary system of wage fixation after 1900, they also became a key player in the workplace negotiation of equal pay. Many feminist scholars have analysed the arbitration system and its impact on women workers. Some have written on the militancy of hotel workers, back of house.[14] The story of equal pay within the hotel industry has never been told.

The struggle for equality

The first federal award achieved by the Liquor Trades Union was handed down in 1914. It defined a barmaid as any woman employed in the bar for more than two hours a day, and set a maximum of fifty hours per week, with wages (not less than 2 pounds a week) at 75 per cent the barman's rate (of 2 pounds 15 shillings a week). Barmen worked fifty-four hours in straight shifts. Any employee male or female working more than ten hours a day was to be paid at time and a half, with a half-day holiday each week, and two weeks holiday leave a year.[15] State industrial tribunals in Queensland, New South Wales and Tasmania followed the precedent. Yet in Western Australia in 1911, in the second state to enfranchise women before Federation, barmaids were given equal pay, a matter so unremarkable at the time that it went unnoticed in the press. The year before bar workers in Western Australia had organised into a Barmaids and Barmens Union (which only recently disappeared).[16]

For all the undoubted advantage it brought to the women working in Western Australia as barmaids, equal pay as awarded did not grant them full status as workers because of the terms on which it was granted. In other words, although 'equal pay', as granted by the Western Australian Industrial Commission, gave barmaids wages commensurate with men's (the rate for the job), it did not grant these women economic citizenship by giving them 'the right to work' at that occupation. Indeed, the award specifically stated that it was an undesirable occupation for women and that they had been granted equal pay in the hope they would be forced out of work. The President of the Court drew attention to the longer hours barmen worked (fifty-six compared with the barmaids' forty-eight) 'but in view of the fact that, in my opinion, serving at the bar is a very unhappy position for a barmaid to occupy, I thought it would be as well to give her at least the same wage as a barman'. He continued, 'and if the effect of making no distinction between the wage is that barmaids are more or less abolished in hotels, I think the result will be a good one'.[17]

This Western Australian decision predated the federal Rural Workers Case by one year, the rationale behind the latter decision being much the same, although less explicitly stated. The Rural Workers Case was heard in the federal arbitration court in 1912. On that occasion Justice Higgins awarded men's rate of pay to women who were employed doing work that men usually did. His judgment sex-typed jobs as men's or women's as he upheld the principle that men had first prerogative in the workplace. Women were not to be employed at cheaper rates that could displace men from work. Similarly, the award granting Western Australian barmaids equal pay endorsed the idea that the work was really men's work, but if women were going to be employed doing it they should not be paid at a rate that would jeopardise men's employment.

Efforts to extend the principle of equal pay to other workers in the Western Australian hospitality and catering industry were not successful. In 1913 when the Hotel, Club, Caterers, Tea Room and Restaurant Employees Union tried to claim equal pay, the President of the Court responded by pointing out that a man was bound by law to support his wife and family and his wage was based on that obligation. 'Do you consider that the single girl should be paid the same wage as the man with a wife and children to support?' he asked the union advocate. 'If they have the same work to do, then they are entitled to it', the union representative replied. 'In this court we have had a long struggle to establish the principle that a man's wage should be based upon his responsibility', another justice chimed in; 'No man is going to be reduced to the wage and the earning capacity of a single woman so long as the law says it is his duty to support his wife and educate his children', concluded the President of the Court. 'I think he ought to get more in view of that obligation.' Despite the fear alluded to by the union in argument that women working for a lower rate at the same work would displace men, the claim for equal pay was, on this occasion, rejected.[18]

Here the court showed how determined it was to uphold men's privilege, to maintain masculinity in the workplace, through the language of wages (a low wage was feminising). It was the maintenance of the differential *between* male and female wage rates that marked out sexual difference. Men (with responsibilities) had to be paid more. To be paid the lower rate was tantamount to becoming a (single) woman (without responsibilities). Masculinity was defined as having responsibilities, femininity as being a responsibility. There was no attempt to match this gendering with the circumstances of real workers; men who were or were not married, women who did or did not have family responsibilities. The wage was a system of meaning, of social ordering, imposed on workers by the legal authority of compulsory arbitration, that restored sexual difference and shaped the expectations of men and women not only in the workplace but in all other areas as well.

Nevertheless, once equal pay was awarded to barmaids in Western Australia it was never removed because of the legal nature of the arbitration system and the way judgments were made on the basis of precedent in relation to the evidence argued before them. For example, when the Barmaids and Barmens Award was being renegotiated in 1918, one of the justices hearing the case, Justice Daglish, remarked, 'I do not agree with this award, but it is based on the award issued in 1911 when the court was very differently constituted.' He went on to make clear that conceding 'equal pay' did not concede women as equal (to men) workers: 'It has been shown in the evidence that the work is not equal, the barmen carrying out certain work in addition to that which barmaids do ... I am doubtful whether the equality of pay is justified, but as it was not challenged at the issues, and as no evidence was given to support differential treatment, we cannot be surprised that the court has followed the principle adopted in 1911.'

Having established the precedent, it was possible for the industrial tribunals in other states to follow suit, although they did not do so. When refusing an application from the Queensland branch of the union for equal pay to be made part of the state award in 1921, the judge declared he was not convinced of its merits. Although the union made equal pay a constituent part of its claims, there was no further move on it until 1941.[19] How heavily the union pushed industrial tribunals to award equal pay is unclear.

'Equal pay has long been advocated by the Trades Hall Council', wrote Sara Lewis, Secretary of the Women's Branch of the Victorian Hotel and Caterers Employes Union, to the *Labor Call* in 1913. Women unionists had organised a meeting because they felt the Victorian Trades Hall was not doing enough 'to advance the cause of women', but members of the Trades Hall Council thought allowing women to pursue their own equal pay campaign 'was putting too much power in the hands of women unionists', and they were unwilling to agree to it. 'This attitude of domination is greatly to be regretted,' Lewis said, 'the Trades Hall Council seek to show women they are entirely dependent by seeking to crush any independence shown by them.' Male trade unionists were more concerned to preserve the privileges attached to masculinity.[20]

Although barmaids in Western Australia received equal pay in 1911, it took another thirty years and the exceptional circumstances of world war before barmaids in the other states got to put the case for equal pay. In the meantime a lower rate of pay made women attractive to employers, especially in times of economic downturn. When the depression hit, a barmaid could do quite well compared with many others.

The Depression

The 1930s were harsh times for workers as the Depression hit Australia very severely. Men's employment was most affected because their wage rates were higher and they worked in the industries (like building and mining) that were most acutely curtailed. The Depression was hard on the pub trade. As a way of boosting custom threepenny counter lunches, a feature of nineteenth-century pub life, now returned in Victoria, New South Wales and Tasmania (Queensland hotels wouldn't touch them). However the emphasis in pubs was on drinking and, with a 30 per cent unemployment rate, cash for drinking was not readily available. Beer consumption per head of population decreased, and about 5 per cent of hotel businesses went bust.[21]

'I seemed the only one among my friends who was doing all right', one barmaid was able to reflect afterwards. She survived through a combination of government assistance and some casual work, 'scratching all the time to make ends meet'. Finding work in the 1920s had been relatively easy, she'd had a sequence of jobs, but now it was hard. It was the employers' day. 'Limiting myself to one meal a day, I walked myself footsore looking for a job ... No longer able to afford the price of a paper, I walked into the city each morning and took my place in the queue of unemployed, eagerly waiting my turn to scan the situations vacant advertisements ... posted on the wall.' She found some casual work then landed a full-time job in a slum pub, 'rats or no rats' she would have stayed, but the fear of being caught by the government and losing both the dole and her children drove her to a housekeeping job in the country. 'There was more and more unemployment and the police began to make it tougher for those on the dole ...'[22] There was also evidence of employers trading after hours and therefore, simultaneously, illegally overworking their bar employees.[23]

The difficulties of the times made sexual difference in the workplace once again an issue. Women workers were perceived to be a threat to men's prerogative of paid employment. Removing women workers seemed a logical solution. Laws were passed against married women teachers and similar constraints were raised in relation to bar workers. In

Figure 6.2 Barmaids in the saloon bar of the Imperial Hotel, West Maitland, New South Wales, *c.* 1939. Notice the man looking through the hatch. (Tooth & Co. Ltd, Dep. no. Z223/144 (p19), Neg. no. 5351, NBAC/ANU)

August 1931 the Queensland branch of the Liquor Trades Union carried a motion supporting extension of the system of barmaids' registration that was in place in Victoria and South Australia to the rest of the country. The Queensland branch had been pushing for this since 1923 when an amendment was proposed to the Queensland Liquor Act. At that time the union wrote to the parliamentary Labor Party on 'the advisability of also making provision for the registration of bar-maids throughout Queensland'. It resurfaced again as the Depression bit.

In 1930 the union led a deputation to the Home Secretary on the question of registration and it was discussed at the union's meeting in April. One member, a barmaid at the Australian Hotel, Miss McDowell, had been visiting hotels, speaking to the barmaids and getting them to sign a petition, probably against the idea of registration. When pressed by the union Secretary as to why she was obtaining signatures McDowell refused to answer. The Secretary clearly thought she was coercing barmaids, and said so, at which point McDowell interjected saying it was 'a deliberate lie' and he was 'a rotten liar'. She refused to withdraw her remarks. The meeting decided to hold a referendum on the issue of registration, to ballot all barmaids who were financial members of the union and the Secretary 'strongly condemned the actions of the opponents to registration' and their methods of obtaining signatures. Although Miss McDowell again spoke against the motion it was carried by a large majority. A month later the Secretary reported that 208 ballot papers had been issued for members to vote. The union Secretary reported that twenty-two (roughly 2.5 per cent) of the barmaids employed in Brisbane had ten years or more experience, and another member of the executive spoke in favour of the system. Only Miss McDowell (who again refused to answer questions directed to her by the Secretary) spoke against the measure. Unemployed barmaids who were financial members were to be included in the ballot. Details of the voting procedures were laid down at a subsequent meeting: all barmaids eligible to vote were to be notified in writing, and voting was to be conducted in the Trades Hall from 1 to 31 May. When the results of the ballot were known (98 against registration, 82 for, with 2 informal votes – a majority of 16 against) the Secretary claimed they indicated that the signing of the petition was not a true reflection of the barmaids' opinion on the question.[24] Unfortunately no further details about the incident and the way the issues were argued are available.

Attempts were also made to remove women employees who were married. The Queensland union strongly protested against the employment of married couples in bars. In addition there were frequent discussions about the principle of 'one man one job', an issue that seemed to be of particular concern to women in the industry. On one occasion a woman was invited to outline her views to the meeting of members.[25] There was also an effort to have a clause stipulating 'one male to one female' written into the Bar Attendants Award being negotiated in 1929.[26] In Western Australia the metropolitan council of the Australian Labor Party complained to the LVA that married barmaids were being given preference in employment, thus keeping 'hundreds of single girls ... on the border line of starvation, while the husbands of most of the married barmaids are in employment'. The Victorian branch of the Liquor Trades Union urged the state government to tighten up the registration system to remove the 'hundreds of women working on other persons' registrations'.[27]

Meanwhile the employers – the LVA – of Victoria, New South Wales and Tasmania wanted longer hours and reduced wage rates for all employees and they took their case to the arbitration commission. In what the LVA's official newspaper called a 'brilliant exposition of [the] case for the trade', the employers argued that the fall in business due to the Depression meant they could not continue to pay existing award rates. They pointed out there had been a drop in consumption, and that customers were more likely to buy bottles for home consumption than drink in the bar, where the publican made more profit. They claimed liquor trade employees were treated better than those in any other industry and claimed that agreements reached between the LVA and the union in 1919 and 1928 had been made under duress. A 10 per cent cut in wages for all workers as a 'cost of living adjustment' in 1931 was not enough and in 1932 they wanted a further 10 per cent cut in the wages set by the 1928 Liquor Trades Award. The arbitration commission thought their claim was fair and reduced wages accordingly. Barmaids were allowed a margin of 25 shillings on top of the basic award rate, 'to cover dress expenses as well as skill, etc.' Once the the cost-of-living adjustment was made and the 10 per cent cut was applied, they were left with a net wage of 2 pounds 16 shillings from a 1928 wage of 3 pounds 10 shillings. Barmen were left with 3 pounds 11 shillings from a 1928 prescribed rate of 4 pounds 15 shillings.[28]

In 1930 the union proposed a forty-hour week while the employers wanted a forty-four hour week. By 1935 things were sufficiently improved for the union to decide to put a case to the arbitration court for restoration of two weeks holiday a year, the limitation on bar attendants' hours to between 8.00 a.m. and 8.00 p.m., and for equal pay for equal work. The following year they were again pushing for a forty-hour week for bar attendants.[29] Varying hotel trading hours became a key issue for the union. In 1941 they opposed the move to alter trading hours in Queensland pubs, and in 1946 a mass meeting of bar attendants in Brisbane protested against the twelve hours a day, six days a week allowed as trading hours. In 1945 the union had proposed hours should be amended so that pubs were open from 10.00 a.m. to 7.00 p.m. weekdays and 8.00 a.m. to 12 noon on Saturdays. They pushed simultaneously for a reduction in hours and equal pay. In 1947 Queensland bar attendants won their forty-hour week. Equal pay took a while longer.[30]

World War II

The outbreak of war was a turning point for women behind the bar. The severe shortage of male labour caused by men's enlistment in the armed forces increased opportunities for female employment in pubs as it also opened up non-traditional workplaces. To deal with the particular 'manpower problems' created by war and the large influx of women workers moving into traditionally male occupations, the Australian government set up an alternative institution to the arbitration court to deal with the question of male and female rates of pay. Under this Women's Employment Board, women doing 'men's work' got 'equal pay' during the war (and women doing traditional 'women's work' did not). The special circumstances of wartime conditions (particularly the shortage of

Figure 6.3 A barmaid at work in wartime Sydney. Pettys Hotel, Sydney, 6.00 p.m., 1941. Photograph by Max Dupain. (Courtesy of Max Dupain Exhibition Archive, Jill White Photography, Sydney)

male labour) was used to justify women's employment, and attention was drawn to the special skills women brought to the workplace.

In 1942 the LVA applied to the Women's Employment Board for permission to employ barmaids in Victoria because there was a shortage of male labour and the number of women working in the industry had successfully been decreased by the legislation brought in at the end of the last war. A count taken in 1936 had found that only 700 barmaids were still employed from a total of 4100 who had registered at the last date for registration in 1920.[31] They could not be replaced without approval of the Women's Employment Board, and the licensed victuallers assured the board any women now employed would be paid full male rates and their employment would be limited to the duration of the war. The LVA's application was supported by the Liquor Trades Union. The Secretary of the LVA also said the idea that girls increased the volume of liquor sales in licensed premises had never been valid but 'in these days of rationed liquor it would not matter whether sales were made by a Venus or a slot machine'. The government urged that the minimum age for any women employed behind the bar should be 30 years.[32]

The WCTU opposed the move. They wrote to the Women's Employment Board asking them not to grant the application as the liquor trade
was a non-essential industry and there was a shortage of women for war
work, 'so much so that a move has been made to induce married women
to take up the work'. They thought it was more important for mothers to
be taking care of their children than for girls to be employed in selling
intoxicating liquor, and they pointed out that there were advertisements
in the paper from unemployed barmen seeking work.[33]

In these circumstances, the Liquor Trades Union put forward its case
for barmaids. First, they had to persuade the Women's Employment Board
that women should be allowed to be employed as barmaids, given that
earlier legislation had banned them. The union argued on grounds of the
wartime labour shortage and the detrimental effect this was having on the
industry. In putting the case for the Queensland Liquor Trades Union to
the board, one speaker alluded to the 'cruel statement that appeared to
come from the Queensland State Court [of arbitration] that the Union
desired equal pay for the sole purpose of doing something detrimental to
the barmaids'. He was emphatic 'that that has never actuated us in any
application we have made. We believe in the principle ... for the protection of the men and the protection of the women, that that labour is
displacing men already in the industry, and at least the employer should
not be able to show a profit.'[34] Here 'equal pay' was being used as a tactic
in male unionists' battle with the male employers. The union argued that
'war has shown that the labour power of women is not to be despised in
its valuation ... Nobody can deny that barmaids in Queensland are doing
the same work as men and in the same quantity, and with the same
efficiency as barmen.' The precedent in Western Australia was then drawn
on by the union, as equal pay had operated there for a long time and had
not, according to the union, been to the barmaids' detriment.

The union argued both ways, that employers preferred men if they
could get them but the war was making this difficult, that there were
certain phases of the work that were rougher and therefore more suitable
for men, but that, in fact, the work was more suitable to women. 'The
woman has a personality, she has a charm of her own ... which is of
value to her employer. She is cleaner, and ... will keep better order in
better style than the man. There are certain things we have to leave to
common sense and knowledge of the Board ... in most phases of the
occupation a woman is more suitable than a man.' This was a dangerous
argument for the union to put if they wanted to preserve men's right over
the work and they quickly followed up, I think most tellingly, with 'she
is not one whit inferior in regard to the amount of money or profit that
goes into the employer's till because of her services as against the services
of the barman'.

The union feared that, to the employers, workers were interchangeable, and yet had to concede this if they were to keep the labour market open at a time when an acute labour shortage was threatening the whole industry. The union needed to keep jobs in the industry even if it meant pushing women into the openings. Pushing women forward threatened turning it into women's work and devaluing wages. Their problem was to preserve their wage rates when their very jobs were under threat. Hence, their support for equal pay.

The federal government addressed the problem of barmaids' employment as part of its wartime measures on liquor control. The federal solicitor-general was called in to advise the government that the Commonwealth could make regulations differentiating between states, as the Victorian and South Australian premiers were concerned to preserve the existing laws. The Prime Minister was unmoved, according to the *Age*. He 'said that they held tenaciously to ideas of moral conduct which had geographical boundaries. He spoke plainly on the manpower needs of the war effort, and showed little regret that it might eventually be necessary to override the State legislation.'[35]

The Women's Employment Board gave permission for barmaids to be employed in South Australia, but no women under 30 were to be employed. Justice Foster, in giving his decision, said 'there were special objections to the employment of women in particular industries, of which employment in hotel bars was one. However, the war was a grave reality, the need for the greatest effort was paramount and considerations which in peace time would be almost unanswerable were today overborne by the fact of war.' Neither the employers nor the Union 'was anxious that women should be recalled to the work', he said, 'but both appreciated the grave needs of the present emergency ... Hundreds of men in the industry might be released for war work, but if the industry was not to cease – and there was no official suggestion anywhere that it should do so – then it must be carried on with the aid of women.' The terms under which women were to be employed were particularly revealing. 'The parties', said Foster, 'had agreed ... that the work of barmaids equalled in all respects that of barmen – equal in productivity and efficiency – and that therefore ... the rate of payment ... would be 100 p.c. of the rate of payment to adult males, that the hours would be 44 per week with the same rate for overtime as were now enjoyed by males; that there would be no period of probation and that in order to safeguard the well-being and interest of the women employed they would become members of the Union.' But no women under 21 were to be employed and all women wishing to be employed had first to get permission from the Deputy-Director of Manpower in the state.[36] By September this last requirement was dropped. The Deputy-Director in South Australia had refused to register women as barmaids, so the clause was deleted in a subsequent judgment. An amendment of the National Security (Employment of Women) Regulations issued on 2 September, stipulated that approval was now needed by the federal Minister for Labor.[37]

The Women's Employment Board also granted equal pay for 'female bar attendants' in Victoria for the duration of the war.[38] The LVA had scored another victory. Expressing their approval of the decision, a spokesperson for the LVA said that hotelkeepers wanted to be in the same position as any other industry in being able to to employ women in wartime.[39] However, the board was careful about their choice of words, given the connotations that had previously been associated with 'the barmaid'. 'Barmaids' were paid women's wages, and had been employed and consequently had their employment stopped by legislation because they were barmaids, that is, women working as women. The sex-typing of the job meant 'women' could not become 'barmen'. So the terminology 'female bar attendant' kept the job 'bar attendant' as appropriate men's work that women were now doing, but it enabled the women doing it to be paid men's wage rates, consistent with the arbitration court's 1912 decision that women doing men's work were to be paid equal pay. This was the decision the Women's Employment Board took on all wartime occupations where women did work that had been designated men's work before the war. And because 'equal pay' was granted outside the arbitration system, it didn't become a precedent for postwar wage rates. Nor did the board's decision to employ barmaids in South Australia survive the war years.

At war's end

In 1948 when the Liquor Trades Union put a claim for equal pay to the arbitration court claiming that a precedent existed in Victoria and Western Australia, the court rejected it. 'In NSW, Queensland and Tasmania there are varying rates for barmaids assessed mainly on the value of their work to the employer as compared with that of a barman', Commissioner Morrison said. A rate of 74.6 per cent of the barmen's wage had been set by the court in 1919, and of 73.5 per cent of the barmen's wage in 1926, 'having regard to the women's basic wage and the value of the services rendered. That is the principle I have followed in fixing the barmaids' rate in this case.' The commissioner then spelled out the 'value' (skill) of the barmaid. 'I agree with the Union that a barmaid must be a capable business woman who attracts custom by her personality and ability', he said. 'Above all she must be honest. Her honesty is really the true measuring rod in determining the value of her services.' Honesty was clearly an important attribute in an occupation where so much cash was handled by the worker, and depletion of the stock was not immediately visible. Surreptitiously sampling the boss's goods quickly led to dismissal. The commissioner, though, did not explain how 'honesty' was specific to women workers: perhaps it was self evident. Women did not drink the way men did; they were not likely to have a team of their footy mates pressing them for free drinks. Nor did the commissioner say how this 'honesty' was to be measured against the barmen's (unspecified) skill (of greater physical strength for the occasional tougher jobs?).

'I have, therefore, fixed a wage calculated on the relative value of her services to that of a barman', Commissioner Morrison stated. For authority, he once again referred to the precedent of previous decisions and their importance in establishing relativities between male and female wages: 'This principle was acquiesced in by agreement and adopted by [Justice] Higgins ... in 1919', he said.[40] Principles changed slowly in this forum.

Yet in 1949 Victorian barmaids did get equal pay, almost by accident. In 1949 the High Court of Australia abolished the Women's Employment Board Regulations, which had been in force for the war's duration, thus restoring the state laws (in Victoria and South Australia) permitting 'only women who were registered barmaids before 1920, or certain relatives of licensees, to serve liquor'. It was estimated that more than a thousand women in Victoria were affected by the judgment. But the government was in no hurry either to force barmaids to leave their jobs or to alter the law in recognition of the wartime changes.[41] Alleyn Best has explained this in his *History of the Liquor Trades Union in Victoria*. I have relied on his account. Abolition of the wartime National Security regulations and the Women's Employment Board Regulations removed the only legal basis on which women could be employed in hotel bars in Victoria. The prewar law prohibiting the employment of barmaids was, therefore, once again operational. Consequently any attempt to enforce the law could lead to their being sacked en masse. For a while nothing happened. The LVA was not anxious to lose barmaids' services. Male labour was hard to obtain and the women were valued employees. Despite the dire predictions of the temperance lobby, 'the bars where females were employed had not degenerated into cesspools of vice'. Indeed barmaids had become motherly figures: they had become the 'grey-haired ladies' who 'would not draw a second glance when passed in the street'.[42]

Just before the High Court decision, a federal arbitration court judgment had renewed the wartime wage status of equal pay for Victorian barmaids, but reduced that of South Australian barmaids back to 75 per cent of the barman's rate. This was the new relativity for female wages in all other industries under the new minimum wage set for women by the

Figure 6.4 By the mid-twentieth century, Victorian barmaids were no longer young: Mrs Sharkey had been a bar worker for fifty years, *Argus* Magazine, 21 December 1951. (La Trobe Collection, State Library of Victoria)

arbitration court, but there is no explanation for why Victorian barmaids were given favoured treatment, not only with other workers, but with barmaids in other states, a situation that continued to exist for another twenty years. Temperance advocates in Victoria were not pleased with this outcome and petitioned to have prewar conditions reinstated. Licensed victuallers wanted barmaids but did not want to pay them equally, especially when publicans in other states were not required to. The Liquor Trades Union went into battle. An industrial dispute erupted in Victorian hotels in December 1949, just in time to disrupt the Christmas trade, and went to the arbitration court for judgment, to the same commissioner who had granted them equal pay just the year before. Here was a federal industrial tribunal setting award wages and conditions in contradiction of state legislation. The union was unmoving, and by 1949 the Australian Council of Trade Unions had also endorsed the principle of equal pay even if they were not actively campaigning for it as the Liquor Trades Union in Victoria was doing. Early in the new year, on 12 January 1950, Commissioner Morrison handed down his ruling: equal pay for Victorian barmaids on condition that the old system of registration under the 'Barmaids Permit Committee' continue to operate under the old rules. The union and the employers did not hesitate, and Victorian barmaids now joined their Western Australian counterparts in being paid equally with men.[43]

'Equal pay for equal work' was a slogan that barmaids could use more effectively than other women workers because they worked alongside men, often in the same workplaces, but even so their work was still construed as gender-specific, and of less value. In that sense their work was never fully equal, because of the value that was attached to the worker. Female bar attendants did 'women's work' because they were not men: the 'skills' that were attached to the work in the arbitration court were gender attributes. The duties barmaids performed were construed as more domesticated, cleaner and more orderly, their 'value' as feminine, their 'charm' and 'honesty' were more service-oriented attributes. The arbitration commission forced arguments to be made that would characterise the work as the same as men's work, but the history of barmaids' work had defined it as domestic, sexualised labour and this was not abandoned lightly. During the war the union had even gone to great lengths to represent the occupation as particularly well-suited to women, but not so as to make it 'women's work'. It is significant that when discussing equal pay and the substitution of female labour for male in hotels in 1942, the Women's Employment Board avoided the derogatory feminised terminology of 'barmaid' in favour of 'female bar attendant'. 'There seems to be no tenderness about the use of the word [in the Licensing Act of Victoria]' the government representative in the discussions declared.[44]

In contrast to the barmaid, men's work as barmen was not sexualised. Nor was it highly paid. The wages for barmen were low compared with other men's work, for barmaids they were high compared with other women's work, and the differential between male and female rates was, therefore, less than in other occupations. The boundaries of sexual difference were less pronounced in this language of wages than industrial tribunals were subsequently to institutionalise (through wage differentials and through the sexual division of labour) in other workplaces. Conse-

Figure 6.5 Men and women working together, Harbour View Hotel, Millers Point, Sydney, 1952. (Tooth & Co. Ltd, Dep. no. Z223/159 (H), Neg. no. 5299, NBAC/ANU)

quently, sexual difference was constantly being re-established in hotel workplace agreements. Union representatives and industrial tribunals both enhanced the status of barmaids and even paid them equally as men, while simultaneously reinforcing the sexual difference that constituted the work behind the bar. There is therefore a connection between the early efforts to abolish the work of barmaids and arguments conducted in the industrial tribunals and the labour movement over the issue of equal pay. Clearly employers wanted to employ women although it was not a women's industry or solely a woman's occupation. Nevertheless while men also did bar work, there were distinctions drawn between men and women behind the bar. Arguments put to the industrial tribunals emphasised the difference while simultaneously arguing for equal pay on the grounds of equal productivity and efficiency.

Yet the special circumstances of war had released prohibitions that could not now be turned back. The end of the war years brought a return to prosperity and an increasing demand for women's labour as the shortage of male labour continued despite the return of men from the front.

The hoteliers' association pointed out that even America was now restoring women to work behind the bar.[45] When the Women's Employment Board was disbanded in 1949, and it looked as if barmaids in Victoria were once again to be prohibited, the Liquor Trades Union called a strike, the Conciliation Commissioner overrode the state law and the barmaids were reinstated with equal pay. Nevertheless, continuance of the registration system meant that 'a whole grand period in Victorian hotel history' looked as if it was coming to an end. Without a change in the licensing laws, which in principle prevented women working behind the bar, 'women who have reigned in the bar-room for over a century' were going to give way to men. 'Take a last look at them, you earnest drinkers, for one day you will be able to tell your grandchildren how you were actually served beer by a woman – by a real live licensed barmaid', a Melbourne journalist wrote. But it was to take until 1973 for the registration of barmaids to disappear. By then pubs had undergone significant changes.[46]

In the 1950s and 1960s changes in pub culture, trading hours and drinking customs affected the nature of the workplace and brought renewed demands for equal pay, equality of treatment and access to work and leisure for women in front of as well as behind the bar. To understand these changes it is necessary to look first at the conditions that prevailed during the era of early closing.

CHAPTER SEVEN

'Beer, Glorious Beer':[1]
Pub Culture and the Six o'clock Swill

Licensing laws which stipulated trading hours were also important in shaping the work behind the bar. They set the length of the working day as well as its routines. And they shaped demand. In the first two decades of the twentieth century those forces that restricted women's work as barmaids in certain states simultaneously forced pubs to close at 6 o'clock in the evening, although other states allowed pubs to stay open till 9.00 or 9.30 p.m. This legislation was brought in during World War I, according to several historians, because of concerns about the drunken behaviour of soldiers and as a patriotic move to preserve the nation's resources.[2] However this does not explain why it was extended in 1919, nor why it lasted more than forty years. That history has not been explored. In restricting the hours in which customers could be served, early closing created a pub culture unlike any other. It created 'the rush hour' that became known as 'the six o'clock swill'. And it created conditions of work that were very difficult.

Six o'clock closing changed the whole culture of drinking, the physical layout of hotels and the nature of the work in pubs, particularly the relationship between bar attendant and customer. With early closing, pubs became 'no more than high-pressure drinking-houses' rather than the 'centres of entertainment, discussion, and business' they had been before 1920. 'The singing groups, the strolling players, the exhibitions that had been a vital part of pub life before the war, were stilled ... Their place as the centre and hub of community life had been destroyed.'[3] Those who felt it most were women – the workers who served behind the bar, the drinkers to whom the public bar was off limits, and the wives at home whose husbands staggered in from work unfit for further socialising.

Writing of her experiences as a barmaid in Sydney during the 1920s and 1930s, Catherine Edmonds Wright, under the pseudonym 'Caddie', wrote of 'the shouting for service, the crash of falling glasses, the grunting and shoving crowd, and that loud, indistinguishable clamour of conversation found nowhere but in a crowded bar [which] beat in on my brain until all my actions became mechanical.'[4] Work under these conditions was not easy. The emphasis was on speed of service and cleaning up afterwards. 'The rush and crush did away with any pretence at amiability and real personal contact between the publican, or even the barman, and the customers. In a flurry of shirt sleeves, spilt froth, slapped-down change, and swished dish cloths, glasses of beer were slid two or three at a time along the wet counter-tops as fast as they could be pulled.'[5] For barmaids and barmen the work was a nightmare: 'It was a long time before I learned to handle that evening rush with any degree of skill', Caddie said. 'The first arrivals crowded against the counter, less fortunate ones called above their heads, late comers jostled and shouted and swore in an attempt to be served before closing time ... We were all flat out serving ... My head was splitting, my feet were killing me' and at the end of the day 'I fell into bed and dreamt of public bars in the rush hour.'

The most obvious changes to pubs were, at first, physical. Pubs 'which had found their tiny bars adequate for anything from twenty to a hundred years, now had to be disembowelled to make room for the herds pressing for a place at the bar'. Thus hotels themselves had to change. From being 'a building in which the bars were physically only a small part of the whole' they changed to buildings where bars formed by far the greater part, 'occupying practically the whole of the ground floor and often the basement area as well'. Reflecting the new emphasis on pubs as drinking establishments, 'the ground floor was occupied almost entirely with bar space. The entrance to the public bar with its long winding counter moved away from the corner to the sides but the bar itself, much enlarged, still occupied the picked position'. Interior finishes were designed 'for quick easy cleaning rather than comfort'. Walls were tiled to five or six feet, the front of the bar counter was treated similarly, linoleum floors were laid, 'chrome-plated fittings, such as bar-rails which needed a minimum of attention, replaced the older brass ones which needed daily polishing, and glass shelves hung on fittings in front of unbroken mirrors ousted their dark-polished, wooden predecessors behind the counter'. The work of the bar staff was also implicated in the new technology. 'Beer-pulls, slow and tiring, were replaced by chromed taps set below the counter-level from which the beer poured continuously and effortlessly as fast as the bartender could pick up the glasses. Stainless steel sinks under the counter and drip-trays compulsorily sprinkled with potassium permanganate to prevent unscrupulous trailing of stale beer into fresh glasses were introduced.'[6] Bar staff complained the potassium permanganate left purple stains on their clothing.

Beer consumption increased 31 per cent in New South Wales between 1910 and 1920, and the reduction in hours that hotels were now open meant that most of this (an estimated 90 per cent) was occurring between the hours of 5.00 p.m. and 6.00 p.m. 'The bars, which had been adequate to cope with the demands made on them before the war, were choked as hordes of thirsty men struggled to contribute their share to the national beer-drinking average in a fleeting sixty minutes.' To cope with the changed demands 'every possible area that could be spared ... was converted to bar space, either public, private, or saloon'. Bar counters were modified: service was sped up by eliminating the uprights that held the upper shelves and instead supporting them from the ceiling. This left the counter-top clear. It was then covered with linoleum – a material new in the 1920s: 'cheap, easily fixed and cleaned, and soft, thereby reducing the likelihood of breakages'. Anything that cluttered up space was ousted; games like darts were banished, and billiards rooms were taken over as bar space.[7]

Photographs taken for Tooth's brewery (see, for example, Figure 7.1) demonstrated the changes: the new materials were visible, and the bar dominated all. It was now even longer and circular because refrigerator cabinets were located underneath.

Figure 7.1 Public bar of the Century Hotel, George Street, Sydney, *c.* 1941. An example of a circular bar. Notice the barmaid standing, obscured, in the doorway. (Tooth & Co. Ltd, Dep. no. Z223/144 (p6), Neg. no. 5346, NBAC/ANU)

Most significantly the customers now were unequivocally male. The public bar was off-limits to women customers even where they were allowed as workers. The masculinity of drinking and pub culture was enshrined in law. The legislation stipulating hours of opening also stipulated pub spaces: how many bars, and who was to drink in them. Aboriginal people were forbidden to be on licensed premises or to

ONE OF THE SAME PERSUASION.

"*A glass of beer, please, dearie!*"

"*We don't serve ladies here. I'm sorry!*"

"*I ain't no lidy, dearie. I'm just a barmaid, same as you!*"

Figure 7.2 'One of the same persuasion', cartoon from the *Bulletin*, 2 April 1925, depicting the contradictory status of barmaids in society. (La Trobe Collection, State Library of Victoria)

purchase alcohol. Women were to drink in 'Ladies Lounges' physically separated from the public bar, even if they were barmaids frequenting another pub or returning after hours as customers. This created the absurd situation where barmaids were allowed to serve in the public bar, yet not allowed to drink in them out of hours, as customers. The unarticulated assumption was, as the *Bulletin* so astutely captured (see Figure 7.3), that by being in the public bar, the barmaid could not, by definition, be a 'lady'. Women who had access to the privileges of male space lost the special status accorded women confined to feminine space.

By the 1920s 'the barmaid' was being represented as a serious working woman, superior and demanding of respect. In the drawing in Figure 7.2 she is authoritative, positioned more highly and taller than the customer seeking a drink, her expression is condescending. Her style of dress, fashioned according to 1920s mode, is glamorous and modern, consistent with the representations of the 1890s barmaids, but she is mature, sophisticated and powerful, a career woman. The woman customer, a barmaid from an earlier era, is reminiscent of nineteenth-century images of the impoverished working-class, the Irish, and the convict women of the early years of the colony. There is perhaps even now the suggestion that barmaids will turn to drink as they get older.

With reduced hotel trading hours, people drank more at home. Then, with a further reduction in beer consumption because of the Depression, the breweries embarked on an advertising campaign, targeting women to encourage them to drink beer. They focused on drinking in the home, promoting beer as an aid to domestic and romantic bliss. And they set about changing the image of their pubs, intending to give them and their product a modern, forward-looking image.[8] In the 1930s most pubs were suburban locals, only a few large accommodation hotels existed, and these were in the centres of the capital cities. It had been nearly fifty years since any hotels of this type had been erected, and during the Depression little new building occurred. When it did, only the breweries were in any real position to take advantage of the cheaper costs. The hotels they built reflected the austere conditions of the times: 'hygienic and efficient but in its sterility ... cold, hard and insipid' was architect J. M. Freeland's opinion. With the outbreak of war in 1939, all new building ceased.

The impact of World War II

World War II brought restricted hours of trading (6 o'clock closing) and a shortage of liquor supplies in all states.[9] But the war also challenged pub practices and brought them into disrepute. Firstly, because liquor supplies dried up (whisky was unavailable and beer was in short supply), city publicans in Sydney controlled custom by turning the beer on for no more than an hour a day; in two half-hour sessions or one one-hour session; a way of handling the crisis that did not endear them to customers. Some licensees exploited the shortages to maximise profits. Bottled beer was unavailable except for specially favoured customers or friends of the publican, a situation designed to cause resentment, and draught beer might go off in the public bar but continue to be available at a higher price in the saloon bar. When that too supposedly ran out, customers might be offered beer out of bottles at a 50 per cent higher charge.

The Western Australian branch of the (newly retitled) United Licensed Victuallers Association (ULVA) tried to accommodate the demands of all classes of customers. It urged licensees to resist calls for closing on Saturday afternoons as this was the time when the vast majority of workers observed their weekly half-day holiday, an especially valuable recreation time for those workers who finished after 6 o'clock and could not take advantage of weekday trading. But it did suggest staggering hours, or closing for one day of the week, and serving servicemen on leave with spirits only during the hours that civilians were at work. They urged licensees to 'make their best endeavours to provide beer during those hours when the greatest numbers of workers aim to quench their thirsts', past experience of local requirements being 'adequate to establish when the needs of the public are greatest'.[10] As Freeland pointed out, 'during the war, the pubs acquired a reputation for high-handedness and profiteering, deserved or not, for which they were to pay dearly come peace and the time of retribution'.[11]

The war also brought new freedoms for women. Jobs in traditionally male areas of employment opened up, and the lucky few women able to take up these opportunities were also paid men's wages, which gave them increased spending power. Other women, influenced by the new consumerism and advertising campaigns of the thirties, sought pleasure and sexual adventure outside the constraints of peacetime inhibitions. The contradictions of wartime – austerity and sacrifice coupled with new freedoms and opportunities – helped redefine femininity and relations between the sexes, which made itself felt in pub culture after the war.

'That hotels in Australia are being given greater patronage by women is something that is not confined to the Commonwealth' but was also happening in England, the *Hotel Review of Western Australia* pointed out in December 1943. There, men taking women out to a pub usually chose the one with the best furnishings, including the most comfortable seating accommodation, thus pressuring licensees to cater for women. During World War I (because of a No Treating Order), English women had taken to ordering their own drinks in licensed houses, so were accustomed to using pubs on their own account, not just in company with male partners. The article concluded with an observation from Australian experience:

Figure 7.3 Men and women drinking together in the lounge bar of the Metropolitan Hotel, West Maitland, New South Wales, *c.* 1943. (Tooth & Co. Ltd, Dep. no. Z223/145 (p139), Neg. no. 5349, NBAC/ANU)

'You cannot make people sober by making them uncomfortable. We all need change ... Public houses to which a man can take his wife ... have a glass of beer or wine, or lemonade, in pleasant and comfortable surroundings are a real boon ... [to] the sum total of happiness.'

This was clearly a portent of things to come. A discussion in the *Hotel Review of Western Australia* about the desirability or usefulness of long bars versus short bars contained an observation from a Glasgow correspondent about 'the increasing custom brought about by the war of men and women drinking together [which] should result in sweeping changes where and if possible. The "bar parlour" one day will be superseded by comfortable public lounges and as a result there should be less of what [is] called "perpendicular drinking"'. The article concluded that 'changes in design [largely] evolve through changes in customer habit'. In January 1945 the *Hotel Review of Western Australia* carried a headline 'Women's Right to Drink'. A publican had refused to allow a man, having purchased it in the public bar where women were not allowed, to carry a schooner of beer out to his wife sitting in their car. The publican felt entitled to restrict his supplies for his usual customers, and the ladies lounge was at the time closed, so he asserted he was not at that time serving women. The court upheld the woman's complaint that she had been refused service, an offence under s. 118 of the Western Australian Licensing Act. Publicans were now worried that women consumers might develop in such numbers that their demands could not (or not easily) be met while restrictions on supplying their 'regular consumers, particularly the workers [associated] with heavier industry' were in place. Clearly they disliked the idea of serving women if men were going to miss out.

In October that year the Western Australian branch of the ULVA ran a major article from an English newspaper on whether there should be separate bars for men and women. The 'remarkable increase in the numbers of women customers has created a demand among men for accommodation from which women are excluded', the paper reported. This was a new demand, different from the separate bars that had existed for women prior to 1914, when it was women who had desired seclusion when drinking. 'Local ... customs about how and where women shall and shall not drink', once very rigidly observed, had been broken down during the war and they anticipated future changes. As to separate bars, the English newspaper thought this would be a pity. 'Woman's advent to full rights of entry into public houses without loss of caste has brought with it an advancement in the status of the public house itself. The presence of women unquestioningly has a restraining and beneficial in-fluence on the company present ... In those areas where women have not yet attained to this right – by common local consent – it will be found, almost without exception, that the public house itself lags behind in advancement.' The fact that women wanted to patronise a particular establishment was a sign that it had the qualities to which a public house should aspire. The article concluded 'we hope and believe that brewers, in the coming reconstruction period, will not encourage the suggestion of the setting aside of portions of licensed premises for the exclusive use either of men or of women'. Perhaps the most striking aspect of this article is the way it was reprinted without comment by the Western Australian hotel-keepers' association, who clearly saw much of con-temporary relevance in the argument. A year later they printed a list of suggestions for hotels that wanted to attract women as guests (e.g. 'pay attention to lights ... for reading in bed'). There was, however, no allusion to opening up public bars to women drinkers.

In 1944 the ULVA of New South Wales appointed a special committee to consider the place of the hotel in postwar reconstruction. One of the ten major points it addressed was the provisions that should be made for female clientele. No answers were provided but the ULVA was concerned to have a place in any decisions that were to be made about hotels after the war. They were aware that the problems of wartime rationing had had a detrimental effect on customer goodwill. The ULVA report concluded that the criticism and abuse and customer cynicism that resulted was inimical to the trade and would have repercussions when peace and normal custom were restored.

Later that year the Western Australian hoteliers' journal called for 'a new era of hotel architecture' with postwar reconstruction. Most particularly they were concerned at the prevalence of darkened or opaque glass in ground floor windows of pubs, 'giving the impression that there is something being done within their walls which must be concealed from view'. Hotels, they said, should be built to provide brightness and airiness if the old stigma against pubs was to be broken down. They commended the Continental idea of beer gardens and open-air cafes where patrons could consume alcohol at tables next to the pavement. '"Planning" for the immediate post-war period in most large urban areas must for the moment be confined to determining policy rather than to preparing a schedule of licensed properties which will require "alteration"', the *Brewers' Journal* had declared. The fundamental, paramount question was one of forward vision, 'What is the public-house of the 50's going to be like?' They pointed to the social changes in drinking practices brought about during more than four years of war: people were using more licensed houses and more people were drinking beer yet the amount of alcohol consumption had gone down. In the future, 'alcohol will be taken, much more than in 1939, as the accompaniment to social intercourse than as a means of securing a temporary alleviation from life's stress and strain'. Pubs would be treated 'as a place of rendezvous rather than as a drink shop', and public houses must be prepared to provide customers with beverages other than alcohol, especially on those mid-week days when patronage was low.

The Australian Temperance Council was also trying to influence wartime, and subsequently postwar, practices. If the elimination of alcohol was not to be attained they urged cabinet to restrict trading hours, remove 'wet' canteens from service messes, and reduce the production of alcohol to 1941 levels. But the ULVA was adamant that 6 o'clock closing even during wartime conditions was undesirable, 'considering the number of cases involving sly-grogging and illicit sales of liquor that have recently been before the courts and the fact that these illegal practices have developed and become pronounced only since six o'clock closing has been operative'. Even the daily press, according to the Western Australian branch, found it necessary to point out 'that six o'clock closing established a custom which had degenerated into a gluttonous swill of liquor between 5 and 6 o'clock of an evening'. It induced quick drinking which was 'neither convivial or congenial, and sends a man staggering home who would not have staggered home in other or more seemly

Figure 7.4 'Suitcase Parade': Adelaide women assembled outside Parliament House protesting to keep 6.00 p.m. closing, 1938. (SSL:MB10324, Mortlock Library, State Library of South Australia)

circumstances'. Again comparisons were made with circumstances in England and contrasts drawn between leisurely social drinking and 'habits of standing at a bar … shouting order to the barman or barmaid above the prevailing babble gulping beer until the hour touches six o'clock'. Liquor reform after the war 'should legalise drinking of light beers and wine with lunch and dinner. It should encourage leisurely, sit-down drinking in [lounges] or on lawns according to circumstances and the weather.' This would lead to 'less illicit trading … less drunkenness and possibly, in the long run, less drinking'. The presence of American servicemen also led to comparisons with the situation in the United States, one small example dealt particularly with Victorian hotels, but the observations made were pertinent nationwide. Early closing resulted in hurried and excessive drinking and was not in the best interests of the trade: hotels closed 'at the very time when it would be most convenient for the majority of people' to use them and meant conditions in Australia approximated those prevalent in the United States during prohibition.

Sir Keith Murdoch, head of Australia's biggest newspaper organisation, also had his say. Hotels could be educational, he thought, if opportunities were available, as they had been previously, for the critical discussion, debate and analysis of the news covered in the press. With early closing 'there is no time to talk in either country or city hotels in Victoria; there is not time to get a drink in comfort'. On the other hand, the French inn was the clearing-house for ideas: 'it was in the little country inn that you best learnt what France is thinking'. After the war when restraints were removed from newspapers, he hoped to see them similarly removed from drinking.

The war thus ended with a feeling that the era of 6 o'clock closing must be past. Postwar reconstruction promised the possibility of change when building once again commenced, liquor supplies returned to levels commensurate with demand, and governments passed new liquor licensing laws. 'Generally it is accepted that in future there are likely to be far more licensed victuallers ... than was the case in 1939', the *Brewers' Journal* announced at the end of the war, and catering in licensed houses was going to take on new significance. Wartime experiences affected people's expectations of life afterwards. The return of prosperity and full employment boded well for the future of the hotel trade.

Mobilising the labour supply

In November 1944 the ULVA in Western Australia paid tribute to the women who 'have done and are doing a great job' in keeping the industry going. 'When the history of the hotel trade in Australia comes to be written', they said, chapters would have to be devoted to 'the wonderful contribution' women had been making, 'courageously carrying on' under wartime difficulties, 'in many cases at the expense of their health'. Wartime conditions, such as staff shortages and rationing, meant that 'many womenfolk are working unduly long hours and undertaking duties which in normal times would be turned over to men engaged for the purpose' but doing so 'in the hope of relief in the not far distant future'. This tribute was clearly also a statement of expectation that women would relinquish their work once men wanted their jobs back.

One wartime licensee was Mrs James Gleeson, of the Drouin Hotel in rural Victoria. She was the subject of a photograph (Figure 7.5) that was part of a documentary series taken during World War II. This is not an impromptu shot, it has been carefully staged to capture the character of Mrs Gleeson's relationship with her clientele. Mrs Gleeson, dressed smartly but discreetly, her hair swept up in a business-like style, conveys an air of brisk, efficient competence, a businesswoman serving the customers on whom her success relies, sharing their jokes as she simultaneously attends to their needs. She is positioned at the centre, with

Figure 7.5 Mrs James Gleeson, licensee of the Drouin Hotel, Drouin, Victoria, 1944. (National Library of Australia)

several of the men looking directly towards her, suggesting the economic success and community status associated with running a local hotel: there is little sense here of the work involved.

The end of the war did not see conditions in the industry change overnight. Lifting manpower restrictions did not ease the position of back-of-house staff to any degree, and at war's end the position was 'desperate'. There had been a dearth of hotel employees since the conditions in the industry had declined in the mid-thirties. Postwar reconstruction promised an available labour supply for hotels through the new immigration program but a shortage of staff numbers was only part of the problem. The ULVA also began calling for the professional training of staff. Usually this was back-of-house – kitchen, cleaning and catering – staff. 'Since the war ended, it has been my experience that the need for organised training of our staff is greater than ever before', the Catering Adviser to the Victorian branch of the ULVA declared in 1947. Unlike other countries, Australia had never had training schools for waiters, waitresses, stewards and housemaids, although since 1937 apprentices had been learning cooking and the Rehabilitation Scheme for ex-servicemen was training chefs. On-the-job training by management was no longer acceptable because of increased expectations of standards from guests, yet the industry was facing a limited labour market because employees had sought fresh fields of employment. The New South Wales government announced in 1946 it was setting up a new school for training cooks and waiters 'and possibly hotel management'. 'Hotel-keeping today is a profession', the *Australasian Post* announced in July 1957; very often it was considered to be an unskilled trade, but its tradition indicated otherwise.

In contrast to back-of-house staff, bar staff were more easily obtained and 'very largely supplemented by discharged servicemen'. The ULVA reported there appeared to be 'no shortage of individuals prepared to take positions in bars'. And no wonder. In 1948, at a time when the male basic wage in Western Australia was 6 pounds 15 shillings a week, and the female basic wage was 3 pounds 13 shillings a week, barmaids and barmen received 8 pounds 2 shillings and another one pound 10 (30 shillings) a day overtime rate for Sunday work, when the basic daily overtime rate for men was one pound 5 shillings (25 shillings) and for women was just on 14 shillings (i.e. less than half what a barmaid could earn). The immediate postwar period also saw the introduction of the forty-hour week for hotel staff, and generous provisions regarding annual holidays, leading one state arbitration commissioner to point out when the Barmaids and Barmens Award was being amended in 1947 that 'barmaids and barmen already receive unusually generous terms ... and are probably better off than any other class of worker to whom the judgement [on annual leave] has been made applicable'.[12] Of course award rates set in legal contracts had to be enforced and this was difficult to police in the many small hotel businesses.

To help their members understand their obligations under the Re-Establishment and Employment Act, which regulated the reinstatement of service personnel into their old occupations, the ULVA published details of the Act in their journal in the last few months of 1945. The difficulties of re-absorbing discharged service personnel back into civilian employment led the ULVA to urge patience and understanding in the handling of staff: 'We read a lot in the press of what must be done for the returned serviceman and woman. True a debt is owing to them; they have earned a just reward of utmost consideration ... yet don't overlook the faithful service rendered by the employee during the war years ... These people kept the men in the front line supplied ... and it was also their efforts which assisted materially in making Victory possible.' This was also perhaps a recognition that antagonising employees who had kept the industry going could be foolish given the continuing labour shortage. Only about 33 per cent of women discharged from the services were eligible for employment, a figure the ULVA found 'rather disconcerting.

It was hoped that with release of women from the services, much more house staff would be available reasonably soon. Therefore,' they said, with how much sincerity is impossible to ascertain, 'little as the prospect sounds pleasing, many female employees in various fields of industry must be replaced by male staff. The male, the breadwinner of the family, ... must be given preference if the position is one that a male worker is eligible to do.'

Female staff employed during the war because of the shortage of male labour now found themselves facing displacement and a return to prewar wage relativities. However in 1949 the arbitration commission set a new minimum wage for women at 75 per cent of the male rate. Most cleaning and domestic tasks in hotels would remain women's work but bar service was one area where men and women were interchangeable and barmaids were thus able to argue for equal pay more effectively than most women workers. As we saw in chapter 6, for Victorian barmaids it worked.

With changing employment conditions and a continuing demand for back-of-house staff, the question arose in Western Australia, where particularly restrictive state legislation had controlled and curtailed Aboriginal people since the turn of the century, of employing Aboriginal women as housemaids, kitchenmaids or generals. The *Hotel Review of Western Australia* pointed out, in answer to questions raised by licensees about the legality of employing Aboriginal workers around licensed premises, that licensees could legally, under s. 151 of the Licensing Act, employ Aboriginal people under certain conditions, with the consent in writing of the Chief Protector, although it was an offence to supply them with alcohol or 'to allow any Aboriginal native to remain on or loiter about the licensed premises'. Serving liquor from behind the bar was obviously out of the question while state laws on Aboriginal drinking remained in force. That Aboriginal women could, and later did, become barmaids is indicated by the fact that in 1962 'coloured bar girls' were the centre of a union dispute in north Queensland.[13]

Licensing laws under review

By 1950 Australia was in a very conservative mood. Robert Menzies' conservative Liberal Party had been elected to federal office the year before and much of the population was trying to establish a family life according to an ideal that two decades of social dislocation and economic shortages had rendered chimeric. Not everybody endorsed the ideal, nor did they find it an easy one to live up to in practice, but a lot of lip service was paid to it. Public discussions about women's work were also couched in familial terms. Now 'the barmaid' became a mother figure: 'motherly, neatly-dressed women', sometimes 'widows with grown children'. Far from being a sexual lure the barmaid was now 'the "other woman" who never wrecks a home'. Indeed in her ability to keep a husband's confidence of his troubles she was a positive asset in keeping marriages together. And 'if more mothers, and fathers ... had as broad and practical a knowledge of the world as barmaids fewer sons would start misguided lives of alcoholism'. They looked after their customers: minded their money, stopped serving them, especially the young ones, if they were drinking too much, and gave their lifetimes to serving the public, this 'in a service-starved community'.[14]

In this climate the previously mentioned story of *Caddie: A Sydney Barmaid* was published. Caddie's story is a rare autobiography of a barmaid in Australia. It enjoyed enormous popular success when it appeared and in the 1970s was made into a film starring Helen Morse, which also enjoyed popular success. It was written as the story of a struggling single mother in Depression Australia, battling for her children: 'a simple account of how a woman earned her keep and her children's keep in the bar of one pub after another', 'not from choice, but because I was broke and needed the money to support myself and my two young children'.[15] Caddie was 24 when she got her first job in a Sydney bar, the first time in her life that she'd been in one. 'In 1924 not only was it forbidden by law for women to drink in a bar, but no woman who valued her reputation would have dared put her nose even into a Ladies' Parlour. To most respectable Australians a barmaid was beyond the pale.' She described her feelings: 'Indeed I felt that morning as I took my place behind the long counter – imagining every eye on me – that I had put myself on the outer.'

'Not that I really had any choice' were Caddie's key words about her move into bar work in the decades between the two world wars. Caddie did not present herself as a pleasure-seeking woman: presented to readers in the 1950s, hers was the story of a mother, of her 'willingness to sacrifice everything' for her children, and of her struggle 'to remain "respectable" and give her children the chance in life she never had'. Thus her experience as a barmaid was written to arouse the readers' sympathy for a lone mother's 'gallant struggle [as] a young untrained woman to rear two children decently', forced by life's circumstances to take a job in a pub, 'the most corrupt and corrupting legal occupation Australia knows'.

Fortuitously, it was 'pure chance that this story ... should appear as a personal case history to the Royal Commission on Liquor in New South Wales', which sat during 1951–52, and exposed the opprobrious conditions under which the liquor trade was conducted.

Novelist Dymphna Cusack, who wrote the introduction to the book, exploited the connections between Caddie's story and the government inquiry then under way quite shamelessly. No doubt this accounted for some of the book's popularity. It may even have been why it was written. *Caddie* revealed in graphic narrative form, through the eyes of a woman and her children, the stark realities of Australia's pub culture, 'the most uncivilised drinking conditions in the world'. But it also revealed the differing representation of 'the barmaid' at mid-century. As 'the barmaid' at the turn of the century was the focus of temperance campaigners seeking to reform the liquor trade, so in 1953 Caddie's experiences behind the bar were used in a campaign to reform Australia's pub culture. In 1900 in temperance literature 'the barmaid' was presented as a sexual lure, a seducer of young men and drunken customers, a victim not of larger economic forces but of unscrupulous employers, doomed to end her days as a prostitute.[16] While the dust jacket on the book had Caddie dressed in 1890s fashion, in the 1950s 'the barmaid' was presented as a maternal figure. Caddie was 'respectable', a loving mother, 'an essentially decent human being', an unwilling participant in pub practices, 'her whole life-struggle was a conflict between her essential decency and an environment that would have debased a woman of lesser quality'. English pub practices were different, Dymphna Cusack explained: there, wives accompanied husbands to drink, chat and watch matches of darts and dominoes. Thus 'the English barmaid is more like the hostess of the assembled group', she said, 'than her Australian counterpart whose job, because of the deplorable conditions surrounding it, is despised by the "respectable" community, whatever her personal character may be'. The Sydney barmaid in the 1950s was still a victim of an unscrupulous liquor trade. Ironically the conditions that Caddie's story exemplified, and that the 1952 royal commission found to be so appalling, were brought about by those very laws sought by similar reformers at the turn of the century.

In 1924, in becoming a barmaid, Caddie had subjected herself to the unrelenting male gaze – 'imagining every eye on me' – in a forum where no other women were allowed, and she had thereby put herself 'on the outer'. This feeling of being 'on the outer' of respectability is not, however, conveyed in the stories she subsequently tells of the working-class communities in which she lived in suburban Sydney. Nor is it supported by press characterisations of barmaids working in city hotels in this period.[17] 'There is often an inverse relationship between disposable income and decent behaviour', one bar worker said recently. Given a choice between 'arrogant ... merchant bankers' in a 'yuppy bar' and 'retired wharfies' in a traditionally working-class suburb, it's obvious which she preferred. 'You're still the barmaid, but that's not someone who's lower than them, if you know what I mean.' There was no snobbery, no class superiority, but there was gender-specific language that rankled.[18]

Caddie too recalled being subjected to sexual innuendo and overtures from customers, and sometimes to abuse, to being treated 'as though she was scum'. Some men thought it 'awfully smart to insult a woman behind the bar', she said, and it was not the barmaid's fault. Learning to deal with it was all part of the job, 'learning to be popular with the customers while keeping them at a distance ... learning to smile ... [being] always bright, always smiling', and never taking your own troubles to work. 'I learned to put the boss before sentiment ... I was there to make money and I made it. If an inch off the bottom of my skirts meant an extra 5s a week in tips, I was prepared to put up with the boss's idea of "Art" ... Above all, I was a good listener, I avoided voicing an opinion wherever possible.'

This recognition of and negotiation of sexuality in the workplace was very careful. 'I took an interest in them, knew what they liked to drink.' This clearly made regulars feel special, but like a good mother, 'I treated them all the same.' In return customers treated the barmaid with respect and an expectation that others do the same. 'There were limits to a barmaid's geniality', Caddie reported, and there were times when a customer overstepped the mark. Yet turning back an insult also had to be done within the unwritten rules of pub culture, the rules set by the customers. Treating the barmaid with respect also meant the barmaid had to tolerate a considerable amount of sexual innuendo and banter, to control the limits of that exchange, without antagonising either the transgressor or the other customers. A particularly vivid account of one such occasion when a customer effectively and loudly imputed she was a prostitute conveyed clearly the exigencies of the job. 'I was flabbergasted – but only for a second. I knew that every eye was on me.' Leaning over the counter she returned the insult in the same loud whisper it had been delivered. 'There was a burst of laughter and one little fellow said [to the transgressor] "Well, you did ask for it."' Relief was clearly felt all round, hard feelings were banished.

There was a positive side to the sexual connotations of bar work. Working behind the bar brought Caddie into contact with several men keen to show her a good time, and it paid her better wages than she was able to get in any other employment in the decades before World War II. For other women, too, seeking work behind the bar was a desirable option, not a lack of choice. 'I wouldn't take any other job now,' one reported, 'I like this work too much.' Another thought working behind the bar after the war was better than it had ever been: 'The hours are shorter and the money higher.' And a third said 'I've loved every moment of my life in the bar.'[19] Clearly where a barmaid worked made a lot of difference to her enjoyment of her job. Shirley Mellor, who was elected Secretary of the Liquor Trades Union Queensland Branch in the early 1980s, started work in a Brisbane city pub in 1959 because she was offered the job by the owner of the pub she frequented with her husband, and it was more interesting than the office she then worked in.[20] But although Queensland had segregated drinking customs, it did not have the iniquitous '6 o'clock swill' that was such a characteristic feature of pub culture in the southern states from 1916 onwards, that made pubs such an unseemly place, especially for women.

As we've already seen, under the National Security Regulations, most states had brought in 6 o'clock closing during World War II. In the 1950s this came under review. Western Australia, for example, extended trading to 7 o'clock even before the war's end, heralding that, in keeping with a resolution adopted by the Western Australian Parliament in 1942, a further move towards restoration of 9.00 p.m. closing was coming.[21] Queensland also had later closing before the war's end: there the Liquor Trades Union opposed the move to 10 o'clock closing that was mooted in 1941.[22] Tasmania had 10 o'clock closing as early as 1937. New South Wales, Victoria and South Australia retained the early closing law that had been in force now for thirty years. For the first time in the 1950s the spotlight was on the drinking culture associated with 6 o'clock closing. Caddie's story was presented as part of a process to bring about change. As she said of that 'six o'clock swill', 'it was a revolting sight and one it took a long time for me to take for granted. The smell of liquor, the smell of human bodies, the warm smell of wine, and on one early occasion even a worse smell, as a man, rather than give up his place at the counter, urinated against the bar.' This was not uncommon, and she described another occasion when a man 'vomited where he stood' in the bar and then just continued drinking.[23]

While there were clearly many people like Dymphna Cusack and Catherine Edmonds Wright (Caddie) campaigning to change the culture, it was a slow process. First they had to change the laws on trading hours. In 1947 New South Wales held a referendum on closing hours but the result was in favour of retention of 6.00 p.m. closing. This was 'an astounding result', with 'very serious consequences' for the industry, according to the ULVA. It had made their opponents appear much more important in the eyes of the public than if the vote had never been taken, one spokesperson pointed out. But perhaps it was also an expression of public reaction to the unscrupulous practices of the war years for he went on to say that now 'The retail section of the Trade will have ... to prove to the public that the hotel is for the public's convenience. The service given must not be just service over the bar. The hotelkeeper must ... supply meals, accommodation and other amenities', he said. Although it was a 'severe set-back', they just had to 'play the game by the public'. Another claimed the result would not defer 'the plan of liquor interests and hotel property owners to bring Australian hotels up to overseas standards'. The impact on New South Wales' reputation as the liberal state was seriously jeopardised. 'The next New South Welshman who tells me that [Victorians are very conservative] will be in danger of having mayhem committed on his person' one jocular Victorian asserted.[24]

Similarly, Victoria in 1955 voted to retain 6 o'clock closing. There the temperance lobby was still very powerful and it was not until they changed their attitudes towards drinking that early closing disappeared from Melbourne pubs. Victoria thus became a focus of attention in the 1950s in a way that other states, even South Australia, managed to avoid. Bringing the Olympic Games to Melbourne in 1956 also brought its drinking laws into the spotlight. In that year journalist Reg Leonard observed that nowhere in the rest of the world was there 'anything as revolting and disgusting as what we call the six o'clock swill. The daily demonstration of piggery is something that no other country in the world can match.'[25] It became something of a tourist attraction for visitors to Victoria but locals were not particularly amused. In a book published at the end of the era of the 6 o'clock swill, Melbourne-based journalist and author Keith Dunstan described drinking during the period from the point of view of the bar customers:

One would leave the office at, say, 5.20 p.m., gather four or five friends and reach the hotel bar by 5.30 p.m. ... a large room with a cold, lavatory-like atmosphere, but filled with pushing men ... no seats, no tables, no stools, no clutter that might interfere with high-speed action. There are only thirty precious minutes left and there are five in one's school, and as a point of honour each man must shout, that is every man must buy a round of drinks. Can it be done in time? There is a large clock on the wall, invariably set fast, because the police come aound at 6.00 p.m. to make sure the bar is cleared ... time ticks away, tension mounts and mounts ... Getting everybody his last shout becomes a desperate affair. There are special men and ladies on for the peak panic, eight or even ten immensely skilled barmen and barmaids, all equipped with the latest pluto taps on plastic hoses, an invention designed for dispensing beer at frightening speed, but they cannot cope ... you know this barmaid pretty well, and she serves you first, but then you have to get your five glasses back to your mates against the wall ... you try to pass the glasses overhead ... the mob is getting desperate ... so they shove, but as the beer rains on them out of your full glasses they do not even notice ... At 6.15 p.m. the crowd, after their thirty minutes or so of tension, would be out on the footpath, many reeling. Constitutions that have not known food for five hours or more need to be strong to take five beers in 30 minutes on an empty stomach.[26]

Photographers saw the 6 o'clock rush hour and Australia's drinking culture as a subject to be captured on film. What their photographs show is that, while it was bad for the customers, it was even worse for the workers. The photographs in Figures 7.6 and 7.7 are taken from behind the bar, showing clearly the working environment.

In the photo of the public bar of Melbourne's famous Scott's Hotel (Figure 7.6), the clock on the wall shows it is nearly 6.00 p.m. The size of the crowd indicates a high noise-level and a lot of demand. The barman is serving, all three barmaids are bent over pouring beers. Nobody is chatting to customers in a relaxed way, the emphasis is on high speed

Figure 7.6 Five minutes to 6 o'clock in the front bar of Scott's Hotel, Melbourne. (Royal Historical Society of Victoria)

and constant demand. There are no stools for patrons to sit on, no chance for the bar staff to get off their feet. No time or inclination for personal details to be exchanged between staff and customers. This is a well-dressed city crowd, probably comparatively well-behaved, but still there must have been spillages, there are slops from spilled drinks visible on the floor behind the bar. Beer was like salt water on shoe leather, union advocates argued in the arbitration court hearings.[27] Looking at this photo, one can almost smell it.

Under the impact of immigration from Europe and the United Kingdom, Australian drinking practices in the 1950s were being assailed by expectations of more sophisticated behaviour. New enlightened attitudes towards drinking led to new demands for liberalised licensing laws. After the war, while the consumption of beer in England steadily dropped to less than 13 gallons a head, beer consumption in Australia steadily increased. In 1944, it averaged 13 gallons per head, in 1946 it had risen to 15, in 1948 to 17, in 1950 to 20 and, by 1955, to 24.[28] These figures were no doubt boosted by an increase in consumption by women. Yet the Australian pub culture being condemned in the 1950s was not only a product of increasing consumption, it was also a product of the out-moded licensing laws that had enabled publicans to exploit the desire for alcohol above all other considerations, and had developed a culture of masculine drinking customs inimical to 1950s ideals of family life. The sexual differentiation of Australian pub culture of which the 6 o'clock swill was the ultimate manifestation was about to be renegotiated.

Still, change was slow in coming and the lead was taken by those outside the industry, the judiciary, journalists and governments. Governments desiring change instituted inquiries that effectively enabled them to bypass a popular vote. In response to concerns raised about corruption in the retailing of beer through the pubs, the New South Wales government established a royal commission to inquire into the provision and distribution of beer through retail outlets. This was the beginning of fundamental changes in Australian pub culture, and the place of women within it.

The Maxwell Royal Commission, 1951–53

The royal commission under Justice Maxwell – with W. G. Dovey as senior counsel and his son-in-law, future Labor prime minister, E. G. Whitlam, as junior counsel – began sitting on 30 July 1951. It addressed itself to all aspects of liquor trading in New South Wales, most notably the tied-house system of hotel ownership, which had grown in strength during the period of Depression and war. Evidence was taken from over four hundred witnesses, from the licensing court, public servants, police and other authorities, local government officials, representatives of trade, breweries and spirits merchants, the Temperance Alliance, publicans and private citizens. The commission's report, presented to Parliament three years later, pointed out that there were 2028 hotels in New South Wales (618 in the city, 1410 in country areas) or one hotel to every 1566 persons, compared with one hotel to every 803 persons in 1920. Of these, individuals owned 975 (856 of these in the country) and brewery companies (mainly Tooth & Co. and Tooheys) owned 884 in fairly equal distribution between the city and the country.[29] More significant than ownership, however, was the number of tied houses. Sixty-nine per cent, or 1400 hotels, were tied to the two major breweries, over 1000 of these were tied to Tooth & Co. alone. Maxwell didn't find any particular disadvantages to the existence of a tied-house system, though he found the ULVA's 'powerful advocacy' of the system needed to be treated with caution because their 'enthusiasm could be, if not begotten, at any rate nurtured, by a sense of dependence, and ... the appearance of gratitude to the brewery benefactors could evidence a lively sense of favours to come'.[30] He was clearly very sceptical about the brewers. His solution was to focus on the licensing laws as the means of regulating the industry, and not to worry about restraint of trade provisions.

Maxwell found that 'the liquor licensing laws have for long been a field for serious malpractices not only by unlicensed persons, but by the holders of publican's licences. The evils established served to stress the importance of the work of the Licensing Court', he said, and he urged that attention be paid to raising the status of the licensing court. Maxwell's most significant finding was, however, the appalling conditions under which men were permitted, indeed forced, to drink. 'I am satisfied ... there are evils associated with 6 o'clock closing which ought not be tolerated in a civilised community', Maxwell said. He was particularly scathing about the duplicitous practices of pub owners. 'I have little doubt that licensees (either tenant or manager) will in many ... instances, favour the retention of 6 p.m. closing,' he said, 'because the return from the sale of liquor is obtained more quickly than with the burden of supervision and added labour involved in later hours.' This was a position based solely on the licensees' self interest, and so arguments from the industry for retention of early closing were given no more credence than arguments against an extension of hours from the Temperance Alliance, who really wanted to close hotels altogether, and were hoping for a return to the local option referendum of 1928. 'There can be no doubt upon the evidence that in the metropolitan area conditions associated with 6 o'clock closing are deplorable; apart from any other consideration, a refusal to attempt some reform involves, in my opinion, the conscious perpetuation of a clearly established evil; in addition the present closing hour encourages sly grog and after-hours trading at "black market" rates.'[31]

Maxwell was weaving a fine line of distinction between the licensees who saw more monetary gain in retaining the existing hours and the ULVA members who 'appeared to favour' later closing, with a break late in the afternoon, such as was the practice in the United Kingdom and on the Continent. Maxwell said 'appeared to favour' because of the careful terms of the resolution they presented. In the 1947 referendum the 'yes' vote for 9.00 or 10.00 p.m. closing was the majority vote in the country areas, where individually owned pubs predominated, while retaining 6.00 p.m. closing was the majority decision in the metropolitan area where tied houses predominated. These results indicated, perhaps, not only rural–urban differences in access to pubs at different times of the day, but also the economic self-interests of the suppliers of the liquor, the breweries. Closely related to the problem of the hours pubs were open was the design of bars, Maxwell pointed out. An improvement in

Figure 7.7 'Perpendicular drinking' Saturday lunchtime at the Bondi Beach Hotel, Sydney, 1951. (Tooth & Co. Ltd, Dep. no. Z223/158 (B), Neg. no. 5359, NBAC/ANU)

conditions was not just going to come with an extension of hours 'if the present typical bar continues'. 'There is clear need for provision for drinking at tables or seated – as against what is described as "perpendicular" drinking, for better facilities than very large bars, less secrecy and more openness attendant upon the present layout of many bars and in addition, greater provision for either gardens or open air bars.' He was in no doubt that opposition to the idea of open-air drinking in gardens came 'from the self interest of those who would be required to make provision for them' but he also pointed out that the licensing court had the power to order such additional accommodation to provide such facilities should it choose to exercise it.[32]

Maxwell appeared particularly bemused by the temperance advocates. When Reverend C. H. Tomlinson argued that 'so-called moderate drinking caused divorce and impaired the national character', that 'later trading will enlist more and more immoderate drinkers … and will introduce women more and more into drinking', Maxwell pointed out that Tomlinson's example of Tasmania (where later trading hours already existed) didn't gel with the evidence. Smyth, Queen's Counsel for the ULVA, asked Tomlinson directly, 'you would prefer the existence of the pig swill and the 4 to 6 o'clock rush if you cannot have prohibition?' to which Tomlinson replied, 'Yes.'[33]

By pointing the way to override the power of the manipulative hotel-keepers as well as the temperance lobby, and by demonstrating that no less alcohol was consumed just because the amount of time in which to drink it was restricted, Maxwell's report led the way to entirely new drinking practices in Australia. It was partly to bring Australian practices in line with more enlightened English, and by now even Scottish and indeed New Zealand, practices that laws were being liberalised. It was also in response to new demands from consumers. Indicative of the shift in public opinion that had occurred since the war was the fact that, where the New South Wales population in the referendum in 1947 had voted overwhelmingly to retain 6.00 p.m. closing, the Maxwell Royal Commission in its report of 1953 came out solidly behind 10.00 p.m. closing. This was enacted in new legislation that came into effect in February 1955.

Now only Victoria and South Australia dragged the chain. It was not until the mid-sixties that they followed suit, setting up their own royal commissions and extending trading hours. While historians have not thought to ask why these laws should have remained in place for over forty years, neither have they yet investigated why, having lasted so long, the edifice should at last crumble, in a little over a decade between 1955 and 1967. When it did so, the impact was dramatic.

CHAPTER EIGHT

'In Praise of Splendid Gels':[1]
Sex, Skill and Drinking Culture

The atmosphere of pub culture created by the 6 o'clock swill and segregated drinking did nothing for the reputation of barmaids or their enjoyment of their work. However, with the end of early closing came a transformation in pubs that threatened their very existence.

The biggest challenge to the overwhelming masculinity of mid-war pub culture, and the niceties of the 6 o'clock swill, came from the licensed clubs. They also employed bar staff. In the Liquor (Amendment) Act of 1945, introduced into the New South Wales Parliament by Premier William McKell, the restriction on club liquor licences that had been in effect since 1906 was abolished and the number of clubs subsequently rose from 85 to 253 within a year, and to virtually 400 within another two years. Licensed clubs were free to sell liquor to their members outside hotel hours, and when they also began introducing poker machines (at first illegally) their numbers increased even further. In 1955 alone nearly four hundred new clubs opened, in 1956 the government introduced legislation legalising poker machines, and within six more years the number of clubs in New South Wales had risen to 1285, with hundreds of thousands of members. Similar though smaller increases occurred in other states. Queensland legislation restricted the growth of clubs but by 1963 had 422 clubs and the number of hotels had declined by 250 compared with 1943; South Australia had 476 clubs, Victoria 246, and Western Australia 213.[2]

The expansion of the clubs was one explanation for the collapse of the old pub culture. Yet clubs had been established to meet a demand from the drinking public, a public that was not universally male. Their growth was facilitated by new licensing laws that posed a direct challenge to old-style drinking practices in pubs. They were symptomatic of a new climate of expectation. The clubs provided to their members what the hotels did not: comfortable, luxuriously carpeted and curtained surroundings, tables and chairs, games-rooms, sporting and swimming facilities, dancing and entertainment. And although actual drinking areas may have been segregated, club premises and facilities were not exclusively male. Although women were not usually full members, they could be associates, and wives and girlfriends could accompany their men or enjoy the facilities on their own. Whole families could go to the local club, drink together (usually at fairly cheap prices) and watch the entertainment, in New South Wales have a flutter on the poker machines, and all in 'comfort, quietness and respectability'.[3]

A survey undertaken in 1957 by Asher Joel Advertising for the ULVA in New South Wales found the public wanted large lounge bars and sit-down drinking, which the clubs were providing but pubs were not. Most particularly they wanted quietness when they drank. The survey revealed that only 11 per cent of drinkers preferred the public bar compared with 53 per cent who preferred either the saloon bar (16 per cent), lounge (22 per cent), or beer garden (16 per cent). The largest number of those preferring the public bar were over 60 years old.[4] Nearly a third of people preferred to drink in mixed company, another 21 per cent didn't care, less than a quarter preferred male company only and, again, one-third of those were over sixty. But most people (71 per cent in total; 69 per cent of the men and 75 per cent of the women) thought women should be excluded from hotel bars.[5] Given the simultaneously expressed preference for mixed drinking, this result was a reflection on the culture of the pub rather than a statement about appropriate femininity. The licensing laws restricting pub hours were only part of the problem, but they were a significant factor and the first change that was required.

The growth of Australian clubs was symptomatic of larger social changes that were occurring in the 1960s, as pubs and the prerogatives of masculinity they enshrined underwent a transformation. The changes began in the 1950s with the extension of hours in licensing laws, for along with later trading went the idea that drinking was a universal pastime to be shared with women companions. Commissioner Maxwell had described it as 'a most unedifying spectacle to see a wife waiting on the footpath for her husband to come out of an hotel bar sometime after 8 p.m., and then both necessarily going in late to a picture-show. Under my suggestion,' he said, 'both sexes would be permitted to partake of liquid refreshment prior to attending the evening shows.'[6] The end of 6.00 p.m. closing was also the beginning of the end of the exclusively male public bar.

Then in 1965 the royal commission in Victoria under Justice P. D. Phillips, QC, handed down its report on the liquor industry in Victoria. Phillips found that the amount of alcohol consumed in Victoria was no less than it was in New South Wales where drinkers had longer to consume it, but the rate of drunkenness in Victoria was proportionately greater and the amount of drinking done away from hotel premises was greater. He recommended the extension of trading hours to 10.00 p.m.

and more liberal licensing laws for restaurants, which were subsequently enacted in legislation. Two years later, South Australia at last followed suit.[7]

The end of early closing in Victoria was heralded by the press as 'a breath of fresh air ... a social revolution'. The *Age* predicted 'a social upheaval' as the trend towards hotel entertainment sped up and a 'new breed of hotel patron – the husband and wife or mixed couple' became common. Not since the advent of television had anything so momentous occurred but it would be many years before the real effects were evident. The *Herald* published a photo of a male bar attendant pouring beer for a female patron, just to demonstrate how the old order was changing.[8] The first evening of late trading was, however, a bit of a let-down, as it had been in New South Wales ten years earlier. Journalists seemed surprised at how quiet the bars and pubs around Melbourne were. When Adelaide finally caught up with the rest of the country, it seemed a non-event. Yet in ending 6 o'clock closing South Australia brought a revolution: first it reinstated barmaids' legal right to work, another catch-up measure. But just as it had in 1908, South Australia led the country with another innovative licensing law that had just as profound an effect as its 'wowser' law at the turn of the century. South Australia introduced the 0.08 limit on blood alcohol readings to curb drink-driving, breath-testing to be done by the police using a breathalyser. It was only a matter of time before the other states followed. The breathalyser was the most revolutionary change to occur in postwar Australia in the eyes of those in the trade.[9] In the 1960s pub culture was under siege from many directions. From now on pubs were to fight for their survival.

The 1960s brought important changes to hotels as tourism became increasingly important. 'The first and most fundamental matter to keep in mind is that an hotel is intended to provide accommodation, food and drink,' Chairman of the Queensland Licensing Commission reminded licensees. 'All too often ... the licensee concentrates on the liquor side of his business and displays little real interest in either accommodation or meals ... Guests should be welcomed', he said, attention paid to their comforts, standards of service improved, 'as is done in many motels'.[10] For with increased prosperity came car ownership for many more Australian families, and motels were starting to compete for the accommodation trade. Now that workers had three and four weeks annual leave, 'Could anyone really have foreseen the effect on hotels that would come with an economy bursting at the seams, with the motor car ... greatly improved aircraft ... and finally, with the leisure time to travel!', the Vice-President of the Queensland branch of the Australian Hotels Association said.[11]

Although in retrospect it was easy to account for the growth of tourism, and to see all too clearly its potential, hotels were simply not geared to meet these new developments when they arrived, the Vice-President said. They were located in towns, rather than on highways, were built to meet travellers' needs of a different era, licensing laws inhibited their movements, the buildings were old and outmoded, and all these factors gave their competitors an advantage.[12] The first motels were built in Australia in 1950 and by 1958 had begun to move into country towns to challenge the hotels for trade. With their growth the accommodation facilities of pubs became even less attractive to customers. 'The motels which scorn the gilt fittings, the liveried attendants, the wandering cigarette girls and myriad other costly services traditional of first-class hotel accommodation ... [are] smiling and exuding confidence', one newspaper reported. Motels were set to take over the accommodation industry.[13]

Now the old combination that had made Australian pubs distinctive – the accommodation and liquor provisions – were split in two. Accommodation was being provided separately by motels which didn't have a liquor licence, and liquor was being provided by licensed clubs which didn't have to provide accommodation. In Tasmania the licensing court found that 112 of the 269 hotels in the state were only just paying their way and the hoteliers' association set out to discover why so many of their number should be making small profits by setting up a research program into the economic and social considerations of the industry. The licensing court thought it was because Tasmania had a higher ratio of hotels to population than any of the other states and that better roads and better motor cars meant many small towns were bypassed by travellers, thus there were hotels surplus to requirements.[14]

By the 1960s hotels were beset by many problems because they had ignored the accommodation sector of the trade during the war years, 'the get-rich-quick beer-swill era', and because of government regulations inhibiting their modernisation. 'The hotel industry has become a political football', the *Australian Financial Review* claimed, 'with the liquor laws a battlefield patrolled regularly by temperance groups ... among the most efficient pressure groups in Australia.' The Victorian government was 'absolutely timid to the point of sabotaging the hotel industry', the consequence was that hotels were 'forced to provide dining and accommodation facilities in order to have the privilege of retaining their licence'. Hotels would continue to lose out to motels until governments realised the value of tourism and industry members started to act with more thought for the good of the industry.[15] The Liquor Trades Union in Tasmania, too, recognised the importance of the tourist trade, and called for 'more liberal licensing laws' to make Tasmania 'as a tourist state ... more attractive to tourists'. It was the duty of the government to ensure that comparable and adequate facilities were provided.[16]

Training the staff

As a sign of the changes, the ULVA in 1959 became the Australian Hotels Association, and they turned their attention to improving their service. The first line of defence was their staff. 'The importance of training for employees has become increasingly apparent in recent years as industry has become more complex and the public taste more discriminating', the *QHA Review* announced in September 1964. 'The shortage of skilled employees has reached serious proportions in ... the hotel industry, and action to remedy this position is urgently needed.' Trade training at the technical college was available for employees in other industries, but while it remained unavailable to hotel industry employees (i.e. cooks, waiters and waitresses) the hotel industry could not 'fulfil its vital role in the rapidly expanding tourist industry ... becoming increasingly import-ant as a major Queensland industry'.

Rules for bar staff posted up in Brisbane's leading hotel in 1952 give a good indication of employer expectations of their front-of-house staff. The first rule was honesty: tills were not to be incorrect. The second rule was honesty: employees were not to shout (treat) customers or give away any of the hotel's goods. The third rule was honesty: staff were neither to rob the customer nor their employer by buying their personal popularity in the bar. Rules 4, 5 and 6 related to cleanliness: of glasses, counters and eating habits. Rules 7 to 11 covered relationships with customers: cour-tesy, deference, memory of orders taken and change to be given, 'try to be pleasant at all times'. Rule 12 was industry specific: 'memorise all prices and be familar with all lines'. Rule 13 was about personal clean-liness and general appearance; rules 14 and 15 about avoiding waste of alcohol, 'in making profits for your employer you earn your own wages'; and rule 16 was 'every employee must work amicably with the rest of the staff'.[17]

Two years later the *ULVA Review* printed 'Rules for the man behind the bar':

1 He is courteous and attentive, and makes each customer feel, by his attention and service, that his business is directly responsible for the success of the establishment.
2 He never pushes a drink towards a customer.
3 He returns each bottle to its proper place after using it so he can reach for it without wasting time when another call comes for the brand.
4 He sees that the label on the bottle is turned so that it can be seen by the patron when pouring.
5 He keeps his glasses sparkling.
6 He keeps his counter spotless, wiping it dry at every opportunity.
7 He is careful about his personal appearance, makes sure his fingernails are clean.

8 Takes extreme care not to serve anyone under age.
9 He avoids [dis]agreements with trouble makers.
10 Makes it plain to known 'touchers' [people looking for free drinks] that they are not wanted on the premises.
11 Does his best to keep the atmosphere pleasant.
12 Avoids familiarity in talking to a patron when he is with others. Never mentions patron's last visit unless patron himself brings up the subject.
13 Avoids any appearance of listening in to a conversation between patrons.[18]

Where earlier definitions of barmen's work had emphasised their heavier duties compared with barmaids' work, here there was no effort to differentiate barmen from female bar attendants. The specifications of tasks and duties were identical. 'The ideal barman is a man with three hands, a set of extra eyes, and a telepathic mind,' the *Hotel Review of Western Australia* claimed in October 1953, 'else he couldn't serve so many drinks so fast so well.' The extra eyes were used to detect customers awaiting service, to attend to the customer's needs immediately. 'He has the uncanny ability to recognise his customers' moods of the moment ... If the patron wishes ... silent reverie, he is left alone. If the customer prefers to be chatty, the ideal barman will swap endless banter and never seem bored by it. Puddles of moisture ... he wipes ... up as fast as they appear. He empties ash-trays the way he breathes – automatically – and almost as often.'

After these attentions to personal relations and clean service, came skills of the trade. 'His crowning virtue is his fetish for preparing mixed drinks by the book ... [he] never experiments with the time-tested standard recipes.' The ideal barman had personal attributes in addition to his service and trade skills. He was 'not a university graduate, but he is well read and intelligent. He is at once politician and diplomat, judge and jury. He can be friendly without being intimate. He can flatter his customers without being false. He can be humble without being servile. He can be silent without being aloof, or talk at length without being garrulous.' These characteristics were clearly desirable not just in employees but were also required in the licensee. 'His wealth may not be large, but his popularity with his customers is enormous.'[19] What was missing from this description of the barworker's skills was the negotiation of sexuality in the workplace. This would undoubtedly be different for male and female workers, as it would be in gay bars, heterosexual pubs, licensed clubs and city pubs compared with rural, suburban, waterfront or college campus pubs. But it was a hidden skill that employers could not easily train their staff in. Nor, perhaps, readily acknowledge.

There was no suggestion in the 1950s that schools were needed to train bar staff, that came considerably later.[20] In the 1960s bar staff still received their training on the job. Just as the anonymous barmaid who wrote her autobiography in the 1890s had been taught by her boss, Shirley Mellor remembers that when she started as a barmaid in 1960, she was taught by her boss how to pull a beer – 'it's all in the flick of the hand'. The 1890s barmaid's boss had told her 'It's like billiards: some get into the way of it all at once, while others make a very poor attempt, and never become proficient.' Shirley, too, said, 'You can tell within a very few minutes if someone is going to be able to learn it.' Her boss also told her the unwritten rules that she passes on to new staff today: don't sleep with the boss, and don't believe what the customers say: 'with every beer they drink you get more beautiful'.[21]

Training was also being done through industry publications. 'The business of a barman does not begin and end with taking orders, pouring the drinks, and receiving payment; it consists of a great deal more than that', an article in the *Hotel Review of Western Australia* said. Conduct, bearing and manner while on duty at the bar had a direct bearing on the sales made and staff were enjoined to 'be friendly but not flip. Cultivate a smooth manner. Work quickly and neatly. There is no excuse for slopping drinks or splashing water. A good memory is as important to a barman as it is to the front clerk of an hotel. Get to know your regular patrons and greet them pleasantly and courteously ... get to know their favourite drinks ... Handle complaints courteously.' The staff were to cultivate these skills because the bar's reputation 'for fine drinks and courteous service' was how it attracted trade, and it just as quickly lost both this reputation and its patrons if the service was not right. Bar attendants were told to never show impatience; never hurry a customer; never let your moods interfere. 'Above all be tactful. No job in the world requires more tact.' A piece from an English newspaper on 'The Barmaids of London', reprinted in the *Hotel Review of Western Australia*, confirmed the importance of personal attributes for bar staff but gave it a gender dimension that sounded like the *Brewers' Journal* defence of barmaids at the turn of the century: 'Contrary to the belief of many teetotallers she does not indulge much in flirtation or general sentimentality, though she will respond with a smile to a compliment that is sincere. Her chief characteristic is good humoured commonsense. She soundly assesses all sorts and conditions of men.'[22]

Equal pay at last

The Liquor Trades Union welcomed new changes in liquor trading laws. The 1960s also brought significant changes in working conditions. In 1962 the union demanded a thirty-five hour week for its members because of

Figure 8.1 Barmaids campaigning for equal pay, Newcastle, NSW, 1962. Notice that on the first placard, under the call for 'straight shifts', one woman has written 'not straight skirts'. (Courtesy of Jeni Thornley)

automation in the breweries.[23] In January 1965 a new federal award was handed down in the arbitration commission, covering employees in south-eastern Queensland, New South Wales, Victoria and Tasmania, reducing to 20 the age at which young women could be employed in bars, reducing the spread of bar attendants' hours to ten, and prohibiting them from scrubbing or washing tables and floors though not from just wiping them down to keep them clean.[24] While the legal drinking age was 21, the age at which women could start work behind the bar was restricted.[25] This was followed three years later, in 1968, by an even more important decision – equal pay. It was 'the greatest overall gain ever' the Tasmanian branch of the Liquor Trades Union claimed.[26]

Extension of pub trading hours impacted on both customers and workers. Bar attendants' working conditions had been developed in relation to the restricted hours of opening set by the licensing laws. Now that these were extended, extra shifts were needed, overtime payments were inadequate and the union wanted a new award with a five- rather than six-day week, and straight shifts. An air of militancy prevailed. 'Brisbane hotel bar attendants are to become better organised and more union conscious in future', the *Courier-Mail* reported on 18 February 1967. It was estimated there were about 1000 bar attendants in Brisbane city and about 1400 in the south-eastern division of Queensland. There had been a stop-work meeting the day before of about 200 bar attendants, 90 per cent of them women, demanding increased margins to bring their pay into line with men's, straight shifts of eight-and-a-half-hours instead of ten, shift allowances, and increased rates, pro-rata sick pay and holiday pay for casuals. They condemned as 'paltry' the offers received from the employers and decided to hold at least two special meetings a year to discuss grievances.[27] However, the employers, the Australian Hotels Association, at first refused to negotiate. In July a four-state hotel strike was called, covering 40 000 workers. Barmaids pressed their claim for equal pay: 'We have to clean up behind the bars, mop up, arrange bottles – and these are things barmen won't do. Why should we get less?'[28] Industrial disputation continued for over eighteen months before the union could finally claim victory. By January 1968 a new award gave hotel-workers a five-day, forty-hour week, and new penalty rates for working after 7.00 p.m.[29] The 1968 Hotel Award also brought in equal pay for barmaids, although not for other, back-of-house, staff. It brought general wage increases for lower paid female employees back of house and, in achieving equal pay for bar attendants, pointed the way, said the union's journal, to their 'determined goal of equal pay for all'. That, however, had still to be fought through the tribunals in different states.[30]

Equal pay had been a long time coming. Victorian barmaids had won it in 1949, Western Australian barmaids back in 1911. Now it was time for the rest of the country to catch up. It was not until 1969 that the federal arbitration commission finally granted all other Australian women workers equal pay for equal work although too few did the same work as men to take advantage of it. Barmaids could, and they had.

The 1968 federal award also reduced the minimum age at which barmaids could be employed in Victoria from 25 to 21, in other states to 19, and allowed one under-21 year old for every three adults employed.[31] This, with the return to 10.00 p.m. closing, also led to the employment of more casual staff. Indicative of this were changes in the union membership. In 1963, when Victorian pubs still closed at 6.00 p.m., the Victorian branch of the Liquor Trades Union was mainly a manufacturing-based union of some 3000 members. Twelve years later the branch numbered 8000 members of whom a majority were in service occupations, and by the 1980s the membership was largely casual and female.[32] The coming of equal pay thus brought contradictory outcomes.

Equal pay meant equal terminology ('bar attendant'), equal duties, equal hours. A 'bar attendant' was again defined as 'any person usually employed for more than two hours in any one day or night in supplying or dispensing or mixing liquor in any portion of the licensed premises including sale of liquor from the bottle department'. It did not just mean

Figure 8.2 The Tasmanian branch of the Liquor Trades Union takes pride in the earlier achievement of equal pay, with a front cover photo of staff at the Brisbane Hotel, Hobart, celebrating equal pay for barmaids, January 1968. (Courtesy of the Tasmanian Branch, Australian Liquor, Hospitality and Miscellaneous Workers Union)

serving behind the bar, or serving draught beer, or mixing cocktails, but clearly anything to do with the retail sale of alcoholic beverages, whether bottled or not. This differed from the United States' definition where 'barmaid' was a term sometimes used to describe a woman who served liquor, at other times a woman who mixed liquor (a mixologist).[33] 'Barmaids' no longer had differentiated tasks or value – or did they?

Defining the skills

'Barmaids' could never be fully equal to 'barmen' while sexual difference was built into the categorisation of the worker. The campaigns and laws passed against barmaids at the turn of the century had established barmaids as a 'different' category of worker. This knowledge was still part of the public's perception although it re-emerged at different times. The pressure on women to perform their sexual difference from men was very great and never far below the surface. Yet at the same time customers really expected efficient service and properly pulled beer. There were at times conflicts between these demands that created intolerable pressures on the women behind the bar. Always they were in front of a public, subjected to scrutiny, as Caddie reiterated several times, 'with every eye on me'.

'Spend a few hours behind a bar and you'll find, strangely enough, that it's the continual smiling at customers that takes its toll more than anything else', journalist Sally Lindsay reported in the Brisbane *Telegraph* in 1967. Having tried the work herself, she came away, she said, 'impressed at their stamina and speedy service. Most customers ... were appreciative of their skill, too.' While they made claims about wanting barmaids to look at, or flirt with, most customers conversed with each other, groups kept pretty much to themselves and it was only when they were drunk that barmaids got to hear all the customers' marital and work problems. 'There are plenty of regulars who drink right through the 6 o'clock swill without even seeing the barmaid' the *Bulletin* had once claimed. 'Not many have long conversations with us because we're so busy with the large numbers of people, but occasionally we have a chat', one barmaid reported. The bar workers themselves liked the work as a way of meeting people, some were prepared to go out with customers, others preferred serving older men, but all were aware of it as hard work. 'We're on our feet on a cement floor', and they were constantly on the go.[34] On another occasion the *Telegraph* interviewed several bar workers, both male and female, about their work and why they did it. Virtually all revealed they liked meeting people, one (male) pointed out the opportunities to work up to running your own hotel, one (female) said the pay was good, and several spoke of the chance to do something different from their usual occupation of nursing or office work.[35]

In the mid-1970s the Liquor Trades Union reported women in tourism occupations were paid more than women in manufacturing. The opposite was true for men.[36] Bar work was undoubtedly a service occupation, and therefore people-oriented. Interpersonal skills were required. Bar attendants were expected to remember patrons who came to the bar regularly and have their drink ready without even being asked for it. 'As soon as he comes in I just get him a Bundaberg rum and a beer chaser', one barmaid said of one of her regulars. 'He's been having that every day as long as he can remember' (and he had been going to that bar for twenty years).[37] Another defined 'a good barmaid' as 'somebody who, if you're a regular drinker, knows what you want without asking', is able to 'read' customers, 'knowing when to talk to them and when not to', being able tactfully to deal with disorderly drunks or disagreeable customers who don't want to pay for their drinks, and can prevent conflict before it gets out of hand.[38] Regulars would go to one pub because of a particular staff member and would follow a bar attendant from one place of work to another if need be. A special relationship of service could be developed and nurtured by an especially skilful bar worker and the sex dynamic of this was not unimportant. Many women working behind the bar preferred to serve men, and many men customers preferred to be served by women. There were also men who refused to have women anywhere near a bar, even serving. They insisted on all-male spaces, with male bar attendants. The Royal George Hotel in Fortitude Valley, Brisbane, was one such hotel. The proprietor acknowledged he therefore had a higher wages bill but this was more than offset by the extra trade his all-male serving staff attracted. There was no suggestion this was a gay bar: only that it was a predominantly industrial area and male bar attendants had been used in the public bar for the 113 years of the hotel's history. The workers, particularly the older men, liked it that way. The head barmen had been there thirty-two years. Women bar attendants served only in the private bars and lounges.[39] Scott's in Melbourne, the longest continually licensed hotel in the city in the 1950s, was similarly 'a masculine haven', had for a hundred years been 'a man's hotel', 'where gentlemen (without ladies) can eat, drink, and talk business ... talk that only a man could really understand'. Scott's not only kept women out of the public bar, it also opened a 'Men Only' cafeteria where only male waiters were employed.[40] Pubs responded to their respective clienteles. That was the only immutable rule. The employment of casual staff interfered with this kind of relationship between clientele and staff.

Trouble in the bar from patrons and between patrons was always a possibility. Shirley Mellor knew she occasionally had to throw a trouble-maker out 'by the seat of his pants', but she could do so because men would never hit a woman. They might take a punch at a barman but not at a barmaid. The other customers would ensure she was safe. 'They were always very protective of the barmaid.' Eileen Dillon, at 23, was Tasmania's youngest licensee when she first got a licence: 'many a strong man who "kicked over the traces" found himself being ejected by an equally strong Eileen' the *Mercury* reported when she'd retired in March 1965. By this means order and control were maintained in the bar. The presence of a woman curbed men's behaviour, not only because she was a mother-figure, but because chivalrous codes of masculinity prescribed the boundaries that men themselves policed.

In a detailed study of bar work and bar workers undertaken in the late 1970s, Sandra Grimes found that 'skilled bar staff exhibit[ed] a range of skills bordering on the diplomatic, for dealing with a variety of difficult behaviour as part of their everyday work'.[41] She explored the differences between male and female workers in the bar, and found that 'bar work entails a complicated and largely undefined range of requirements, not suggested by the largely unskilled routine tasks associated with the work'. 'Elements of discretion, disguise or subtlety' were highly personal in their individual style and manifestation; there was 'a need for a high degree of flexibility ... with reference to customer expectations of sociable involvement', which could change within a short space of time even with the same customer. 'The core characteristics of bar work, regardless of differentiations among bar staff, entail service, sociability and social regulation.'[42]

Sexual difference was obviously important in the manifestation of these subtle, discrete elements of the work, and the performance of sexuality was part and parcel of customer expectation. Dress – 'wearing a snug-fitting black dress to set off her blonde hair'[43] – was not only part of the job, but very much part of the public representation of 'the barmaid'. But it was over-emphasised as knowledge of what a barmaid was. Dress here was again indicative of the public representation across the bar, and the invisible reality behind it. 'Although barmaids do not wear uniforms', as airline stewards and waiters did, they 'all wear scuffs or sneakers below counter level as a matter of course', the reporter in the Brisbane *Telegraph* reported. Out of sight of customer expectations, barmaids' reality as workers was visible only to each other. Similarly, being able to keep the bar clean while customers were resting their glasses on it was no easy task, 'knowing that a seasoned drinker rarely likes anyone moving his glass ... With a swoop of her right hand she literally takes a glass of beer out of the customer's hand, holds it aloft for five seconds, and then wipes the bar vigorously with a cloth with her left hand. That sort of thing takes courage!' the reporter observed, 'But laughing uproariously and sharing jokes Pat made it seem like nothing.'[44]

'Making it seem like nothing' was a very valuable attribute in a workplace that depended on customer satisfaction and pleasure for continuing business. Invisibility and performed sexuality have been characteristics bar work has shared with other service work that women have done. The overriding feature of bar work that was beginning to break down in the 1960s was the exclusively male clientele of public bars and saloon bars. Mixed-drinking venues meant women's expectations as customers were also beginning to shape the workplace environment and the nature and meaning of the work. It was selling to male customers that had distinguished bar work from retail sales in other shops in earlier decades. Like secretarial work, sex-specificity was built into the definition of the worker because of the nature of the workplace: in the office the sex-specific (male) executive generated a sex-specific (female) assistant providing necessary services.[45] In pubs, sex-specific (male) customers seemed to require sex-specific (female) serving staff. However, this was not the case in restaurants or hotel dining-rooms. Clearly other dynamics were operating in the bar workplace.

One important distinguishing feature of bar work, that was not true of restaurant or dining-room service, was the personal relationship customers and bar staff could build up. The ability to relate personally to customers – to remember regulars' preferences, to chat when required, to smile, to share a joke, to keep men's secrets, to quieten down a trouble-maker and restore a peaceful environment, to make customers want to return and make this pub their regular watering-hole – while simultaneously skilfully pouring a beer in the way customers demanded, handling change deftly and honestly, and keeping the bar counter clean, required a high degree of interpersonal skills and work-based competence. Sexuality was a minor but not invisible player. Femininity required artful disguise. So, too, did being a barmaid. The bar counter was a barrier that helped preserve the artifice. Behind the bar, below the counter, barmaids' footwear spoke of the drudgery and sheer physical strain of being on your feet all day, amidst spilt beer and water, at the beck and call of demanding customers who must always be greeted with a smile. After four hours, no wonder 'constant smiling at customers wore a bit thin'.[46] Bar work has always been very labour intensive, not highly paid, and women in most states have not been able to command the same level of wages as male workers. So, while women performed the skills of femininity behind the bar, they also performed the economic and power dynamics of sexual difference: they provided a cheap source of labour that entertained, soothed, encouraged, titillated and perpetuated the identification of the work as women's, and of women as service providers usually to men. Now that, too, was changing.

Women become the customers

The 1950s had seen the beginning of the dismantlement of a pub culture that had been in place for half a century as the licensing laws gradually eroded the spatial arrangements of drinking practices. Between 1957 and 1972 state laws prohibiting Aboriginal people from drinking were also liberalised, although Aboriginal people could, and did, still experience discrimination from individual pub-owners.[47] The 1960s saw the challenges to exclusively male drinking customs coming from a new youthful generation of drinkers who took it for granted that women were also customers, and by the 1970s ideas of sexual differentiation were coming under renewed challenge from a recently revitalised feminist movement for women's liberation. Not surprisingly, the public bar was one of the first sites of feminist insurgency. 'Complicated patterns of repression and guilt coupled with a hedonistic abandonment of social prescriptions' had characterised Australian men's drinking patterns, feminist Anne Summers claimed, which meant they preferred getting drunk 'without the restraining presence' of their wives and girlfriends.[48]

In the 1960s the drinking market in Australia was beginning to change as the postwar baby boomers came of age. By the end of the decade, 'the swinging sixties', youth culture, more enlightened attitudes to the place of alcohol consumption, a demand for wine and more sophisticated concoctions (rum and coke was made popular by the Beatles) all challenged the traditional drinking culture of the pub, which was built around beer. Women demanded to be served as customers.

The first sign of change on the horizon in Queensland came in 1963, when about 200 women wanting to attend an art exhibition in a pub were turned away by the licensee who thought it would be an offence under the Liquor Act for women to enter the private bar where the paintings were hung. The Licensing Commission Chairman pointed out there was no offence in a woman merely being in a bar. 'This aspect had not been considered because it had been felt that if women could not be supplied with liquor there would be no reason to enter the bar.'[49] In 1965 Merle Thornton and Rosalie Bognor, 'two married women ... and each the mother of two children', tested this advice when they walked into the public bar of the Regatta Hotel in suburban Brisbane, and asked to be served a lemonade. Immediately someone called the police. When they were refused the lemonade, the women took out a thick dog-chain and padlocked themselves to the foot-rail. Several men bought beers for them, their husbands distributed pamphlets urging that women be allowed to drink in bars, and the police took their names, pointed out that the Licensing Act clearly stated that women were not allowed in a public bar, then discreetly removed themselves rather than create a scene.[50]

The episode was small, low-key but extremely significant in its timing and purpose, and it got press and television coverage. The demonstration, Rosalie Bognor pointed out to the journalists present, had followed after a deputation of women to the minister concerned had not persuaded him to alter the Licensing Act to allow women into public bars. Earlier that month Queensland had undertaken a major overhaul of its liquor laws, sweeping changes were introduced, mainly to do with the consumption of food and liquor together (e.g. for later hours in hotel dining rooms and on Sundays for restaurants). It deleted the prohibition on the supply of liquor to women in rooms with direct access to bars, but otherwise did not liberalise the drinking restrictions on women in a public space. Thornton and Bognor thus took action themselves. The forty or so men in the bar at the time canvassed by the journalist admired the stand of the women; the licensee, on the other hand, opposed their presence. A week later they tried again. In company with another eight women, dubbed 'Brisbane's "bar-room suffragettes"' by the *Courier-Mail*, they approached three different hotels, where 'men cheered them as they entered; offered to buy them drinks and gossiped with them on a "man-to-man" basis over a glass of beer'. A male bar attendant at one pub refused to speak to them or any of the reporters in the party, but the police refused to come in response to calls that male sympathisers were buying the women beer; 'And nobody tried to stop them' the article was headlined. One customer in the public bar when the women entered was reported as saying he was 'all for it. They can do it in New South Wales – why can't they do it here?' Consequently, Merle Thornton claimed, it had been 'a great victory for women's rights'.[51]

Four years later, Marjorie Stapleton, 'equipped with a cold bottle of beer and the courage of my convictions', strode into another Brisbane hotel (this time to the saloon bar) and 'demanded the services that until then had been the unique prerogative of the men of Queensland!' Stapleton was exploiting a loophole in the law that effectively enabled women to be in the bar provided they brought in their own unopened bottle. The publican cheerily opened it for her, 'seven terrified men put down their beers and disappeared into the middle distance', but the licensee quickly warmed to the idea, 'there should be more of it', he said, 'I like it', and soon Stapleton was drinking with about twenty men, 'all of whom agreed that women would be welcome in saloon bars so long as there was one bar kept for men only'.[52]

The law made it quite plain, the newspaper report pointed out, that women were not barred from public and saloon bars; nor were they barred from drinking there; it was, however, illegal for someone to supply them with liquor, whether that be the hotel staff or any of the other bar patrons. By this time the discussion had shifted to one of equality between the sexes. 'In drinking equality of the sexes is a joke', a headline in the Brisbane *Sunday Truth* had proclaimed the month before Marjorie Stapleton took her stand. Because women were only permitted to drink in Ladies Lounges they had to pay extra for their drinks, even though 'simply because they are women most of them are on smaller wages than men'; men not only got their drinks cheaper but the conditions of the

Figure 8.3 A rare photograph of Aboriginal and white, men and women, drinking together, Broome, Western Australia, 1953. (Battye Library, 816B/TB679)

Saloon Bars where they drank were far superior. 'Equality is a joke' reporter Terry Ryan wrote. 'Who can justify a situation where women who sit on peeling rickety chairs and use tins for ashtrays pay more than men who sit on plush stools with carpet under their feet?' the article said. The situation could be rectified either by pubs lowering lounge prices or by the government changing existing laws and allowing women to drink in saloon and private bars alongside men, but equality 'always will be [a joke] while discrimination like this exists'.[53] A week later the new Lennons Hotel opened its new saloon bar, the Stockyard Bar, to women and served them drinks at the same price as the men. The barriers were coming down. 'We are now on our way to equality', reporter Lesley Johnson concluded.[54] Aboriginal women were similarly pushing against discrimination. In a small country town in Victoria, with a reporter and photographer from the major metropolitan daily in tow, two Aboriginal women charged the licensees of the local hotels with race prejudice as they went from pub to pub seeking service, only to be turned away without explanation.[55]

Obviously, drinking in pubs alongside (white) men was a highly symbolic act and women's demands to be treated equally as customers a major challenge to the culture. Being refused service in a public bar may seem 'a small thing perhaps to the uninitiated woman, but to your frenetic feminist, a barb in the delicate buttock', a Sydney woman said. A protest in several Manly beachfront pubs, that involved chanting, banging on the bar, 'seventeen or so women seated on the floor, demanding a drink, refusing to be moved', led to the arrest of four of them and some quite heated interjections from the pub's male patrons 'roused as much by our gender as our din'.[56] Although it was being led by women themselves, it is also clear that there was support from men for whom, for whatever reason, older drinking customs had no appeal. At the same time Australian pubs were being celebrated and mythologised by other men, in popular culture and academic studies alike.[57] In 1966 journalist Craig McGregor celebrated drinking as a 'determinedly egalitarian activity, the great social leveller' that allowed Australian men 'to indulge in the mateship ritual which has been one of the persistent motifs in Australian History'. And J. M. Freeland wrote his now very well-known history of the Australian pub, in which he mythologised it as 'linoleum counter-tops patterned with beer-rings ... cold tiles, chrome, glass, buxom genial barmaids, groups of singing bawling customers ... football arguments ... smoke ... roll-neck sweaters, dirty dungarees, and hacking jackets ... voluptuously-shaped bottles ... jostling shoulders ... battalions of up-ended glasses'.[58]

Ockers and the creation of national myths

'Buxom genial barmaids' had a central place in this mythologising. By the 1970s a resurgence of Australian nationalism called ockerism, which celebrated drinking and a boorish masculinity, had taken up 'the barmaid' and sexuality was once more her principal characteristic. 'The Australian barmaid is one of the chiefest ornaments of our society', two such ockers, John Hindle and John Hepworth, declared. In an attempt at humour, they defined 'the barmaid' as 'Boozers' laborer. Wise counsellor. A cheerful voice in time of trouble. Minister of first aid and comfort. Tolerant but firm chider of the faller by the wayside. A licensed premises wife. Ministering angel. Pal.' They went on to say that 'any good barmaid is in fact a sort of wife to a great number of men'.[59] Although ockerism contained elements of self-mockery, this description was dangerously close to the definition of a common prostitute as a woman who had sexual intercourse with many men. Hindle and Hepworth carried the analogy further: 'generally the relationship is platonic ... nonetheless it is a deep and intimate relationship, perhaps made stronger by the fact that it is reserved for the special and comforting environment of the pub itself'. They then described how 'the barmaid' met their needs. 'It is easy to see why the barmaid really becomes No. 1 wife' for it was 'much more amiable' after a particularly heavy drinking bout 'to be greeted by a sonsy bird ... than to confront the cold bum and burnt toast of the nuptial bed and table ... The polyandry of the pubs is one of the closest-knit human relationships you will find in modern society ... a relationship likely to last a lifetime.'

Ignoring the skills barmaids had as workers, which had been pointed out by women journalists, publicans, unionists and barmaids themselves for over a century, Hindle and Hepworth concentrated on one identifiable feature. The one 'outstanding physical attribute of the barmaid ... is (without in any way being sexist)', they hurriedly added, 'that she has what can only be called, not to put too fine a point on it, tits.' In an extraordinary leap in this fantasy they claimed, 'these seem to go along with the environment and the avocation. If they haven't got them when they start, they grow into them ... It is in the nature of the barmaid species to lean *forward* over the bar when bending a sympathetic ear. This calls for a generous bosom. And since it calls for a generous bosom ... if they haven't got it – they grow it!' They concluded 'Nature is indeed wonderful.' And then in a very odd shift to a militaristic metaphor, they claimed that if ever Melbourne was invaded and occupied by enemy forces, 'it would be to the barmaids of Melbourne we would look'. Similar to the Parisian bar girls who maintained the honour of Paris during the German occupation, 'our splendid Melbourne bar girls could be relied upon to guard our honour likewise'.

Hindle and Hepworth's 'In Praise of Splendid Gels behind the Bar' was part of a book on pub culture that was the last of a spate of such publications beginning in the mid-1960s but really reaching their peak in the 1970s. Their characterisation of barmaids as wives with proper bosoms, 'the generous warmth of their bodies' instead of cold reproving bums, was consistent with J. M. Freeland's 'buxom, genial barmaids' and other representations of this period.[60]

Publications mythologising drinking practices, 'boozing out', 'pub crawls' and what we generally associate with ockerism in Australia, dominated the study of pubs and pub culture in the decades after 1960, and is indicative of a national preoccupation with pubs that was not in fact confined to celebrating ockerism. Some studies were more academic in their approach but still they were subjecting pubs to a scrutiny that was new at that time and which subsequently disappeared from view. Even though they might well have been parodying ockerism, such a cluster of publications reveals a degree of anxiety in the culture about the signifi-cant social changes that were occurring and raises questions about the time and circumstances that gave rise to them. Australian pubs were under serious challenge in the 1960s from competitors for the hospitality and tourist trade – the new motels – and from competitors for the entertainment trade – the licensed clubs, which had extended drinking hours and the attraction of poker machines. In the 1950s eating out in Australia meant eating in hotel dining rooms. In the 1970s licensed restaurants were replacing hotel dining rooms and grocery stores were attracting custom away from hotel bottle shops. Pubs reliant on a traditional clientele were therefore forced into a degree of self-examination and the adoption of new measures in order to be competitive.

By the end of the 1970s, as the Australian Hotels Association pointed out to the New South Wales parliamentary inquiry on liquor trading, 'more and more younger women who drink are preferring to do so in hotels' because of 'the influences of equal pay for women and a more liberal attitude by male drinkers to women in bars. Indeed the modern, multi-services hotel has increasing appeal for young marrieds to accompany their husbands to hotels, providing opportunity for relaxation together and strengthening their family bonds.'[61] In keeping with the new demands for higher standards and altered drinking practices to bring Australia into line with other parts of the Western world (the United States hotel industry had undergone dramatic transformation before 1920), pubs, their services and service providers, therefore came under public scrutiny. Many of the pubs were owned by breweries which undertook major design renovations.

But the traditional clientele of public bars reacted to the changes with outpourings of nostalgia for a lost masculinity, a lost masculine space where the presence of 'the barmaid', in an absence of other women, had helped define their masculinity. Hepworth and Hindle and their middle-class peers were doing more than exploring pub culture. They were actually creating a public knowledge about pubs and the role of women within them that not only bore little relationship to the actuality of pub work from the point of view of the women serving, but was also an attempt to create and celebrate a national culture out of men's desires. 'The wife', the 'pal', with the ample bosom, warm body and sympathetic ear, whose presence in the pub was what made pubs worth visiting, as a warm and safe environment away from home, was disappearing under challenges from economic competitors for the trade, and from women demanding (and achieving) equal pay as workers in pubs and access as customers to the same space that male customers had historically occupied.

The pub was thus being celebrated as a site of masculine pleasure in Australia, with no attention paid to women's drinking customs. 'There has never been any correlation between Australian women's frequenting of hotels and their willingness to drink', Anne Summers pointed out. Statistics on women's alcohol consumption showed that Australian women were much more likely to drink than their American counterparts and the rate of alcoholism among women was rising.[62] Segregated drinking cultures, however, also rendered this invisible. Woman was central to the mythology of the pub but not as drinking companion. Along with the 'voluptuously-shaped bottles' went the presence of 'The Barmaid', as provider of service, commodified and sexualised, 'buxom' and 'genial'. In this way 'the barmaid' was woven into the nation's culture, but not as worker, desiring subject or agent of her own history. Women's presence in this celebration of pub culture was invisible except as objects of desire to this masculine gaze.

A 'disreputable occupation'?

Thus the 1970s feminists attacked segregated drinking customs and unequal wage rates. They drew attention to pub culture and, in Anne Summers' words, the 'disreputable occupation' of barmaid.[63] Sexual harassment – the issue of how women working behind the bar were frequently subjected to sexual innuendo and lewd conduct – became the subject of scrutiny in the 1980s.[64] While the concern was reminiscent of the old WCTU concerns about why bars were unsuitable places for

Figure 8.4 Women drinking at the Kings Head Tavern, Kings Head Bar, Elizabeth Street, Sydney, *c.* 1970s. (Tooth & Co. Ltd, Dep. no. Z223/159 (K), Neg. no. 5359, NBAC/ANU)

women, the focus in the late twentieth century was on men's improper behaviour. Sandra Grimes argued that the sexual code of harassment inflicted on barmaids may be a means of communicating that women bar workers are 'sexually loose' in order to free up men's behaviour; it 'enables customers to engage in rapid transformations of behaviour from, for example, abuse to flattery, while simultaneously maintaining a service relationship. In other words, whatever customers may do when they are drunk, it will not matter' because the usual 'civilising' restraints that good women impose are absent. 'The process of sexual objectification is the mechanism which permits these transformations. Once objectified, persons acquire a kind of social invisibility, they must remain in the background, not to be listened to, addressed or taken into account.' Thus barmaids are kept in their place and men are freed to perform their uninhibited masculinity in the undisturbed circle of other men.[65]

Once women gained access to the public bar as customers, and had equal pay as workers, the boundaries of sexual difference in pubs had to be re-negotiated. The terminology 'barmaids' disappeared from the language of industrial awards, to be replaced with the gender-neutral terminology of 'bar attendant'. Except in Victoria where a minimum age of employment still applied to women employees, there was no sex distinction on wages and conditions. But hotels were feeling the pinch of the reduction in trade. In 1963 some Sydney and Brisbane barmaids were required to wear tight-fitting hipster slacks or matador pants; by the end of the 1970s pubs were seeking the services of 'topless barmaids' and 'exotic bar girls'. Negotiating the sexuality of the workplace took on new meaning for women working behind the bar.

Melbourne journalist Kate Nancarrow encountered the pressures being imposed on bar staff and later wrote of her personal experience of the 'topless barmaid' phenomenon. As a 19-year-old newly accredited bar attendant she had, years earlier, arrived in the north Queensland city of Townsville to work in the public bar with two other women. 'I like to think we offered something akin to a European *salon*', she said wryly, 'offering stimulating conversation to the patrons who treated the bar as a second home.' Her perception was at odds with the customers' view: 'It's possible,' she said, 'they just wanted beer.' There were two other barmaids, one who was nearly 50 and had worked at the pub a long time. Like Shirley Mellor's first work colleague, who hadn't liked 'flighty barmaids', Kate Nancarrow's also 'didn't tolerate young flibbertigibbet barmaids. It was a job and a job to be done well.' They worked hard, on their feet 'for hours on end surrounded by a sea of drinkers desperate for a refill and all prone to punch-ups when they'd had too much'. The owners, too, had their expectations: 'the unspoken pressure on the barmaids to keep cheerful and smiling to drag in the customers was enormous'. It then, however, 'got significantly worse' when the competing pub, the swishest pub in Townsville, went topless. 'The owners of our pub responded ... by asking [us] to wear bathers in the bar. Nothing as tasteless as a string bikini, they said, just a one-piece swimsuit with plunging neckline. No-one batted an eyelid at [the older woman's] exclusion from this opportunity to earn an extra 10 cents an hour.' The younger women hesitated, the owners 'upped the offer' if they'd go topless, and still the older woman wasn't included and the younger women hesitated.

Nancarrow felt the pressure, she said, because she was in the running for The Barmaid of the Year competition where contestants were given votes by their customers. 'I was busily showing off my dexterity at the beer taps, my creativity in arranging the $1 bar meals and my style with the bar towels', she said, and the votes were beginning to come in. She agonised about whether she'd get more votes topless, and whether she could live with herself 'in a future life that I suspected wouldn't always be lived in a sea of beer swill'. It was getting hard to be cheerful with the mounting pressure and she feared that being grumpy and tired would lose her votes. In the end, both younger women said no, and Nancarrow still won the competition, 'beating a bare-breasted rival' and contributing some funds to a local charity. It wasn't a big deal, 'but it was a title and it was mine' she said with some pride. Nevertheless, the consequences were scarring, she recalled, and she resigned her job and returned to Melbourne.[66]

Nancarrow's story was told in the 1990s in response to the material success of supermodel Elle Macpherson who 'kept appearing more and more with less and less on', and at a time when not only topless barmaids but nude table-top dancers were increasingly popular in city pubs at lunchtimes. Once again women workers behind the bar were performing and negotiating the boundaries of commercialised sex under the unrelenting powerful male gaze. But Nancarrow's story – told with a wry sense of bathos – is also a story of triumph. Her skill in serving competently and efficiently ('carrying four beers in one hand') under the tutelage of the older experienced barmaid, according to her definition of the requirements of the work, were what was ultimately sought, and appreciated, by her customers.

Work behind the bar has always contained that paradoxical mix of the real and the imagined. Like the theatre, the pub is a place of fantasy and allure where customers go to relax, enjoy and escape. Fantasising 'the barmaid' has been part of that culture of enjoyment that has mystified and obscured the skills demanded of the workers while simultaneously rendering their workplace a space for sexualised encounters they have had both to repel and attract. Yet 'the barman' has not been fantasised in the same way. Women's negotiation of the public spaces where men congregate in convivial enjoyment and contest with other men[67] is part of what defines femininity. All service industry workplaces and occupations carry within them the potential for sexual allure.[68] Service is by definition eroticising. The sexualised fantasy of 'the barmaid' has been a particularly enduring one, perhaps one even sometimes shared by the women workers as it has masked the actuality of their daily grind behind the bar.

The industry transformed

The three decades between 1960 and 1990 saw major changes in the nature of the hotel industry in Australia. Old landmarks like Scott's were demolished and replaced by big new international standard hotels in the central business districts of major cities as multi-national corporations moved in. There was also an expansion in the labour market. In all there were now between 110 000 and 130 000 employees in the hotel industry throughout Australia, the majority in New South Wales (34 000) followed by Queensland (24 000) and Victoria (22 000). Yet a large proportion of the jobs were casual, seasonal or part-time, and a disproportionate number of senior management positions were the preserve of full-time male staff. Sixty per cent of the workforce were women and only 57 per cent of it was full-time (two-thirds of whom were male).[69] In 1953 the licensee of the Carlton Club Hotel in Hobart had said he would prefer to pay overtime to his permanent staff rather than employ casual staff, 'because they take a greater interest in the work'. And the branch president of the union had said there was not enough money in casual work to enable a person to live on it.[70] Similarly in the United States in the 1970s, the proportion of women working behind the bar had increased dramatically. Historically kept out of the work by the union, in 1940 women held only 2.5 per cent of bartending jobs in the United States, by 1970 they held 21 per cent, by 1980 44 per cent, and by the end of that decade were nearly half of all bartenders.[71] Expansion of the industry had increased women's participation in it but employer demands for flexibility and cheap labour meant casualisation of the workforce, and a declining industry made women more vulnerable and more susceptible to employer demands to exploit their sexuality.[72]

In Australia in the 1980s the trend towards increasing female employment and casualisation of the labour force behind the bar continued even more dramatically than it had in the 1970s: there were 30 000 members of the Victorian branch of the Liquor Trades Union, the overwhelming majority of whom were service members, many of them casual and female.[73] In 1987 there were 26 756 bar staff employed in 'accommodation establishments' throughout Australia; of the total full-time bar staff, 3688 were men, and 2841 were women. There were almost equal numbers of bar attendants (2058 men:2258 women) but many more men were Head Bar Attendant (898) than women (239). The figures for part-time/casual staff were 7241 men, compared with 13 000 women. Mobility in the industry was high. In the majority of establishments employees stayed between six months and two years, and about a quarter stayed between two and five years.[74] Not surprisingly it was among the least unionised of all Australian industries, something the Tasmanian branch of the union had been aware of in 1962.[75] At that time a deputation of both hoteliers and union leaders had called on the state Premier to complain about licensed clubs using voluntary labour and destabilising the hotel industry, and the union had embarked on a concerted campaign, 'an all-out drive', to unionise all hotel workers in Tasmania. Now the 1980s brought deregulation and further competition.[76]

Brewery workers no longer dominated. A survey of their membership undertaken by the Liquor Trades Union (1983) demonstrated that the workforce was overwhelmingly female (women comprised 60 per cent of hotel workers and 80 per cent of motel workers), casual (61 per cent of hotel staff, 44 per cent of motel staff) and younger than the workforce in general. They were therefore more likely to be single and to have a higher level of education. Casual part-time workers on average worked only fourteen hours a week. Only 43 per cent worked more than thirty hours per week. The union was concerned not only that a high proportion of this casual staff worked only a few hours a week, hardly enough to earn a sufficient income and thereby compelling workers to hold down multiple jobs, but also that the vulnerability of the industry meant even those jobs were at risk. Bar attendants and waiters were the most numerous occupational category, 72 and 77 per cent of them, respectively, were employed on a casual basis.[77]

Big multi-national hotel chains were not always pro-union, but hotels in Australia were still mainly small businesses. In South Australia in 1990, 72 per cent of hotels employed fewer than twenty people. It was in these small workplaces, that were difficult to organise, that women were concentrated.[78] This made regulating conditions in the industry, and ensuring award conditions were adhered to, difficult. The 1990s promised change. A new federal award in 1990 – 'the first time we have got away from unskilled rates of pay' – augured well; tips were no longer an important component of the pay packet, and employers were realising that transient staff cost them more.[79] But it was the bosses who had changed most. Now they were managers with tertiary credentials, in the city pubs if not in the suburbs and country areas. In 1992 women licensees and managers in the Australian Hotels Association began to organise among themselves to increase women's profile in the industry.

Coincidentally perhaps the hotel industry at that time was held to be on the verge of collapse, even in its 'death throes'. The reduction in the number of hotels that had occurred during the previous thirty years was now fully evident. 'The history of the industry in Victoria begins with harsh regulation and concludes with sweeping deregulation', John Pasquarelli wrote in the Melbourne *Herald-Sun* in February 1992. Identifying himself as a 'small businessman and former country Victorian publican' it was, he said, 'sadly, the passing of a very real part of Australian culture'. A combination of factors was responsible. Deregulation of the industry had increased competition – there were 3500 new licences in Victoria going mainly to bar/cafes and restaurants – while labour costs, licence fees and sales taxes for hoteliers had increased. Added to these were a downturn in the economy and a rise in the price of the beer: 'it is no wonder that for the first time a significant number of publicans are going bankrupt, lessees are walking away from their landlords, and many hotels are closing, never to open again'. What had begun at the turn of the century as a short-term compensation fund for publicans being deprived of their licences under the Licences Reduction Board, had become, by the 1990s, 'a crushing and iniquitous tax'. Publicans, he said, in trying to compete against licensed restaurants which had low capital investment, or supermarket chains operating also as liquor outlets, were 'playing uphill and kicking against the wind'. It was easy to identify an establishment that was going down, he said. 'The first symptom was a large sign indicating "as much pasta as you can eat – $4". When "topless barmaids" and "lingerie ladies" are advertised, the death throes are beginning!' The implications for the thousands of staff within the industry were devastating, Pasquarelli said: 'The traditional hands-on publican is being replaced by managers with tertiary qualifications.' Even worse, 'that great hotel heroine, the barmaid, is almost extinct'.

The change in bar staff was a barometer of the enormous social transformation that had occurred in Australian life. 'Once hubs of Sydney life, pubs are now old-fashioned – and empty', Wanda Jamrozik reported in the *Sydney Morning Herald* on Australia Day 1993. Hotel takings were down 20 per cent over the previous two years as changes in drinking patterns took effect. Over 70 per cent of alcohol consumption occurred off the premises, usually at home, only 14 per cent occurred in pubs and another 14 per cent in clubs. 'It's all a far cry from the old days when pubs, and the drinks they sold, were at the heart of Australian social culture.' A new temperance movement was having its impact, but this time it was real, and it was not imposed on an unwilling populace.

Pubs had always been associated with transport. In the early nineteenth century they were built along coach routes. As railways extended into the country districts and throughout the suburbs, pubs were built at the terminus and next to the stations.[80] The automobile changed all that. Motels replaced hotels on country routes, and walking neighbourhoods gave way to dormitory suburbs where residents drove to work each day and to the football, the beach and the pub on weekends. The introduction of breathalysers, random compulsory breath testing and drink driving laws that imposed heavy penalties on offenders, especially young drivers, reduced the amount of alcohol being consumed and changed the places where people chose to drink. The introduction of television and home entertainment systems, and changes in marketing packaged beer, reinforced the trend. One publican openly lamented the changed attitudes to drinking. 'The Drug Offensive has just spent $150 million telling people not to drink', he said. 'People used to drink six beers in an hour. They don't do that any more. I mean, you can't go round advising people to drink more but, fair go ... '[81]

In 1968 the ratio of hotels to population had altered dramatically from the nineteenth century. It was highest for Tasmania at 1:1442 persons, Queensland was 1:1586, South Australia 1:1888, and New South Wales and Victoria had one hotel for every 2000+ persons.[82] If clubs and other licensed premises were included the reduction in numbers would not look so great, the ratio of licences to population was 1:848 in Western Australia and down to 1:959 in Queensland. But the trend was unmistakeable. Australians were, as Tony Dingle pointed out, drinking less over time.[83] As alcohol consumption went down, the public bar declined and customers turned from draught beer to packaged beer readily available in supermarket outlets. Hotels had to expand their food, accommodation and entertainment operations to compete.[84] Once again, as had been the case in the mid-nineteenth century, men women and children were encouraged to patronise them. Suburban pubs even began to build playrooms for children and cater for their birthday parties.

Pubs responded to the changed drinking culture by 'reinventing themselves as sophisticated entertainment centres'. Far from 'the pub', a local where a regular clientele came each evening, these new locales were meeting places that attracted people from all over the metropolitan area. And they were dividing up into different bars with different ambiences for different clienteles within the one establishment: a downstairs open-plan bar for trendy young things, an upstairs restaurant and bar serving more conservative clients, a bar with a pool table in one corner for the chaps. 'The clientele can mix it with the card machines in the front bar, sample the live music in the second bar or sit out back near the barbecue.' Anyone who knew something of nineteenth-century pubs with their little parlour bars for discreet customers, their upstairs private bars, their differentiated clienteles, before the licensing laws turned them into ground-floor, drinking-only establishments, could only have been struck by the irony of this return to pubs as sources of community entertainment.

Licensee Doris Bishop reminisced nostalgically about the time 'when pubs were as much a part of ordinary, everyday life as the post office'. She had been in the business since the mid-1960s and remembered vividly the stark sexual differentiation in the spatial arrangement of drinking. 'We were one of the first hotels to let women go into the public bar', she said. Before that 'We had what we called the sow pen ... a specially walled-off room, more like a cubicle, from where the local women were served by the barmaid through a special hatch.' While women were prevented from entering the public bar, 'Men weren't allowed to go in there.' Women would come in there in the afternoons, 'their hair up in curlers and they would sit in there and have a beer and shell the peas ... Then they'd go home to get the husband's tea ready for when he came home.'[85]

By the 1990s the sense of loss over this pub culture was so great that some patrons even lamented the loss of early closing 'when pub hours were restricted, not to be wasted. Drinking and conversation were both serious and convivial pursuits.' Out of such social intercourse apocryphal tales had been born. Now all eyes were 'fixed moronically on television sets broadcasting race meetings' or were 'twitching with the idiot burbles of poker machines ... the espresso machine, the caterwaul of a video screen or karaoke machine'. Now to get your glass refilled you had to fight for the attention of the bar staff when once no more than an inclination of the head or a wistful gaze would have been needed, 'to press harder would have been an insult to their prideful professionalism'.[86] Indeed, it was a rule for the bar attendant: even while engaging in conversation with a customer at one end of the bar, be always and immediately alert to the needs of those others at the bar. Older women had often been preferred as staff precisely because they were less likely to be distracted from their tasks by individual customers.[87] Older male customers now regretted that loss of privilege their status as customers had enshrined.

Lamenting the loss of the barmaid

'Today, real barmaids are few and far between', Sydney journalist Philip Cornford lamented in 1994. 'Once there was a trinity born in the souls of men – cool bar room, cold beer and a barmaid with great hands and generosity.' In the 1990s 'bar persons' were usually part-time workers and most of them seemed to be male. Cornford attributed this to letting women into the public bars, which he claimed made the barmaids jealous, 'their special preserve had been intruded on; this was a rape of the space where they ruled supreme by their own sex'. Consequently they had voted with their feet, and were 'a sad and irreplaceable loss'.

Cornford's story, with its sexualised language of 'rape' and 'great hands', conveniently blamed barmaids themselves and their women customers, as he attributed the loss of pubs from the city to the loss of 'the pub' as masculine space and its changed purpose as entertainment centre with televisions, video machines and canned music. In doing so he also perpetuated the mythologising of Australian pubs and their barmaids that had begun with Paul McGuire's study of innkeepers in 1952. Barmaids, said Cornford, 'they were the fair dinkum pub legends. You put your money on the bar and they ran the shouts, and you never questioned their judgement as to whose turn it was. Nora, Faye, Junie, may their names live forever.' In a feature article called 'The Pub with *NO* Barmaid' – parodying the old Australian ballad, 'The Pub with No Beer' – the *Australian Magazine* in July 1995 claimed 'their celebrated role in society is fading like a sepia photograph'. The nostalgia, however, was nearly all from the side of the (older male) customers and employers.

Stories – of beautiful barmaids, sharing jokes, returning sexual banter, slipping bank notes down the cleavages of their ample bosoms and letting the customers retrieve it – were part and parcel of the pub culture. Their telling seemed imperative in the construction of memories of a bygone era. Not everyone shared the mourning, the *Australian Magazine* pointed out. Female bar attendants of the 1990s were better educated, expected equality behind the bar, and thought the old-style barmaids 'simply made the best of a bad lot; tolerating segregated bars, sexist attitudes and unequal pay because they had few alternatives'. The respect they had experienced and valued so highly was bought at a high price for whatever else they had to tolerate. 'Ask [today's] bar attendants about bad behaviour and the horror stories flow as easily as beer from a new keg', journalist Richard Jinman said. Bar attendants now knew their rights, did their jobs, and left the social work aspects of bartending to the experts. Many of them were on their way to other occupations. They were multi-skilled 'flexible hotel careerists' and their dress – vests, ties, white shirts – reflected their new equality and careerism. 'It's a much happier atmosphere now,' barmaid Helen Kopcewicz said when she retired after twenty years working at Young and Jackson's hotel in Melbourne.[88]

Barmaids had always needed 'people skills'. Young professionally trained bar attendants in the 1990s had credentials in management, accounting, public relations and labour relations. They were multi-skilled employees developing careers in hotel work for which serving behind the bar was a stepping-stone, or just one of the several skills needed, for the industry. Knowing people, responding to individual customers and their needs, was still the primary skill. Bar staff had to develop defences against bar-pests, personas to protect themselves, and to know what the rules were among their particular clientele. And they had to provide service that was attentive not intrusive. The days when customers were four and five deep at the counter had gone but the 'economic value of old-style service and a bit of panache' had not.[89] Credentials, skills, awards and career paths spoke volumes about professionalism: challenging the old dividing line between 'respectable' and 'unrespectable' is now left to 'the skimpys' who serve or dance topless. Though their work is much more explicitly sexual, it too is still work, a performance provided for the sexual excitement of the customers.[90]

In the mid-1970s the film of *Caddie*, the single mother who had worked as a barmaid to support her children during the 1930s Depression, opened in Sydney at a charity preview. The *Herald* sought out Caddie's daughter who had been 'the pretty little girl who nearly died of diphtheria, and who didn't cry like her brother when Caddie had to leave them at a children's home'. She was now a grandmother herself, and 'like Caddie ... shrinks from publicity'. The daughter maintained the mother's story: 'I used to peer through the crack in the frosted glass at all the men

Figure 8.5 Dressed professionally: 1990s hotelier Jan Potter, Cricket Club Hotel, South Melbourne, 1993. (Jan Potter, 931009/2, photo courtesy of The Herald and Weekly Times)

drinking in the bar ... Mum was terrific, and you could always trust her, and know that at least there was one person you could depend on.'[91] Caddie's de facto husband remembered a different story. 'The legend of Caddie is a myth' he declared; she was 'a born liar, unfaithful and at times wicked'. She had been 14 stone (89 kg), 'a big woman who would never have been attractive ... an affectionate woman but not a very good woman'. 'Caddie, the Sydney barmaid', was both a good mother and a wicked, untrustworthy woman. In the language of the 1890s, perhaps, in hitching up her skirt that extra inch, she was also a 'sexual lure'.

Although the mythologising of the barmaid is open to reinterpretation, 'the Pub' still holds its untroubled place in Australian legend. 'There is no such thing as *the* Australian pub', Douglass Baglin and Yvonne Austin wrote in their best-selling book of pub photographs, they all had a distinct local character: 'there's certainly a plenitude of "boozers", "locals", "sheds", "watering-holes" and even hotels in this vast and thirsty land ... but it would be a brave man, and an even braver woman, who would say that such-and-such a pub is typical'.[92] Their study, first published in 1977 and in its fourth edition by 1989, echoed Paul McGuire's 1952 celebration of the innkeepers who conquered the continent. It was conceived as a 'special tribute to the memory of those men and women who constructed such beautiful buildings and gave to them a personality unique to this country'. At the beginning of the 1990s, such sentiments of national pride in the history of pubs, which denied their racially exclusive and gendered history, still spoke powerfully to the Australian imagination. And some are still reluctant to let 'the barmaid' disappear. Watching one young manager going about her work journalist Richard Jinman concluded, 'It's easy to believe the spirit of the old-style barmaid might be alive and well after all.'[93]

Notes

INTRODUCTION

1 *Northcote Leader* (Melbourne), 24 May 1995, p. 2, 19 July 1995, p. 3; *Herald-Sun* (Melbourne), 12–15 July 1995, and 4 August 1995, p. 74 for Jean Dent Obituary; I am very grateful to Tanja Luckins who found this story.

2 *Daily Telegraph Mirror* (Sydney), 2, 8 November 1995; Interview with Brenda Fletcher, Sydney, December 1995.

3 Brian Hoad, 'Froth and trouble', *Bulletin*, 15 September 1992, p. 97.

4 Richard Jinman, 'The pub with *NO* barmaid', *Australian Magazine*, 22–23 July 1995, p. 28.

5 Judith Walkowitz, *City of Dreadful Delight: Narratives of Sexual Danger in Late-Victorian London*, Chicago, University of Chicago Press, 1992, p. 20.

6 See Ann McGrath, 'Beneath the skin: Australian citizenship, rights and Aboriginal women', in R. Howe, ed., 'Women and the State', *Journal of Australian Studies*, no. 37, June 1993, pp. 99–114; Anne Summers, *Damned Whores and God's Police*, Ringwood, Vic., Penguin, 1975, p. 57 et seq.

7 See Lisa Jacobson, 'The Ocker in Australian drama', *Meanjin*, vol. 49, Autumn 1990, pp. 137–47 for the theatrical representation of these ideas.

8 Paul McGuire, *Inns of Australia*, Melbourne, Heinemann, 1952, pp. ix–x, 84.

9 J. M. Freeland, *The Australian Pub*, Melbourne, Melbourne University Press, 1966, pp. 1, 6.

10 Angela Bennie, 'View from behind the bar: Review of "Barmaids" by Katherine Thomson', *Sydney Morning Herald*, 3 September 1992.

11 For studies of drinking cultures elsewhere see Thomas Brennan, *Public Drinking and Popular Culture in Eighteenth-Century Paris*, Princeton, Princeton University Press, 1988; William B. Taylor, *Drinking, Homicide and Rebellion in Colonial Mexican Villages*, Stanford, Stanford University Press, 1979. I am indebted to my colleague John Cashmere for bringing these to my attention. See also *International Labor and Working Class History*, no. 45, Spring 1994, for several articles on drinking in different cultures.

12 Sasha Grishin, *The Art of John Brack*, vol. 1, Melbourne, Oxford University Press, 1990, pp. 44–7.

13 John McCallum, 'The Doll and the legend', *Australian Drama Studies*, vol. 3, no. 2, April 1985, p. 34.

14 ibid., p. 43 and John McCallum, 'Summer of the Seventeenth Doll', in Philip Parsons, ed., *Companion to Theatre in Australia*, Sydney, Currency Press, 1995, pp. 564–5.

15 Kerryn Goldsworthy, 'Is it a boy or a girl? Gendering the Seventeenth Doll', *Southerly*, vol. 55, no. 1, Autumn 1995, pp. 89–105. See also Miriam Formanek-Brunell, *Made to Play House: Dolls and the Commercialization of American Girlhood*, New Haven, Yale University Press, 1993.

16 Imre Salusinszky, 'What's bugging Olive? A new reading of "The Doll"', *Southerly*, vol. 50, no. 2, June 1990, p. 171.

17 David Hough, 'No tap unturned', *Bulletin*, 26 November 1991, p. 113; Hoad, 'Froth and trouble'; Bennie, 'View from behind the bar'; Gretchen Miller, 'Of pouring, pawing, drinks and drunks', *Sydney Morning Herald*, 1 June 1995.

18 Sarah R. Perkins, 'Behind the Bar', *The White Ribbon Signal* (New Zealand), vol. 8, no. 86, July 1902, p. 1.

19 Ann Mitchell, Temperance and the liquor question in later nineteenth-century Victoria, MA thesis, University of Melbourne, 1966, remains unpublished; on the WCTU there is only the work of Anthea Hyslop, 'Temperance, Christianity and feminism', *Historical Studies*, vol. 17, no. 66, April 1976, pp. 27–49. Both studies concentrate on Victoria. For the United Kingdom, see Ian Donnachie, *A History of the Brewing Industry in Scotland*, Edinburgh, John Donald Publishing, 1979; Peter Clark, *The English Alehouse: A Social History, 1200–1830*, London, Longman, 1983; Brian Harrison, *Drink and the Victorians: The Temperance Question in England, 1815–1872*, London, Faber, 1971.

20 For example, Perry Duis, *The Saloon: Public Drinking in Chicago and Boston 1880–1920*, Urbana and Chicago, University of Illinois Press, 1983; Dorothy Sue Cobble, *Dishing It Out: Waitresses and Their Unions in the Twentieth Century*, Urbana and Chicago, University of Illinois Press, 1991.

21 Peter Bailey, 'Parasexuality and glamour: the Victorian barmaid as cultural prototype', *Gender and History*, no. 2, Summer 1990, pp. 148–72; there is also an unpublished study by V. Padmavathy, The English Barmaid, 1874–1914: A case study of unskilled and non-unionized women workers, PhD thesis, Miami University, 1989.

22 Lenard R. Berlanstein, ed., *Rethinking Labor History: Essays on Discourse and Class Analysis*, Urbana and Chicago, University of Illinois Press, 1993; Ann Curthoys, 'Labour history and cultural studies', *Labour History*, no. 67, November 1994, pp. 12–24.

23 Patrick Joyce, ed., *The Historical Meanings of Work*, Cambridge, Cambridge University Press, 1987, p. 1.

24 Gay Gullickson, 'Commentary: New labor history from the perspective of a women's historian', in Berlanstein, *Rethinking Labor History*, pp. 202–4.

25 See Donnachie, *A History of the Brewing Industry in Scotland*, p. 183.

26 For example, Joan Scott, *Gender and the Politics of History*, New York, Columbia University Press, 1988; Alice Kessler-Harris, *A Woman's Wage*, Lexington, University of Kentucky Press, 1990; also Ava Baron in *Work Engendered: Toward a New History of American Labor*, Ithaca and London, Cornell University Press, 1991.

27 Rosemary Pringle, *Secretaries Talk: Sexuality Power and Work*, Sydney, Allen & Unwin, 1988, pp. ix–x; Jill Julius Matthews, 'Deconstructing the masculine universe: The case for women's work', in Women and Labour Publications Collective, *All Her Labours, 1: Working It Out*, Sydney, Hale & Iremonger, 1984, p. 15.

28 See especially the work of Eileen Boris, *Home to Work: Motherhood and the Politics of Industrial Homework in the United States*, Cambridge, Cambridge University Press, 1994.

29 Pringle, *Secretaries Talk*, p. 90.

30 Lisa Adkins, *Gendered Work: Sexuality, Family and the Labour Market*, Buckingham and Bristol, Open University Press, 1995, pp. 3, 6–7; Adkins is quoting C. Offe, *Disorganized Capitalism: Contemporary Transformations of Work and Politics*, Cambridge, Polity Press, 1985.

31 Quoted in Hilary Land, 'The family wage', *Feminist Review*, 6, 1980–81, pp. 55–78.

32 Boyd Tonkin, 'Icons of the dispossessed', *History Workshop Journal*, 21, Spring, 1986, pp. 157–65.

33 Quoted in Julie Brown, Versions of reality: The production of function photographs in colonial Queensland, 1880–1900, PhD thesis, University of Queensland, 1985, p. 31.

34 Jonathan Bayer, *Reading Photographs: Understanding the Aesthetics of Photography*, New York, Pantheon Books, 1977.

35 Phillip Adams, 'Take a photo to look at life itself', *Weekend Australian*, 12–13 October 1991.

36 Halla Beloff, *Camera Culture*, Oxford, Basil Blackwell, 1985, p. 2.

37 Abigail Solomon-Godeau, *Photography at the Dock: Essays on Photographic History, Institutions and Practices*, Minneapolis, University of Minnesota Press, 1991, p. xxviii.

38   This literature is too voluminous to list but particularly notable recent examples include Boris, *Home to Work;* Vivien Hart, *Bound by Our Constitution: Women Workers and Minimum Wage Laws in U.S. and Great Britain*, Princeton, Princeton University Press, 1994; Ulla Wikander, Alice Kessler-Harris and Jane Lewis, eds, *Protecting Women: Labor Legislation in Europe, the U.S. and Australia 1880–1920*, Urbana and Chicago, University of Illinois Press, 1995.

39   Natalie Zemon Davis, *Fiction in the Archives*, Stanford, Stanford University Press, 1987, pp. 3–4.

40   ibid., p. 5.

41   McGrath, *Beneath the skin*.

42   Marilyn Lake, 'The politics of respectability: Identifying the masculinist context', *Australian Historical Studies*, vol. 22 no. 86, 1986, pp. 116–31; Chris McConville, 'Rough women, respectable men and social reform: A response to Lake's "masculinism"', *Historical Studies*, vol. 22 no. 88, April 1987, pp. 432–40.

1 'NO PLACE FOR A WOMAN'? PUBKEEPING IN COLONIAL TIMES

1   Mayse Young with Gabrielle Dalton, *No Place for a Woman: The Autobiography of Outback Publican, Mayse Young*, Sydney, Pan Macmillan, 1991.

2   Rosa Campbell Praed, *My Australian Girlhood: Sketches and Impressions of Bush Life*, colonial edition, London, Fisher Unwin, 1902, pp. 128–31. My thanks to Patricia Grimshaw for this reference.

3   Alice Clark, *The Working Life of Women in the Seventeenth Century*, London, Routledge, 1919, p. 222; Peter Clark, *The English Alehouse: A Social History, 1200–1830*, London, Longman, 1983, pp. 1, 6, 21; Judith Bennett, 'The village ale-wife: Women and brewing in fourteenth-century England', in Barbara Hanawalt, ed., *Women and Work in Pre-Industrial Europe*, Bloomington, Indiana University Press, 1986, p. 23.

4   Clark, *The Working Life of Women*, pp. 229–30, 233.

5   J. M. Freeland, *The Australian Pub*, Melbourne, Melbourne University Press, 1966, p. 16; see also A. Dingle, '"The truly magnificent thirst": an historical survey of Australian drinking habits', *Historical Studies*, vol. 19 no. 75, October 1980, pp. 228–9.

6   Dingle, '"The truly magnificent thirst"', p. 235; Ian Philip, The development of brewing and beer drinking in New South Wales in the nineteenth century, BA(Hons) thesis, Australian National University, 1979, pp. 3–5.

7   Katrina Alford, *Production or Reproduction: An Economic History of Women in Australia 1788–1850*, Melbourne, Oxford University Press, 1984, p. 195.

8   Freeland, *The Australian Pub*, pp. 20, 22.

9   Alford, *Production or Reproduction*, p. 195; Marian Aveling, 'She only married to be free, or Cleopatra vindicated', in Norma Grieve and Patricia Grimshaw, eds, *Australian Women: Feminist Perspectives*, Melbourne, Oxford University Press, 1987, pp. 119–33.

10   List of names of Publicans at Sydney whose Houses are either of bad fame or injuriously situated … Signed L. Macquarie, Government House, 10th February 1820, Archives Authority of NSW, COD 198.

11   Quoted in Ruth Teale, ed., *Colonial Eve: Sources on Women in Australia, 1788–1914*, Melbourne, Oxford University Press, 1978, p. 34, taken from Hassall Correspondence, Mitchell Library, Sydney, IV, pp. 1607–8.

12   Monica Perrot, *A Tolerable Good Success: Economic Opportunities for Women in New South Wales 1788–1830*, Sydney, Hale & Iremonger, 1983, p. 56.

13   ibid., pp. 113–18, compiled from the *Sydney Gazette*.

14   Alford, *Production or Reproduction*, p. 196; Teale, *Colonial Eve*, p. 32.

15   Alison Alexander, The public role of women in Tasmania 1803–1914, PhD thesis, University of Tasmania, 1989, pp. 101–2.

16   Perrot, *A Tolerable Good Success*, p. 55.

17   ibid., p. 85.

18   Alexander, The public role of women in Tasmania, p. 100; Perrot, *A Tolerable Good Success*, p. 58 gives some examples, see also p. 85.

19   Alexander, The public role of women in Tasmania, pp. 101–2.

20 Teale, *Colonial Eve*, pp. 32, 34; see also Deborah Oxley, *Convict Maids: The Forced Migration of Women to Australia*, Cambridge, Cambridge University Press, 1996; Aveling, 'She only married to be free'.
21 Alexander, The public role of women in Tasmania, p. 103.
22 Clark, *The English Alehouse*, p. 5.
23 Freeland, *The Australian Pub*, pp. 4–5.
24 Clark, *The English Alehouse*, p. 4.
25 Freeland, *The Australian Pub*, pp. 43, 54–5; Mark Girouard, *Victorian Pubs*, London, Studio Vista, 1975, p. 25; Brian Harrison, *Drink and the Victorians: The Temperance Question in England 1815–1872*, London, Faber, 1971.
26 Freeland, *The Australian Pub*, pp. 95, 102.
27 ibid., p. 5.
28 I'm grateful to Baiba Berzins for making available her paper, Women in the hotel trade: The north coast experience, subsequently published in Baiba Berzins, *North Coast Women: A History to 1939*, Sydney, Royal Australian Historical Society, 1996, pp. 104–11. These details are in the Tooth's archives held in the Noel Butlin Archives of Business and Labour, Australian National University, Canberra; a full list of licensees was published as a supplement to the *New South Wales Government Gazette*, 9 September 1870.
29 Report from Hall-Gibbs Mercantile Agency on Licensees of Hotels, Queensland Breweries Papers, John Oxley Library, Brisbane.
30 Paula-Jane Byrne, *Criminal Law and Colonial Subject*, Cambridge, Cambridge University Press, 1993, p. 63.
31 Told in Berzins, Women in the hotel trade, p. 106.
32 Freeland, *The Australian Pub*, pp. 72, 83.
33 ibid., p. 118.
34 Marilyn Lake and Farley Kelly, eds, *Double Time: Women in Victoria – 150 Years*, Ringwood, Vic., Penguin, 1985, pp. 52–60, 86–96.
35 Katrina Alford, 'Gilt-edged women: Women and mining in colonial Australia', Working Paper No. 64, Department of Economic History, Research School of Social Sciences, Australian National University, February 1986.
36 Anne-Marie Willis, *Picturing Australia: A History of Photography*, Sydney, Angus & Robertson, 1988, p. 70.
37 ibid., p. 65; John Tagg, *The Burden of Representation: Essays on Photographies and History*, Minneapolis, University of Minnesota Press, 1988, p. 37.
38 Willis, *Picturing Australia*, p. 66; see also Tagg, *The Burden of Representation*.
39 Pierre Bourdieu, 'The social definition of photography', in *The Field of Cultural Production: Essays on Art and Literature*, Cambridge, Columbia University Press, 1993, p. 80.
40 Freeland, *The Australian Pub*, p. 132.
41 Willis, *Picturing Australia*, p. 66.
42 Alford, *Production or Reproduction*, p. 195.
43 For elaboration of this idea see Abigail Solomon-Godeau, *Photography at the Dock*, Minneapolis, University of Minnesota Press, 1991.
44 Willis, *Picturing Australia*, p. 84.
45 Patricia Grimshaw, ed., *Families in Colonial Australia*, Sydney, Allen & Unwin, 1985.
46 Alexander, The public role of women in Tasmania, p. 102.
47 Quoted in Berzins, Women in the hotel trade.
48 Alexander, The public role of women in Tasmania, p. 102; Young, *No Place for a Woman*, pp. 62, 86.
49 Mayse Young had 'a Groote Eylandt girl' as nursemaid, helper and 'member of the family' for eighteen years, *No Place for a Woman*, p. 106; see also Berzins, Women in the hotel trade.
50 Ann McGrath, 'Beneath the Skin: Australian Citizenship, Rights and Aboriginal Women', in Renate Howe, ed., 'Women and the State', *Journal of Australian Studies*, no. 37, June 1993, pp. 99–114.
51 ibid.

52   *Queenslander* (Brisbane) 5 August 1899, p. 280; 'Woman's work in Sydney', *The Australasian Financial Adviser*, 8 January 1900, reprinted in Alan Birch and David MacMillan, eds, *Australian Business History*, Sydney, Angus & Robertson, 1967, pp. 160–3.
53   Susan Hunt, *Spinifex and Hessian: Women in North-West Australia 1860–1900*, Nedlands, University of Western Australia Press, 1988, p. 56.
54   New South Wales, Census, 1891, p. 295, 'The occupations of the people'; see Desley Deacon 'Political arithmetic: The nineteenth-century Australian census and the construction of the dependent woman', *Signs*, vol. 11, no. 1, Autumn 1985, pp. 27–47 for analysis and regional differences in colonial censuses.
55   Alexander, The public role of women in Tasmania, p. 103.
56   Thomas Brennan, *Public Drinking and Popular Culture in Eighteenth-Century Paris*, Princeton, Princeton University Press, 1988.
57   Freeland, *The Australian Pub*, pp. 80, 82.
58   Chris McConville, 'Rough women, respectable men and social reform: A response to Lake's "masculinism"', *Historical Studies*, vol. 22, no. 88, April 1987, p. 434.
59   Girouard, *Victorian Pubs*; Brian Harrison, 'Pubs', in H. J. Dyos and Michael Wolff, eds, *The Victorians*, London, Routledge, 1973, pp. 161–90.
60   W. A. Sinclair, 'Women and economic change in Melbourne 1871–1921', *Historical Studies*, vol. 20, no. 79 October 1982, pp. 281–2; see also Raelene Frances, *The Politics of Work*, Cambridge, Cambridge University Press, 1993.
61   Jenny Crew, 'Women's work and wages – Britain and Australia Pre 1914', *Journal of Australian Studies*, no. 21, November 1987, pp. 61, 64.

2 'THE PHOTOGRAPHER AND THE BARMAID': NARRATING WOMEN'S WORK

1   Deborah Oxley, 'Convict women', in Stephen Nicholas, ed., *Convict Workers*, Cambridge, Cambridge University Press, 1988.
2   *Queensland Figaro*, 4 July 1885, p. 5, clipping in Queensland Brewery Papers, John Oxley Library, Brisbane.
3   Joint Committee on the Employment of Barmaids, *The Employment of Women as Barmaids*, London, King & Son, 1905, p. 11.
4   Peter Bailey, 'Parasexuality and glamour: The Victorian barmaid as cultural prototype', *Gender and History*, no. 2, Summer 1990, p. 150.
5   Mark Girouard, *Victorian Pubs*, London, Studio Vista, 1975, pp. 27–8; in Scotland, too, the pub was more of a house than a shop until counters were introduced in the nineteenth century, according to two Scottish historians, Rudolph Kenna and Anthony Mooney, *People's Palaces: Victorian and Edwardian Pubs of Scotland*, Edinburgh, Paul Harris Publishing, 1983, p. 6.
6   See articles in the *Argus* (Melbourne) 1856, where no mention is made of this innovation.
7   'Melburnian', 'Social sketches: The barmaid', *Table Talk*, 6 October 1893, p. 10.
8   ibid.
9   J. M. Freeland, *The Australian Pub*, Melbourne, Melbourne University Press, 1966, p. 55.
10   I am much indebted to Hilary Kent for this insight and information.
11   Edward Higgs, 'Domestic service and household production' in Angela John, ed., *Unequal Opportunities: Women's Employment in England, 1800–1918*, Oxford, Basil Blackwell, 1986, ch. 4.
12   *Mercury* (Hobart), 11 June 1856 and 19 January 1860, both reported in Alison Alexander, The public role of women in Tasmania, 1803–1914, PhD thesis, University of Tasmania, 1989, p. 108.
13   Susan Hunt, *Spinifex and Hessian: Women in North-West Australia*, Nedlands, University of Western Australia Press, 1988, pp. 78–9. There were only 286 women counted in the 1881 census of this area; Wendy Brady, Women workers in the Western Australian hotel and catering industry, 1900–1925, BA(Hons) thesis, Murdoch University, 1982, p. 2.

14 Alexander, The public role of women in Tasmania, p. 108.
15 See Wages Book, Hotel Victoria, 1870, Melbourne University Archives; Joint Committee on the Employment of Barmaids, *The Employment of Women as Barmaids*, pp. 2–4; New South Wales, Census, 1891, p. 295, 'The occupations of the people'.
16 Joint Committee on the Employment of Barmaids, *The Employment of Women as Barmaids*.
17 See Shirley Fisher's analysis of domestic servants for the high correlation between Irish female immigration and domestic service in *Rising Damp*, Melbourne, Oxford University Press, 1989.
18 *The Life, Adventures and Confessions of a Sydney Barmaid*, Sydney, Panza & Co., 1891.
19 ibid., pp. 6, 9, 10.
20 *Australian Brewers' Journal*, 20 March 1908, p. 412.
21 'The girl workers of London, II: The barmaids', *Young Woman: An Illustrated Monthly Magazine*, vol. 6, 1897–98, pp. 52–4.
22 'Lucy' quoted in Alexander, The public role of women in Tasmania, p. 110.
23 ibid.
24 New South Wales, Parliament, *Debates*, 1902, p. 4544.
25 *Australian Brewers' Journal*, 20 September 1904, p. 730.
26 *Australian Brewers' Journal*, 20 September 1906, p. 708.
27 Beatrix Tracy, 'The girl in waiting', *Lone Hand*, 1 June 1908, p. 129.
28 Victoria, Statistical Register of Victoria 1895, Parliamentary Papers, vol. II, pt. 2, 1896.
29 Jenny Crew, 'Women's work and wages – Britain and Australia Pre 1914', *Journal of Australian Studies*, no. 21, November 1987, p. 68.
30 Reported in *Australian Brewers' Journal*, 21 March 1904, p. 413.
31 See reports of court cases brought against Martin Wenke, licensee of the Post-Office Club Hotel, Elizabeth St, Melbourne, and against John Kinane, licensee of the Victoria Park Hotel, Collingwood, and a Perth case in 'Adelaide Bar Gossip', *Australian Brewers' Journal*, 21 November 1904, p. 84; 20 July 1904, p. 642; 20 March 1903, p. 413.
32 Women's Employment Agency Report, *N.S.W. Industrial Gazette*, June 1914, p. 1253.
33 *The Life, Adventures and Confessions of a Sydney Barmaid*.
34 Alexander, The public role of women in Tasmania, p. 109.
35 'The English Barmaid', reprinted from *Bonfort's Wine and Spirit Circular* (New York) in the *Australian Brewers' Journal*, 20 March 1908, pp. 411–12.
36 Crew, 'Women's work and wages', p. 70.
37 Brady, Women workers in the Western Australian Hotel and Catering Industry; Louise Walker, Beers, bed and board: Industrial behaviour around the Victorian hotel and liquor industry wages boards, 1900–1914, BA(Hons) thesis, Monash University, 1995.
38 'The English Barmaid', p. 412.
39 Joint Committee on the Employment of Women as Barmaids, *The Employment of Women as Barmaids*, p. 8.
40 Melanie Nolan, Uniformity and diversity: A case study of female shop and office workers in Victoria 1860 to 1939, PhD thesis, Australian National University, 1989.
41 'The girl workers of London', p. 52.
42 John Freeman, *Lights and Shadows of Melbourne Life*, London, Sampson, Low, Harston, Searle & Rivington, 1888, p. 47.
43 'The girl workers of London', p. 52.
44 Tracy C. Davis, *Actresses as Working Women: Their Social Identity in Victorian Culture*, London and New York, Routledge, 1991, p. 76.
45 ibid., p. 83.
46 *Australian Brewers' Journal*, 20 January 1905, p. 215.
47 Reported in the *Australian Brewers' Journal*, 20 April 1904, p. 493.
48 Davis, *Actresses as Working Women*, p. 83.
49 Jan Carter, *Nothing to Spare: Recollections of Pioneering Women*, Ringwood, Vic., Penguin, 1981, p. 38.

50   A barmaid was the first woman buried in the Kalgoorlie cemetery but 'there are few surviving true stories about the early barmaids of Kalgoorlie . . .', Norma King, *The Daughters of Midas*, Victoria Park, WA, Hesperian Press, 1988, pp. 69–71.

51   Carter, *Nothing to Spare*, pp. 38–9.

52   R. C. Harrison, 'Some Hints to Bar Attendants', published by the Licensed Victuallers Association of Western Australia, New South Wales, Queensland and Victoria, 1912, R. C. Harrison Papers, Battye Library, Perth. My thanks to Wendy Brady for locating this source.

53   Joint Committee on the Employment of Women as Barmaids, *The Employment of Women as Barmaids*.

54   Tracy, 'The Girl in Waiting', no. iv: p. 128.

55   Letter from 'Hotelkeeper' to the *Argus* (Melbourne), 8 December 1916, p. 5.

56   Desley Deacon, 'Political arithmetic: The nineteenth century Australian census and the construction of the dependent woman', *Signs*, vol. 11, no. 1, Autumn 1985, pp. 22–47.

57   Brian Harrison, *Drink and the Victorians: The Temperance Question in England*, London, Faber, 1971, p. 39.

58   Girouard, *Victorian Pubs*, pp. 63, 69.

59   Chris McConville, 'Rough women, respectable men and social reform: A response to Lake's "masculinism"', *Historical Studies*, vol. 22, no. 88, April 1987, p. 434.

60   A rare exception is Clare Perry, Real women do shout: Narratives of pub culture, BA(Hons) thesis, University of Melbourne, 1991, and PhD in progress.

61   Davis, *Actresses as Working Women*, p. 86.

62   Joan Scott, ' "L'ouvrière! Mot impie, sordide . . .": Women workers in the discourse of French political economy 1840–1860', in Joan Scott, ed., *Gender and the Politics of History*, New York, Columbia University Press, 1988, pp. 139–66.

63   Kathy Peiss, ' "Charity Girls" and city pleasures: Historical notes on working-class sexuality, 1880–1920', in Ann Snitow et al., eds, *Powers of Desire: The Politics of Sexuality*, New York, Monthly Review Press, 1983, pp. 74–87.

64   Harrison, *Drink and the Victorians*, p. 187.

65   Bailey, 'Parasexuality and glamour'.

66   *Australasian Post*, 20 August 1951, pp. 22–3.

67   *Australian Brewers' Journal*, 20 December 1904, p. 130.

68   Bailey, 'Parasexuality and glamour'.

69   ibid.

70   Brady, Women workers in the Western Australian hotel and catering industry; interview with Brenda Fletcher, Sydney, December 1995.

71   *Clipper* (Hobart), 15 August 1896, reported in Alexander, The public role of women in Tasmania, p. 109.

72   Freeland, *The Australian Pub*, p. 152.

73   Victoria, Parliament, *Debates*, vol. 48, 1885, p. 305.

74   Freeland, *The Australian Pub*, p. 153; see also McConville, 'Rough women, respectable men and social reform'; South Australia, Commission Appointed to Report on the Liquor Laws, Parliamentary Papers, vol. 3, no. 34, 1879.

3 'THE PROBLEM OF THE BARMAIDS': URBANISATION AND LEGISLATIVE REFORM

1   Chris McConville, 'Rough women, respectable men and social reform: A response to Lake's "masculinism"', *Historical Studies*, vol. 22, no. 88, April 1987, p. 434, but he is quoting Mark Girouard, *Victorian Pubs*, London, Studio Vista, 1975.

2   Evidence of William Sandover, MLC, to the Commission Appointed to Report on the Liquor Laws, South Australia, Parliamentary Papers, vol. 3, no. 34, 1879, Minutes of Evidence, p. 47 (hereafter SA Liquor Commission).

3 *The Life, Adventures and Confessions of a Sydney Barmaid*, Sydney, Panza, 1891, p. 19 et seq.
4 McConville has noted that 'respectable' was an attribute deployed in many different circumstances, sometimes also by brothel-owners to describe their own establishments, see 'Rough women, respectable men and social reform'.
5 J. M. Freeland, *The Australian Pub*, Melbourne, Melbourne University Press, 1966, p. 153.
6 Jonathan Bayer, *Reading Photographs: Understanding the Aesthetics of Photography*, New York, Pantheon Books, 1977.
7 SA Liquor Commission, p. 47.
8 Victoria, *Select Committee Upon a Bill for the Prevention of Contagious Diseases*, Legislative Assembly, Votes and Proceedings, vol. 1, 1878, p. 4 (hereafter Vic. Select Committee on Contagious Diseases).
9 Victoria, Royal Commission on Employés in Shops, 2nd Progress Report, Parliamentary Papers, vol. 2, Paper 16, 1883.
10 Victoria, Royal Commission on Employés in Shops, *Report on the Employment of Barmaids*, Parliamentary Papers, vol. 2, Paper 29, 1884 (hereafter Vic. Royal Commission, *Report on Barmaids*).
11 For a further elaboration of this idea see Louise Walker, Beers, bed and board: Industrial behaviour around the Victorian Hotel Liquor Industry Wages Boards, 1900–1914, BA(Hons) thesis, Monash University, 1995; Wendy Brady, Women workers in the Western Australian hotel and catering industry, 1900–1925, BA(Hons) thesis, Murdoch University, 1982.
12 Letter from 'A Barmaid from the Bush' to the *Bulletin* (Sydney), 8 May 1897, p. 7.
13 Queensland, Shops Factories and Workshops Commission, 1891, Minutes of Evidence, p. 195 (hereafter Qld Shops Commission); *The Life, Adventures and Confessions of a Sydney Barmaid*, Sydney, Panza, 1891.
14 Victoria, Parliament, *Debates*, vol. 49, 1885, pp. 1213–30.
15 Evidence given to the Qld Shops Commission.
16 Judith Walkowitz, *City of Dreadful Delight: Narratives of Sexual Danger in Late-Victorian London*, Chicago, University of Chicago Press, 1992, pp. 46–7, 50–2.
17 Vic. Select Committee on Contagious Diseases, p. 4; Meg Arnot, 'The oldest profession in a new Britannia', in Verity Burgmann and Jenny Lee, eds, *Constructing a Culture*, Ringwood, Vic., McPhee Gribble/Penguin, 1988, pp. 46–62 discusses the police surveillance of women in colonial cities.
18 Evidence of George Hill, Question 7287, Vic. Royal Commission, *Report on Barmaids*, p. 5.
19 *Australian Brewers' Journal*, 20 June 1902, p. 530.
20 Qld Shops Commission.
21 New South Wales, Legislative Assembly, Votes and Proceedings, vol. 7, 1888.
22 Queensland, Royal Commission into ... Intoxicating Liquors, Report, Parliamentary Papers, vol. 53, 1901.
23 New South Wales, Parliament, Legislative Assembly, *Debates*, 1890, p. 3733 et seq.
24 Reported in *Sydney Morning Herald*, 17 September 1890, p. 5.
25 Victoria, Parliament, *Debates*, vol. 49, 1885, p. 1247.
26 ibid., vol. 50, p. 519.
27 New South Wales, Parliament, *Debates*, 1902, pp. 4559, 4561.
28 Victoria, Parliament, *Debates*. vols. 49–50, 1885.
29 New South Wales, Parliament, *Debates*, 1883, p. 1342.
30 Laws were passed first in Chicago in 1897, see Perry Duis, *The Saloon: Public Drinking in Chicago and Boston*, Urbana and Chicago, University of Illinois Press, 1983, p. 49; see also Dorothy Sue Cobble, *Dishing It Out: Waitresses and Their Unions in the Twentieth Century*, Urbana and Chicago, University of Illinois Press, 1991, pp. 165–8.

4 'WANTED, A BEAUTIFUL BARMAID': TEMPERANCE AND THE LANGUAGE OF DESIRE

1   Keith Dunstan, *Wowsers*, Melbourne, Cassell, 1968, p. 50 gives 1835 for New South Wales, 1839 for Adelaide and 1837 for Melbourne; there is no general history of the temperance movement in Australia.
2   Ann Mitchell, Temperance and the liquor question in later nineteenth century Victoria, MA thesis, University of Melbourne, 1966, p. 21; Walter Phillips, *Defending 'A Christian Country': Churchmen and Society in New South Wales in the 1880s and After*, St Lucia, University of Queensland Press, 1981, p. 144; Judith Smart, War and the concept of a new social order: Melbourne 1914–15, PhD thesis, Monash University, 1991.
3   Phillips, ibid.
4   Charles Fox, *Working Australia*, Sydney, Allen & Unwin, 1991.
5   *Alliance Record*, October 1885.
6   'An American's opinion of barmaids', *Alliance Record*, 15 December 1882, p. 3.
7   Mitchell, Temperance and the liquor question, p. 51.
8   *Age* (Melbourne), 8 June 1912, reprinted in *Alliance Record*, 1 July 1912.
9   Beatrix Tracy, 'Explorations in industry, no. iv: The girl in waiting', *Lone Hand*, 1 June 1908, p. 128.
10 Mitchell, Temperance and the liquor question, p. 14.
11 *Alliance Record*, July, October 1885.
12 'An American's opinion of barmaids'.
13 Francis Bertie Boyce, *The Drink Problem in Australia: The Plague of Alcohol and the Remedies*, London, National Temperance League, Edwards Dunlop & Co., 1893, pp. 129–40.
14 Article from the *Wimmera Star* reprinted in *Alliance Record*, July 1885, p. 4.
15 ibid., October 1885.
16 ibid., September 1895.
17 Boyce, *The Drink Problem in Australia*.
18 ibid.; J. M. Freeland, *The Australian Pub*, Melbourne, Melbourne University Press, 1966, p. 141.
19 J. G. Barrett at the Australasian Temperance Conference in 1914, *Alliance Record*, 1 July 1914, p. 3.
20 Mitchell, Temperance and the liquor question, pp. 92, 207.
21 *Golden Records: Pathfinders of Women's Christian Temperance Union of New South Wales*, Sydney, WCTU, 1926, pp. 69–70.
22 *Alliance Record*, September 1895.
23 'An American's opinion of barmaids'.
24 *Australian Brewers' Journal*, 20 October 1896, p. 2; 20 April 1905, p. 369.
25 ibid., 20 December 1897, p. 80; 20 September 1906, p. 708; 20 April 1905, p. 369; 20 October 1896, p. 2.
26 ibid., 20 October 1896, p. 2; 20 April 1905, p. 369; 21 November 1898, p. 56.
27 ibid., 20 August 1902, p. 638.
28 ibid., 20 September 1906, p.708; 20 October 1906, p. 22; 20 June 1905, p. 487; 20 June 1905, p. 505; 20 August 1904, p. 666.
29 ibid., 20 September 1906, p. 708; 20 January 1905, p. 200; 20 March 1905, p. 319; 20 October 1902; 20 December 1902.
30 *Bulletin* (Sydney), 25 July 1885, p. 4.
31 ibid.
32 ibid., 4 October 1884, p. 4.
33 ibid., 31 December 1892, p. 5 (Letter from 'Titus Salt').

5 'WHITE SLAVES BEHIND THE BAR': WOMEN CITIZENS, THE WCTU AND THE LAWS AGAINST BARMAIDS

1   Walter Phillips, *Defending 'A Christian Country': Churchmen and Society in New South Wales in the 1880s and After*, St Lucia, University of Queensland Press, 1981, p. 144.

2 For example, Anthea Hyslop, 'Temperance Christianity and feminism', *Historical Studies*, vol. 17, no. 66, April 1976, pp. 27–49; the contest between men's pleasures and responsibilities has been discussed by Marilyn Lake, 'The politics of respectability: Identifying the masculinist context', *Australian Historical Studies*, vol. 22, no. 86, 1986, pp. 116–31; Chris McConville, 'Rough women, respectable men and social reform: A response to Lake's "masculinism"', *Historical Studies*, vol. 22, no. 88, April 1987, pp. 432–40.

3 Ian Tyrrell, *Woman's World/Woman's Empire*, Chapel Hill, University of North Carolina Press, 1991, p. 192; Sarah Dalton, The pure heart: The New Zealand Woman's Christian Temperance Union and social purity, 1885–1930, MA thesis, Victoria University, 1993.

4 *Alliance Record*, October 1902, p. 154.

5 *White Ribbon Signal*, vol. 1, no. 3, January 1893, pp. 34–5.

6 ibid., vol. 1, no. 5, March 1893, p. 73.

7 ibid., vol. 1, no. 8, June 1893, p. 117.

8 ibid., vol. 4 no. 4, February 1896, p. 356.

9 ibid., February 1896, p. 352; vol. 4, no. 3, January 1896, p. 841.

10 WCTU 9th Annual Report, 1896, p. 13; 10th Annual Report, 1897, p. 14.

11 WCTU 10th Annual Report, 1897, p. 23.

12 'Women's work in society …', *White Ribbon Signal*, vol. 4, no. 2, December 1895, p. 322–4.

13 *White Ribbon Signal*, vol. 3, no. 8, July 1895.

14 ibid., vol. 3, no. 2, January 1895, p. 174.

15 ibid., vol. 5, no. 9, July 1897, p. 561.

16 Mrs Phillips, 'Employment of women as barmaids', *White Ribbon Signal*, vol. 5, no. 4, February 1897, pp. 502–3.

17 'The city barmaid', *White Ribbon Signal*, vol. 5, no. 9, July 1897, p. 561.

18 I. G. Noar, 'Domestic Servants', *White Ribbon Signal*, vol. 5, no. 10, August 1897, p. 570.

19 WCTU 7th Annual Report, 1894.

20 *Woman's Sphere*, 10 October 1902, p. 217.

21 Linda Gordon and Ellen DuBois, 'Seeking ecstasy on the battlefield: Danger and pleasure in nineteenth-century feminist sexual thought', in Feminist Review, ed., *Sexuality: A Reader*, London, Virago, 1987, pp. 82–97.

22 Judith Walkowitz, *City of Dreadful Delight: Narratives of Sexual Danger in Late-Victorian London*, Chicago, University of Chicago Press, 1992, p. 52 makes a similar point about middle-class women charity workers in Victorian London.

23 WCTU 13th Annual Report, 1900, pp. 19, 25.

24 WCTU 16th Annual Report, 1903, p. 26.

25 WCTU 17th Annual Report, 1904, pp. 39, 41, 52.

26 WCTU 18th Annual Report, 1905, p. 47; 19th, 1906, p. 38.

27 WCTU 23rd Annual Report, 1910, p. 57; 27th, 1914, p. 31; 29th, 1916, p. 46.

28 A. R. Grigg, 'Prohibition and women: The preservation of an ideal and a myth', *New Zealand Journal of History*, vol. 17, no. 2, October 1983, pp. 144–65, says 'an early 1908 police report stated that there appeared to be an increase in the number of women drinking in hotel bars, particularly in [the major cities]' (p. 157).

29 Edward S. Kiek, *An Apostle in Australia: The Life and Reminiscences of Joseph Coles Kirby, Christian Pioneer and Social Reformer*, London, Independent Press, 1927, p. 206. My thanks to Walter Phillips for this reference.

30 Letter to the Editor, *Daily Post* (Hobart), 3 August 1908, p. 3.

31 Judith Allen, *Rose Scott: Vision and Revision in Feminism*, Melbourne, Oxford University Press, 1994, pp. 150–2.

32 Peter Fitzpatrick, *Pioneer Players: The Lives of Louis and Hilda Esson*, Cambridge, Cambridge University Press, 1995, p. 47.

33 Beatrix Tracy, 'The shop girl', *Lone Hand*, 1 September 1908, p. 529.

34 Beatrix Tracy, 'The girl in waiting', *Lone Hand*, 1 June 1908, pp. 124–30.

35 Gail Reekie, *Temptations: Sex, Selling and the Department Store*, Sydney, Allen & Unwin, 1993.

36   Perry Duis, *The Saloon: Public Drinking in Chicago and Boston 1880–1920*, Urbana and Chicago, University of Illinois Press, 1983, talks about the significance of public drinking in this period.
37   Beatrix Tracy, 'The woman in industry', *Lone Hand*, 1 October 1908, pp. 705–6.
38   'White slaves behind the bar: Some experiences of a dangerous occupation', was an article, supposedly written by an ex-barmaid, published in *Everybody's Monthly* in England, which was reprinted in *Alliance Record*, September 1911, p. 139 and *White Ribbon Signal* (New Zealand), vol. 17, no. 198, December 1911, pp. 11–13. In Australia this term was only used when quoting English sources.
39   'The white slaves behind the bar: Temperance women fight to abolish the barmaid', Sandry Coney, *Standing in the Sunshine*, Auckland, Viking, 1993, pp. 128–9.
40   Reported in *Australian Brewers' Journal*, 20 April 1904, p. 490.
41   *Mercury* (Hobart), 24 July 1908, 1 August 1908; *Daily Post* (Hobart), 6 August 1908, p. 6.
42   *The Disappearing Barmaid: A Turn of the Century Tragedy*, SA, Pump Press, Aldgate, 1967.
43   *Lyttelton Times* (New Zealand), 21 May, 8 June 1911, quoted in Coney, *Standing in the Sunshine*; letter from 'A Barmaid from the Bush', to the *Bulletin* (Sydney), 8 May 1897, p. 7.
44   An insight of Judith Smart's.
45   *Alliance Record*, October 1902, p. 154; WCTU Annual Report 1902, pp. 31–2, 55.
46   J. D. Bollen, *Protestantism and Social Reform in New South Wales 1890–1910*, Melbourne, Melbourne University Press, 1972, p. 10. Richard Broome, *Treasure in Earthen Vessels: Protestant Christianity in New South Wales Society 1900–14*, St Lucia, University of Queensland Press, 1980.
47   *Alliance Record*, October 1908.
48   New South Wales Census, 1901. See also Susan Sheridan, *Along the Faultlines: Sex, Race and Nation in Australian Women's Writing 1880s–1930s*, Sydney, Allen & Unwin, 1995.
49   Kerreen Reiger, *Disenchantment of the Home*, Melbourne, Oxford University Press, 1984.
50   Andrew Markus, 'Legislating White Australia 1900–1970' in Diane Kirkby, ed., *Sex, Power and Justice: Historical Perspectives on Law in Australia*, Melbourne, Oxford University Press, 1995, pp. 237–51.
51   *Alliance Record*, October 1902, p. 154.
52   *Alliance Record*, July 1903, p. 102; October 1908, pp. 151, 154.
53   Rudolph Kenna and Anthony Mooney, *People's Palaces: Victorian and Edwardian Pubs of Scotland*, Edinburgh, Paul Harris Publishing, 1983, p. 29.
54   New South Wales, Parliament, *Debates*, vol. 8, 1902, p. 4561.
55   ibid., pp. 4546, 4557, 4559.
56   ibid., pp. 4558–9.
57   Joint Committee on the Employment of Barmaids, *The Employment of Women as Barmaids*, London, King & Son, 1905, p. 46.
58   ibid., pp. 49–50.
59   For details of the English campaign see V. Padmavathy, The English barmaid, 1874–1914: A case study of unskilled and non-unionized women workers, PhD thesis, Miami University, 1989.
60   South Australia, Parliament, *Debates*, 2 December 1908, p. 441.
61   ibid., pp. 468, 472–3.
62   *West Australian* (Perth), 28 October 1910.
63   *White Ribbon Signal* (New Zealand), March 1911, p. 6; see also Dalton, The pure heart, p. 40.
64   *White Ribbon Signal*, 1 July 1914, p. 171.
65   See Walter Phillips, ' "Six o'clock swill": The introduction of early closing of hotel bars in Australia', *Historical Studies*, vol. 19, no. 75, October 1980, pp. 250–66.
66   President's Annual Address, *White Ribbon Signal*, December 1914, p. 31; see also 1 January and 1 August 1914.

67 This was also true in the United Kingdom, see Joint Committee on the Employment of Barmaids, *The Employment of Women as Barmaids*; Helen Hamley has traced women's labour force participation in The limits of choice: White women, their work and labour activism in Queensland factories and shops 1880s to 1920, MA thesis, University of Queensland, 1992; Melanie Nolan, Uniformity and diversity: A case study of female shop and office workers in Victoria, 1880 to 1939, PhD thesis, Australian National University, 1989, has emphasised the importance of the youthfulness of this labour force; Ray Markey, *The Making of the Labor Party in New South Wales 1880–1900*, Sydney, New South Wales University Press, 1988, pp. 222–3.

68 Reekie, *Temptations*.

69 Sandra Grimes, An anthropological perspective on gender in the workplace: A case study of women working in hotel bars, PhD thesis, University of Adelaide, 1980, found women working in Adelaide who claimed they had always been able to find employment; for New Zealand see Dalton, The pure heart, p. 42.

70 Joan Scott, 'Statistical representations of work', in Steven Kaplan and Cynthia Koepp, eds, *Work in France: Representations, Meaning, Organization and Practice*, Ithaca, Cornell University Press, 1986, pp. 335–63.

71 Joan Scott, ' "L'ouvrière! Mot impie, sordide …": Women workers in the discourse of French political economy, 1840–1860', in Joan Scott, ed., *Gender and the Politics of History*, New York, Columbia University Press, 1988, pp. 139–66.

72 *Westralian Worker*, December 1911.

73 A UK law on women in coal mines was transported intact to the Australian colonies but never separately enacted there, see Andrew Metcalfe, *For Freedom and Dignity: Historical Agency and Class Structure on the Coalfields of New South Wales*, Sydney, Angus & Robertson, 1988.

74 *Australian Brewers' Journal*, 20 December 1902, p. 144.

75 Ian Philip, The development of brewing and beer drinking in New South Wales in the nineteenth century, BA(Hons) thesis, Australian National University, 1979, pp. 58–69; there were investigations into and laws passed against tied houses in other states as well.

76 Nolan, Uniformity and diversity, p. 40 et seq.

77 Women's desires for pleasures associated with drinking are discussed in Mary Murphy, 'Bootlegging mothers and drinking daughters: Gender and prohibition in Butte, Montana', *American Quarterly*, vol. 46, no. 2, June 1994, pp. 174–94.

78 Letter signed 'Hotelkeeper' to the *Argus* (Melbourne), 8 December 1916, p. 5.

6 'WHEN MEN WORE HATS': GENDER, UNIONS AND EQUAL PAY

1 The feminist literature on arbitration is summed up in Diane Kirkby, 'Arbitration and the fight for economic justice' in Stuart Macintyre and Richard Mitchell, eds, *Foundations of Arbitration*, Melbourne, Oxford University Press, 1989, pp. 334–51.

2 Shirley Mellor, Secretary, Queensland Branch, Federated Liquor Hospitality and Miscellaneous Workers Union, interview in Brisbane, December 1995.

3 Alleyn Best, *The History of The Liquor Trades Union in Victoria*, Melbourne, Victorian Branch, Federated Liquor and Allied Industries Employees Union of Australia, 1990. Unless otherwise indicated all details of the union's history are taken from Best; the union's history is also told by Jim Munro in 'History of the Liquor Trades Union', *The Liquor and Allied Trades Union Journal* (Victorian Branch), 1978–1985.

4 In addition to Best see Edna Ryan, *Two-Thirds of a Man: Women and Arbitration in New South Wales*, Sydney, Hale & Iremonger, 1984; W. Nicol, 'Women and the trade union movement in New South Wales: 1890–1900', *Labour History*, vol. 36, May 1979, pp. 18–30.

5 Nicol, ibid., pp. 23–4.

6 Quoted in Nicol, ibid., p. 27.

7 Wendy Brady, Women workers in the Western Australian hotel and catering industry, BA(Hons) thesis, Murdoch University, 1982.

8   Discussed by Diane Kirkby in 'Oh! What a tangled web!' in Verity Burgmann and Jenny Lee, eds, *Making A Life*, Ringwood, Vic., McPhee Gribble/Penguin, 1988, pp. 253–66.

9   Louise Walker, Beers, bed and board: Industrial behaviour around the Victorian hotel and liquor industry wages boards, 1900–1914, BA(Hons) thesis, Monash University, 1995, p. 45.

10   Jim Munro, 'History of the Liquor Trades Union', *The Liquor And Allied Trades Union Journal*, vol. 10, no. 4, 1980, p. 13.

11   Federated Liquor and Allied Trades Union, South Australian Branch, Minutes, Noel Butlin Archives of Business and Labour, Australian National University, Canberra, E 95/2.

12   Federated Liquor and Allied Trades Union, Queensland Branch, Minutes, 3 September 1916, Office of the Federated Liquor Hospitality and Miscellaneous Workers Union, Brisbane (hereafter Qld LTU Minutes).

13   Women's Employment Agency Report, *New South Wales Industrial Gazette*, June 1914, p. 1253.

14   Wendy Brady, '"Serfs of the sodden scone"?: Women workers in the West Australian hotel and catering industry 1900–1925', in Patricia Crawford, ed., *Women in Western Australian History*, Nedlands, University of Western Australia Press, 1983, pp. 34–46.

15   *Argus* (Melbourne), 7 July 1914.

16   See 'Rules of the W.A. Barmaids and Barmen's Union', Federated Liquor and Allied Trades Employees Association papers, Noel Butlin Archives of Business and Labour, Australian National University, Canberra.

17   Western Australia, Boards of Conciliation and the Court of Arbitration, Reports of Proceedings, vol. 10, 1911, p. 117 (WA Branch Federated Liquor Hospitality and Miscellaneous Workers Union, Perth).

18   Western Australia, Industrial Reports of Proceedings of the Court of Arbitration, vol. 12, 1913, pp. 143–4 (WA Branch Federated Liquor Hospitality and Miscellaneous Workers Union, Perth).

19   Qld LTU Minutes.

20   See in particular Raelene Frances, *Gender and the Politics of Work*, Cambridge, Cambridge University Press, 1993.

21   J. M. Freeland, *The Australian Pub*, Melbourne, Melbourne University Press, p. 180.

22   (Catherine Edmonds Wright), *Caddie: A Sydney Barmaid, Told by Herself*, London, Constable, 1953, pp. 186, 249.

23   Qld LTU Minutes, 9 May 1932, 1934.

24   ibid., 22 April, 9 June 1930.

25   ibid., 24 October 1929; 25 August, 14 December 1931.

26   ibid., 14 October 1929.

27   Reported in *Vigilante* (LVA Victoria) 29 April 1932. M. J. Murphy, Secretary (Federated Liquor Trades and Allied Industries Employees Union, Victorian Branch), to J. J. Holland, MLA, 24 October 1933, Federated Liquor Trades and Allied Industries Employees Union, Victorian Branch papers, Melbourne University Archives, Melbourne.

28   *Vigilante*, 10 June, 17 June, 22 July 1932.

29   Qld LTU Minutes, 25 November 1930; 22 January, 26 August, 1935; 14 September 1936.

30   Qld LTU Minutes, 29 July 1941; 11 September 1945; 25 February 1946; 11 December 1947.

31   Reported in the *Argus* (Melbourne) 21 December 1951.

32   *Age* (Melbourne), 5 September 1942, p. 3.

33   Letter from Ada Bronham, General Secretary, to the Editor, *Advertiser* (Adelaide), 9 July 1942, p. 6.

34   Licensed Victuallers Qld v. Liquor Trades Union Qld, Australian Archives, MP 346 1943/44, no. 418.

35   *Age* (Melbourne), 12 August 1942, p. 2.

36   *Advertiser* (Adelaide), 11 July 1942, p. 7.

37   ibid., 3 September 1942, p. 7.

38   Australian Archives, MP 346 1942–47, no. 919.

39   *Advertiser* (Adelaide), 3 September 1942, p. 7.

40 Australian Archives, MP 346 1942–47, no. 919.
41 *Hotel Review of Western Australia*, vol. 6, no. 7, July 1949, p. 27.
42 *Argus* (Melbourne), 21 December 1951 (clipping held in State Library of Victoria, La Trobe Library's HPC Collection).
43 Told in Best, *The History of the Liquor Trades Union in Victoria*, p. 174.
44 Australian Archives, MP 346 1942–47, no. 919.
45 *Hotel Review of Western Australia*, vol. 2, no. 10, September 1945, p. 40; see also Dorothy Sue Cobble, *Dishing It Out: Waitresses and Their Union in the Twentieth Century*, Urbana and Chicago, University of Illinois Press, 1991, pp. 166–70.
46 *Argus* (Melbourne), 21 December 1951.

7 'BEER, GLORIOUS BEER': PUB CULTURE AND THE 6 O'CLOCK SWILL

1   This comes from the title of Cyril Pearl's book, *Beer, Glorious Beer*, Melbourne, Nelson, 1969.
2   For example, Walter Phillips, '"Six O'Clock Swill": The introduction of early closing of hotel bars in Australia', *Historical Studies*, vol. 19 no. 75, October 1980, pp. 250–66.
3   J. M. Freeland, *The Australian Pub*, Melbourne, Melbourne University Press, 1966, p. 178.
4   (Catherine Edmonds Wright); *Caddie: A Sydney Barmaid, Written by Herself*, London, Constable, 1953, p. 8.
5   Freeland, *The Australian Pub*, p. 176.
6   ibid., pp. 175–6, 180.
7   ibid.
8   Charles Pickett, *Refreshing! Art Off the Pub Wall*, Sydney, Powerhouse Publishing in association with Angus & Robertson, 1988; these advertisements appeared in the *Bulletin*.
9   K. G. Laycock, Government interference with the Australian way of life: The control of liquor order of 16 March 1942, BA(Hons) thesis, Australian National University, 1981.
10 *Hotel Review of Western Australia*, vol. 1, no. 3 February 1944, p. 8 (unless otherwise stated the source for material from now on is the *Hotel Review of Western Australia* [*HRWA*], published monthly 1944–50).
11 Freeland, *The Australian Pub*, p. 182.
12 Reported in *HRWA*, vol. 4, no. 8, August 1947, p. 20.
13 *Truth* (Brisbane), 10 June 1962.
14 'Woman's reign in the bar-room is approaching its end', *Argus* (Melbourne), 21 December 1951.
15 *Caddie*, pp. vii, 1.
16 Louise Robinson, Perceptions of barmaids in late nineteenth century Melbourne, BA(Hons) thesis, University of Melbourne, 1990.
17 *Argus* (Melbourne), 1951.
18 Quoted in Richard Jinman, 'The pub with *NO* barmaid', *Australian Magazine*, 22–23 July, 1995, p. 33.
19 *Argus* (Melbourne), 21 December 1951.
20 Shirley Mellor, Secretary, Queensland Branch, Federated Liquor Hospitality and Miscellaneous Workers Union, interview in Brisbane, December 1995.
21 *HRWA*, vol. 2, no. 7, June 1945, p. 10.
22 *Courier-Mail* (Brisbane) 4 September, 9 October, 29–30 November 1941; *Telegraph* (Brisbane), 31 July, 13 October 1941; *Worker* (Brisbane), 9 December 1941.
23 *Caddie*, pp. 8, 113.
24 *HRWA*, vol. 4, no. 3, March 1947, p. 26.
25 *Sun News-Pictorial* quoted in Keith Dunstan, *Wowsers*, Melbourne, Cassell, 1968, p. 108.
26 ibid.
27 *Courier-Mail* (Brisbane), 29 November 1941.
28 Freeland, *The Australian Pub*, p. 183; see also A. Dingle, '"The truly magnificent thirst": An historical survey of Australian drinking habits,' *Historical Studies*, vol. 19, no. 75, October 1980, pp. 228–9.

29   New South Wales, Royal Commission on Liquor Laws in New South Wales, Report, 1954, p. 8 (hereafter Maxwell Report); for the brewers' responses see also Tooth's Brewery, 'Report on Maxwell Royal Commission Report', Tooth's Brewery Collection, Noel Butlin Archives of Business and Labour, Australian National University, Canberra.
30   Maxwell Report, pp. 18, 19.
31   ibid., pp. 16, 87.
32   ibid., p. 87.
33   Reported in *The Mercury* (Hobart), 30 April 1952, p. 3.

8 'IN PRAISE OF SPLENDID GELS': SEX, SKILL AND DRINKING CULTURE

1   John Hepworth and John Hindle, *Boozing Out in Melbourne Pubs*, Sydney, Angus & Robertson, 1980.
2   *ULVA Review*, Qld Branch, November 1959, pp. 39–40, May 1958, p. 11; J. M. Freeland, *The Australian Pub*, Melbourne, Melbourne University Press, 1966, pp. 184–5; Queensland Hotels Association, *QHA Review*, November 1963, p. 51.
3   Freeland, *The Australian Pub*, pp. 184–5; see also *ULVA Review*, Qld branch, May 1958, p. 11.
4   *ULVA Review*, Qld Branch, May 1959, p. 33.
5   ibid., May 1958, p. 41; May 1959, p. 33.
6   New South Wales, Royal Commission on Liquor Laws in New South Wales, Report, 1954, p. 86.
7   Reported in *QHA Review*, May, July 1965; *QHA Review*, March 1967, p. 11.
8   *Age* (Melbourne), 2 February 1966; *Herald* (Melbourne), 2 February 1966.
9   An opinion conveyed to me in a personal interview with Shirley Mellor, Secretary, Queensland Branch, Federated Liquor Hospitality and Miscellaneous Workers Union, Brisbane, December 1995.
10   *QHA Review*, November 1963, p. 33.
11   ibid., January 1967, p. 35.
12   ibid.
13   'Motel versus hotel for accommodation', *Australian Financial Review*, 12 March 1963, p. 16.
14   *The Mercury* (Hobart), 4 October 1967, p. 2; 5 October 1967, p. 14.
15   'Hotels beset by many problems', *Australian Financial Review*, 12 March 1963, p. 17.
16   Reported in *Mercury* (Hobart), 7 June 1969, p. 3.
17   Reprinted in *ULVA Review*, Qld Branch, vol. 2 September 1952, p. 10.
18   ibid., January 1954, p. 22.
19   *Hotel Review of Western Australia*, vol. 10, no. 10, October 1953.
20   Kathy Nunn, *William Angliss College: The First Fifty Years*, Melbourne, Hargreen Publishing, 1990, traces the changes in training hotel staff in Victoria.
21   Shirley Mellor, interview; *The Life, Adventures and Confessions of a Sydney Barmaid*, Sydney, Panza, 1891, p. 11.
22   *Hotel Review of Western Australia*, vol. 7, no. 6, June 1950; vols. 5–7, July 1948.
23   *Courier-Mail* (Brisbane), 11 April 1962.
24   Reported in *QHA Review*, March 1965, pp. 13, 17.
25   See *Courier-Mail* (Brisbane), 26 November 1954 for the legal implications for women staff in the new liquor laws.
26   *Liquor Trades Journal* (Tasmanian Branch), New Year Edition, January 1968.
27   *Courier-Mail* (Brisbane), 18 February 1967, p. 7.
28   *Sunday Telegraph* (Brisbane), 2 July 1967.
29   Told in Alleyn Best, *The History of the Liquor Trades Union in Victoria*, Melbourne, Victorian Branch Federated Liquor and Allied Industries Employees Union, 1990, pp. 205–7.
30   *Liquor Trades Journal* (Tasmanian Branch), January 1968; I'm grateful for material provided to me by Eugene Fry, Secretary of the Western Australian Branch of the Liquor Hospitality and Miscellaneous Workers Union. A series of articles on equal pay began in the *Liquor and Allied Industries Union Journal*, vol. 1, no. 6, 1959.

31 *Liquor Trades Journal* (Tasmanian Branch), January 1968.
32 Best, *The History of the Liquor Trades Union in Victoria*, pp. 197, 213.
33 Dorothy Sue Cobble, *Dishing It Out: Waitresses and Their Unions in the Twentieth Century*, Urbana and Chicago, University of Illinois Press, 1991, p. 287.
34 *Bulletin* (Sydney), 15 December 1954; *Telegraph* (Brisbane), 20 May 1967, p. 14.
35 *Telegraph* (Brisbane), 27 December 1967.
36 Liquor Trades Union, Newspaper Clippings, John Oxley Library, Brisbane.
37 *Telegraph* (Brisbane), 20 May 1967, p. 14.
38 Wendy Bastalich, Gender and skill in Australia: A case study of barmaids, MA thesis, University of Adelaide, 1991, p. 51.
39 *Sunday Truth* (Brisbane), 30 April 1967.
40 *Australasian Post*, 2 August 1951, pp. 22–3; yet the photo taken of Scott's public bar (discussed in chapter 6) does show women at work alongside men.
41 Sandra Grimes, An anthropological perspective on gender in the workplace: A case study of women working in hotel bars, PhD thesis, University of Adelaide, 1980, p. 137.
42 ibid., p. 145.
43 *Telegraph* (Brisbane), 20 May 1967, p. 14.
44 ibid.
45 See Rosemary Pringle, *Secretaries Talk: Sexuality, Power and Work*, Sydney, Allen & Unwin, 1988.
46 *Telegraph* (Brisbane), 20 May 1967, p. 14.
47 Ann McGrath, 'Beneath the skin: Australian citizenship, rights and Aboriginal women', in R. Howe, ed., 'Women and the State', *Journal of Australian Studies*, no. 37, June 1993, pp. 99–114; *Age* (Melbourne), 19 August 1972, p. 3.
48 Anne Summers, *Damned Whores and God's Police: The Colonization of Women in Australia*, Ringwood, Vic., Penguin, 1975, pp. 82–4.
49 *Courier-Mail* (Brisbane), 1 May 1963.
50 ibid., 1 April 1965.
51 ibid., 8 April 1965.
52 *Sunday Truth* (Brisbane), 22 June 1969.
53 ibid., 25 May 1969.
54 ibid., 8 June 1969.
55 *Age* (Melbourne), 19 August 1972, p. 3.
56 Reported in *Mejane* (Sydney), March 1973.
57 Freeland, *The Australian Pub*, is the most academic study; see also F. Barbara, J. Usher and N. Barnes, 'The rules of "shouting" in Sydney public bars', *Australian Journal of Social Issues*, vol. 13, 1978, pp. 119–28; popular studies are John Larkins and Bruce Howard, *Australian Pubs*, Adelaide, Rigby, 1973; John Hepworth and John Hindle, *Boozing Out in Melbourne Pubs*; John O'Grady, *It's Your Shout Mate! Australian Pubs and Beer*, Sydney, Lansdowne Press, 1972; Cyril Pearl, *Beer, Glorious Beer*, Melbourne, Nelson, 1969. This does not include celebratory studies of breweries which began to appear in the 1980s, e.g. Keith Dunstan, *The Amber Nectar: A Celebration of Beer and Brewing in Australia*, Ringwood, Vic., Viking/Penguin, 1987; Suzanne Welborne, *Swan: The History of a Brewery*, Nedlands, University of Western Australia Press, 1987; Mike Bingham, *Cascade: A Taste of History*, Hobart, Cascade Brewery, 1992.
58 Craig McGregor, *Profile of Australia*, London, Hodder & Stoughton, 1966, p. 134. Freeland, *The Australian Pub*, p. 2.
59 Hepworth and Hindle, *Boozing Out in Melbourne Pubs*.
60 Freeland, *The Australian Pub*; and O'Grady, *It's Your Shout Mate!*
61 New South Wales, Parliament, Report from the Select Committee of the Legislative Assembly upon Liquor Trading, 1979, p. 7.
62 Summers, *Damned Whores and God's Police*, p. 83.
63 ibid., p. 313.
64 Susanne Lloyd-Jones, 'You can't sell a beer without a broad': The political economy of sexuality in the hotel industry, B.Ec.(Social Sciences) (Hons) thesis, University of Sydney, 1993; Bastalich, Gender and skill in Australia.

65   Sandra Grimes, 'Across the bar: Women's work in hotels', in Lenore Manderson, ed., *Australian Ways: Anthropological Studies of an Industrialised Society*, Sydney, Allen & Unwin, 1985, pp. 71–3; see also Sherri Cavan, *Liquor License: An Ethnography of Bar Behaviour*, Chicago, Aldine, 1966; Valerie Hey, *Patriarchy and Pub Culture*, London, Tavistock, 1986.

66   Kate Nancarrow, 'Breasting the tape ahead of my other barmaid rivals', *Sunday Age* (Melbourne), 4 September 1994, p. 4.

67   See Thomas Brennan, *Public Drinking and Popular Culture in Eighteenth-Century Paris*, Princeton, Princeton University Press, 1988, for a definition of sociability that includes contest.

68   See in particular Pringle, *Secretaries Talk.*

69   Alan B. Nankervis, 'Servants or service? Perspectives of the Australian Hotel Industry', University of Western Sydney, School of Business, Working Paper no. 73, August 1990.

70   *Mercury* (Hobart), 25 November 1953, p. 9.

71   Linda Detman, 'Women behind bars: The feminization of bartending', in Barbara Reskin and Patricia Roos, eds, *Job Queues, Gender Queues: Explaining Women's Inroads into Male Occupations*, Philadelphia, Temple University Press, 1990, pp. 241–55.

72   See anecdotes and interviews reported in Susanne Lloyd-Jones, 'You can't sell a beer without a broad'.

73   Best, *The History of the Liquor Trades Union Movement in Victoria*, 1990, p. 197.

74   Nankervis, 'Servants or service?'.

75   ibid; *Mercury* (Hobart), 15 November 1962, p. 29.

76   *Mercury* (Hobart), 21 September 1963; 15 November 1962, p. 29. The union's response to deregulation is found in the *Liquor and Allied Trades Union Journal*, no. 3, 1986, p. 15.

77   Victorian Branch, Federated Liquor and Allied Industries Employees Union of Australia, *Employment in the Hospitality Industry*, researched and written by Sara Charlesworth, November 1983 (hereafter 'Charlesworth Report'). There was also a high level of injury. The most commonly reported being 'cuts and burns' and 'backs' and they were most common among bar attendants. No details were provided on how they were acquired.

78   Wendy Bastalich, Gender and skill in Australia, p. 49.

79   Christine Huxtable, General Secretary of the Australian Liquor, Hospitality and Miscellaneous Workers Union, Liquor and Hospitality Division, quoted in Richard Jinman, 'The pub with no barmaid', *Australian Magazine*, 22–23 July 1995, p. 32.

80   Brian Harrison, 'Pubs', in H. J. Dyos and Wichael Wolff, eds, *The Victorians*, London, Routledge, 1973, pp. 161–90 has mapped the location of London's pubs. A similar pattern probably existed here.

81   Reported in *Sydney Morning Herald*, 26 January 1993.

82   Reported in *Mercury* (Hobart), 20 May 1969, p. 4.

83   A. Dingle, '"The truly magnificent thirst": An historical survey of Australian drinking habits', *Historical Studies*, vol. 19, no. 75, October 1980, pp. 228–9.

84   Charlesworth Report.

85   ibid.

86   Philip Cornford, 'Closing time: Sydney's disappearing pubs', *Sydney Morning Herald*, 21 November 1994, p. 6.

87   Shirley Mellor, interview.

88   *Herald-Sun* (Melbourne), 18 October 1993, p. 16.

89   Jinman, 'The pub with *no* barmaid'.

90   Liz Conor, Discursive localities for appearing women, BA(Hons) thesis, La Trobe University, 1992, is now exploring these themes in a PhD thesis in progress.

91   *Herald* (Sydney), 19 April 1976.

92   Douglass Baglin and Yvonne Austin, *Australian Pub Crawl*, 4th edn, Sydney, PR Books, 1989 (first published 1977), p. 5.

93   Jinman, 'The pub with *no* barmaid'.

Index

231